METRO
DOG

METRO DOG

THE ESSENTIAL GUIDE TO RAISING YOUR DOG IN THE CITY

BRIAN KILCOMMONS
& SARAH WILSON

WARNER BOOKS

An AOL Time Warner Company

Warner Books, Inc., 1271 Avenue of the Americas, New York, NY 10020
Visit our Web site at www.twbookmark.com.

 An AOL Time Warner Company

Printed in the United States of America
Originally published in hardcover by Warner Books, Inc.
First Trade Printing: September 2002
10 9 8 7 6 5 4 3 2 1

The Library of Congress has cataloged the hardcover edition as follows:

Kilcommons, Brian.
Metrodog: a guide to raising your dog in the city / Brian Kilcommons and Sarah Wilson.
p. cm.
Includes bibliographical references (p.).
ISBN 0-446-52603-7
1. Dogs. 2. City and town life. I. Wilson, Sarah, 1960- II. Title.
SF426.K489 2001
636.7'0887—dc21   2001017795

ISBN 0-446-67918-6 (pbk.)

Book design and composition by L&G McRee

To Chester, Scotch, Kesl, Sasha, Fawn, Deacon, Lila, Piper, Rama, Abigail, Toby, Flynn—just a few of the wonderful Metrodogs we've known.

Suzannah Valentinetti communes with one of her small charges.

ACKNOWLEDGMENTS

The first thank-you goes to our intrepid and willing photographers, whose work we value tremendously. Christine Pellicano, Joseph Valentinetti, and Shirley Minatelli carried the bulk of the task. Couldn't have done this without you!

Next, our appreciation to trainers Suzannah Valentinetti of Both Ends of the Leash and Tony Kay-Wolff of The Well-Mannered Dog for taking time from their hectic schedules to come in and for agreeing to let me take loads of pictures of them doing what they do well.

Also, our community at Greatpets.com who have taught us a great deal and continue to do so. And to the other dog enthusiasts who agreed to contribute their knowledge and experience to this project.

To all the dog lovers who have come to us for instruction, training, and care through the years. It is your questions and quandaries that got us thinking about these issues and finding solutions that work.

Last, but most important, to all the Metrodogs we've delighted in knowing. If a dog can humanize a human's life, they certainly do, every day, millions of times over.

JOSEPH VALENTINETTI

CONTENTS

Introduction   xvii

1: Finding Your Metrodog   1
     Which Breed?   3
     Beyond Breed   7
     Adopting the Older Dog   11
     Sources   13

2: The Apartment Puppy (Seven Weeks to End of Quarantine)   17
    Setting Up Your Apartment for Success   18
    Countdown to Your Puppy   20
    Housebreaking—The First Steps   20
     Straight Paper Training   23
     Paper Training Before Housebreaking   24
     Straight Housebreaking   24
    Sample Schedule   25
    Food and Water   26

Homecoming: Making the First Day as Easy as Possible   28
The Family Dog   29
Introducing Your New Pup to Other Pets   30
    To an Older Dog   30
    Cat   33
    Other Pets   34
ABCs of Confinement   34
    Crates   36
    Confinement Behind a Gate   41
    Tethered   42
FRAP   43
Making It through the Night   44
Quarantine: Why and for How Long?   46
    Socialization   47
    Sanity Savers: Games for Tired Owners
      and Active Pups   53
    Quiet Time   54
Good Habits: Start Now!   55
    Introducing the Collar and Lead   56
    Controlling Barking   59
    Jumping Up   60
    Mounting Problems   62
    Accepting Handling   63
    Begging   64
    Destructive Chewing   65
    Submissive Urination   66
Dealing with Different Temperaments   68
    Sensitive   68
    Reactive   69
    Bold   70
    Independent   71
    Stable   71

Commands Every Metropuppy Should Know 72
    Sit 74
    Down 78
    Leave It 80
    Out 81
    Come 82

3: Hitting the Streets (End of Quarantine to Seven Months) 87
Impossible Behavior or Normal Puppy? 88
First Week of Walks 89
    Keep First Trips Brief 89
    Let Your Pup Explore 90
    Have Fun 90
    Stick to Quiet Areas 90
    Great Greetings 92
    The Scoop on Scooping 93
Being a Leader Worth Following 94
Handling Common Fears 97
    Frightened of People 100
    Frightened of Objects 102
    Frightened of Other Dogs 103
From Papers to the Park: Getting Your Pup to Go Outside 105
    Plan A—The Gradual Method 106
    Plan B—Cold Turkey 107
    Plan C—For Pups Not Clean in the Crate 109
    Getting Outside Dry 110
    Developing the Urge to Curb 111
    Housebreaking—The Next Steps 112
    Paper Training—The Next Steps 112
    Keys to Handling Inquisitive Strangers 113

City Services 115

    Trainers and Behaviorists 115

    Dog Walkers 119

    Doggie Day Care 120

Indoor Activities 122

    Mental Gymnastics 123

Exercise—How Much and What Kind 125

    No Forced Marching 126

    Keep Your Pup Lean 127

    First Trips to the Dog Run 127

    Game: Treats, Then Retreat 128

    Dog Run Rules for Pups 129

    Why Neuter Your Male Dog? 131

Hitting the Streets: Obedience 132

    Sit 133

    Down 134

    Leave It 136

    Out 137

    Rules of Corrections 139

    Off 140

    Come 141

    New Commands 143

        Wait 143

        Place 144

        Let's Go or Controlled Walking 146

4: Inner-City Youth (Eight to Eighteen Months) 149

    What to Expect from Your Adolescent Canine 150

    Six Steps to a Better-Behaved Dog 151

    Reading Canine Body Language 153

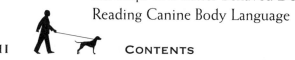

Proper Social Etiquette 159

  Elevator Issues 159

  On the Street 161

    Retractable Leashes 162

  Park 163

  Dog Runs 166

    Dogfights 167

Safe Interactions: Metrodogs and Kids 171

Eighteen-Month-Old Weenies 174

Training Equipment: The Good and the Bad 175

Training for the Inner-City Youth 185

  Advanced Sit 186

  Advanced Down 186

  Distance Down 188

  Down When Moving 189

  Off of Furniture 190

  Place—Continued 192

  New Commands 192

    Move 192

    Stay 193

    Let's Go 196

5: Smooth Sailing (Nineteen Months to Seven Years Plus/Minus) 199

  Health Care 200

    Diet and Nutrition 200

    Dental Care 200

  Beyond Exercise 202

    Dog Sports/Events—What They Are and How to Find Them 202

  Home Alone Success 209

  Taking Your Dog to Work 215

Dogs and Taxicabs — 217
Tethering Near Store — 221
In-Store Manners — 221
Dealing with the Mentally Troubled — 224
Dogs Off Leash on Sidewalks — 225
Metrodog Problems with Solutions — 227
    Too Much Energy — 227
    Couch Hopping — 227
    Separation Problems — 231
    Demanding Behavior — 231
    Barking — 233
    Not Coming When Called — 237
    Dogs Lunging and Barking at Your Dog — 238
    Your Dog Lunging and Barking at Other Dogs/People — 239
    Leg Lifting — 239
    Housebreaking Problems — 240
    Adult-Onset Phobias — 242
        Thunderstorms/Loud Noises — 243
        Fear of Certain Places — 244
    "Good Dog" Aggression: Understanding Late-Developing Aggression — 245
    Dominant Dogs — 247
Continuing Education — 250
    "Off" for the Adult Dog — 252
    Stay—Continued — 252
    Come—Continued — 255
    Pulling on Lead — 257

6: The Older Metrodog (Age Seven Onward) — 261
Life Expectancy — 262
Physical Changes — 264

CONTENTS

Making Life Easier   269
Health Care   269
Games and Activities for the Older Dog   270
More Training?   273
New Puppy?   274
When the Time Comes   275
What Will Happen?   277

Conclusion   279
Resources   281
Index   289

Metrodogs have much more fun!

If you have a dog, other dog owners will talk to you. That makes the city a nicer place to live.

"I could never have a dog in the city! It's so cruel!"

Actually . . .

Metrodogs can have the best of everything. They meet other dogs daily, romp in the park, accompany their owners to stores and cafés. These animals are never delegated to the garage or banished to the backyard to walk around in bored solitude. No two walks are the same in the city. What suburban dog can make such a claim?

Dogs do not need "room to run" as much as they need social interaction and mental stimulation. They don't want freedom in isolation, they want companionship and variety.

In our decades as Manhattan dog trainers, we've seen almost every breed of dog living happily in the most concrete of concrete jungles. From Great Danes to Chihuahuas, almost anything is possible with planning, commitment, and information. "Possible" does not necessarily mean easy. Standards of behavior are higher for city dogs. Leaping on strangers, cutting people off on the sidewalk in a dive for a chicken bone, or barking hysterically at another dog will earn your dog (and you) nasty looks and nastier side comments.

Not only are standards higher, but the routine training can be more of a challenge. Running a puppy out the door when he starts to urinate is one thing in a house, another in an apartment on the twenty-second floor. But, as with anything, there are tricks to making things easier, and we share those tricks and tips here.

So enjoy, don't feel guilty. There's nothing wrong with having a dog in the city, and there are a lot of things right with it.

INTRODUCTION

METRO DOG

ISABEL BACKUS

CHAPTER 1

Finding Your Metrodog

Go to any major city and you will find every imaginable breed living there with apparent ease. Some choices are generally easier than others, and our job is to help you make a decision based on more than looks alone. Whole books have been written on the subject of selection (we've done a couple), but the information here can get you started. For more about this important process, please see our resources section.

Let's start by considering some of the most common questions:

Is it cruel to have a dog in the city?

Not at all. In fact, a well-loved Metrodog can have the best of all canine lives. Surrounded by people, other dogs, and interesting smells . . . it sure beats being in a small backyard by yourself.

When adults, some giant breeds can work well as Metrodogs— if you can accommodate their needs.

DIANE LARATTA

Are small dogs the only choice?

No. While small dogs have some obvious advantages, what size is appropriate for you depends on your location and your lifestyle. If you're not too active, do not live near any parks/dog runs, and think a nice walk around a couple of blocks in the afternoon is plenty of exercise, then a small dog may be the best choice. If you're a jogger who has easy access to a dog run and the time to spend an hour or more a day there, then a larger, more active breed may suit you perfectly. Even the giant breeds have their place, with people who have the space to handle them. Surprisingly, their exercise needs (in adulthood) are less strenuous than those of the smaller sporting breeds, so don't rule out the big dogs.

My apartment is small; what are my options?

Many. As above, if you're near a dog run, you can consider a more active breed. If not, then a smaller dog may be a better choice. Giant-breed adults would fit in energy-wise but perhaps not be the easiest choice size-wise.

I'm gone from eight A.M. until past six P.M.; is that too long?

Yes, this is a long day, but being a city dweller, you probably have some excellent options. Hire a dog walker to take your dog out for a long stroll midday. Consider leaving her in doggie day care. Could you trade off dog care with another owner who works different hours? There are ways to make sure your Metrodog's needs are met.

If none of this is an option, please consider some of the other wonderful companion animals, such as a pair of cats, rabbits, guinea pigs, or smaller birds, all of whom can be loving, affectionate, stay-at-home companions.

METRODOG

LONG EARS, WET BEARDS, AND FUZZY FEET

A Metrodog is exposed to all manner of dirt on his daily walks. Metrodogs with long ears and/or beards that drag on the sidewalk when they sniff or fuzzy feet that can track in the dirt when they come home require more maintenance to keep clean and tidy. Fastidious housekeepers may never be happy. Other people don't give it a second thought. You just have to know your personal tolerance for that sort of thing.

BRIAN KILCOMMONS

In this New York City class, we have a poodle mix, a Bichon Frise, an Australian Shepherd, a Bearded Collie, and an English Springer Spaniel.

Which Breed?

Everyone has a personal preference on breed or mixes. Most of those preferences are based on looks, and looks (beyond the amount of grooming necessary) are not what make a dog easy or not easy to live with. Delve deeper than that. Following are a few things to consider when thinking about which breed to get:

SCENT HOUNDS

Beagles, Basset Hounds, Bloodhounds, etc. tend to be gregarious animals, with low territorial and dog-to-dog aggression. That is good in the city. On the downside, they can be eager garbage eaters and may never come reliably when called. Howling (baying) is a trait that was carefully selected for in these breeds, so don't be surprised by it.

JOSEPH VALENTINETTI

SIGHT HOUNDS

Dogs like Greyhounds, Whippets, and Afghans are elegant animals who also have low territorial aggression and, despite being built for speed, can thrive on one good daily run in a fenced area. Usually this is a quiet group, not known for nuisance barking or being especially good watchdogs. However, few come immediately when called, and all can be a long way away, heading for danger, in seconds.

The active retrievers are always a popular choice, though not always an easy one because of their high exercise needs as young dogs.

RETRIEVERS

Labrador and Golden Retrievers are the most common family dogs. Well bred and raised, they should love all other beings—two or four legged. They appeal to many people who don't take into account the big exercise requirements these dogs have in the first three or more years of life. They also tend to be oral, making chewing and eating garbage common problems.

SPANIELS

The American Cocker Spaniel has taken the spotlight for decades, but the English Cocker, Springers (English and Welsh), etc. are equally charming dogs. Good ones are universally friendly beings; poorly bred ones are not. Their long coat (especially the American Cocker's) requires regular professional grooming.

The "Westie" can make a delightful companion. I'd be happier, though, if this dog were on lead.

POINTERS AND SETTERS

German Shorthaired and Wirehaired Pointers as well as Vizsla and Weimaraners seem the most popular pointers for the city. All three setters (English, Irish, and Gordon) also make their appearance. The issue for these dogs is exercise. Unless you have access to a large fenced area at least twice a day, energy-related behaviors such as barking, chewing, pulling, and jumping can be a problem.

TERRIERS

Jack Russell, West Highland White, Cairn, and Soft-Coated Wheatens are just a few of the popular terriers. Small in size, large in heart, these dogs fit well into many apartments. A correct harsh coat of many terriers sheds dirt surprisingly well, though the Wirehaired Terriers will require professional grooming to stay neat and tidy. Terriers can be feisty, barking a great deal, picking fights with other dogs, and generally being a bit rowdy. Terrier people find this part of their charm.

TOYS

Possibly the most numerous of all Metrodogs, the toys (Yorkshire Terrier, Maltese, Shih Tzu, Pug, Cavalier King Charles Spaniel, etc.) are popular urban companions. A walk around a couple of blocks is enough for most of these dogs, who can get plenty of exercise even in a small apartment. Some require regular grooming. Some are barkers, others more quiet. Do your research; there are terrific companion dogs in the group.

WORKING

For various reasons, some of the dogs in this group are hard to own in the city. The sled dogs (Siberian Husky, Malamute, Samoyed, etc.) crave vigorous daily exercise and can be soulful howlers as well as monumental chewers if bored/underexercised/undertrained. The guard dogs (Doberman, Rottweilers, Great Danes) need strong, consistent leadership to be the best they can be. If they are left undertrained and underexercised, aggression of various kinds can be a problem. The rescue/draft dogs (Newfoundlands, Saint Bernards, etc.) can actually work surprisingly well as Metrodogs if you have room for them in your home. They are something like a walking couch that sheds, drools, and needs long daily walks.

NONSPORTING

A catch-all group of dogs. Generalities aren't useful; research the history of each breed, and talk to breeders and rescue people to find out if the breed (or mix) you are considering would be a good choice.

HERDING

Ranging from the low-to-the-ground Corgis to the ever-popular German Shepherd Dog, this group comprises people-focused, highly trainable dogs. They require vigorous daily exercise, consistent training, and thoughtful management or some can become problem dogs. More than a few herding breeds are sound sen-

 **METRODOG**

sitive, which makes life in the city a poor choice. All types of aggression are commonly present in many of the breeds.

For detailed information on the pros and cons of some of the most common breeds, please see our 1999 book, *Paws to Consider.*

TWO PUPS BETTER THAN ONE?

No. Two pups from the same litter are a "please, no." Two same-sex pups from the same litter can be real trouble as they mature and begin to vie for leadership position. Two pups are twice as much work and trouble. If you decide to go that way, be sure to work with each pup individually daily and take them one at a time around town to socialize. If you aren't careful, they can become overdependent on each other or fail to mature mentally/emotionally. If you have the time and energy to devote to rearing them properly, it can work—but it is more work for all concerned.

What is the most popular kind of dog— the mixed breed. What is he? Who knows. He's loved and loving, and that is the important thing.

JOSEPH VALENTINETTI

Beyond Breed

Once you've chosen a few breeds or mixes to consider, what about the other details? Age? Gender? Watchdog or guard dog?

ADULT OR PUPPY?

Pups are charming and demanding. Are you ready for constant surveillance and round-the-clock teaching for the next few months? Adult dogs bond to you as well as pups (sometimes even better) and are through the more demanding developmental stages. Rescues may have behavioral problems that need resolving.

Whichever you choose, choose carefully. Avoid impulsive choices. Consider hiring a trainer to help you select your dog. Get your dog (pup or adult) from rescues, shelters, or breeders that use formal temperament testing, have policies about not adopting out aggressive dogs, and will take back the animal that doesn't work out.

MALE OR FEMALE?

Your choice. Both are equally wonderful. And since you will be neutering your companion regardless of gender (right?), it makes little difference. If this is your second dog, consider gender more carefully (see following); otherwise, select the dog whose temperament best suits your needs and don't worry about his or her plumbing.

IS THIS YOUR SECOND DOG?

If you are adding another dog to your family, consider the following:

• **Opposite sex.** The chances of having a perfect match are better if your new dog is the opposite sex of your current companion. Yes, plenty of same-sex pairings get along like bread and butter, but if you do not have a strong preference, select the opposite.

• **Different age.** The further apart dogs are in age, the less likely they are to clash. So adding a younger animal to the mix is your best bet, as that dog will probably fall in line behind your current dog.

• **Defers to first dog.** Your second dog should defer to your first, meaning if your first gets between you and the new pup and lifts a lip, the new dog demurs with

 **METRODOG**

head low and eyes averted. A new addition who behaves in this way will not be likely to challenge the first dog.

• **Well-matched temperament.** Being well matched does not mean being the same. A bold pup may be a perfect companion for a less confident older dog. The reverse is also true. Two of the same can be trouble, with two bold dogs getting into more trouble, two reactive dogs reacting off each other, and two shy dogs both scrambling to dive under the bed.

DON'T TOUCH MY DOG

More than once, in the city, we've had people say that they don't want anyone to touch their dog because they want the dog to be protective. If you really want a protective dog (and not just an antisocial, fearful dog), socialize him as much as you can. Let him learn what normal human behavior is so he'll recognize when something is amiss. This way, if that time ever comes, he'll be by your side and not end up in the back room because he is out of control.

WATCHDOG OR GUARD DOG?

For many urban dwellers, fear is the norm. And a good answer to that fear can appear to be a dog trained to attack. What better protection can you have than a best friend ready 24/7 to protect?

Actually owning such an animal is more complicated (and dangerous) than it can appear. First of all, once a dog knows how to fight (and has been taught to enjoy fighting) with a human, she is no longer simply a "pet." Having a dog trained to the high level required for this work demands your time and energy as well— daily. You can't relax about maintaining training. Your insurance company will probably not cover a trained guard dog, so check that.

A better plan is to have a well-trained responsive dog, a dog who is with you at the door, alert but under control. This can be quite intimidating, as people don't know how extensively your dog is trained. A dog who barks at strange sounds or activity, but is not trained to battle it out, is a watchdog, and that is the kind of companion most of us need.

Let's face it, we're all much more likely to hear something go bump in the night than to actually have an intruder in our home. The thing most criminals want more than anything is to go unnoticed, and a barking dog foils that plan. But that bark does not need to be backed up with a bite.

MAKING A RURAL DOG INTO A METRODOG

This is a huge shift for any dog and can be stressful for some, but it is usually doable. Expect some weeks of adjustment issues before your companion adapts fully to her new, unasked-for lifestyle change. Things you can do to make the adjustment easier include the following:

• **Walk her on lead before the move.** Walk her on lead in the country so she gets used to urinating and defecating close to you. Many rural dogs find that aspect of urban life difficult at first. If your dog likes her privacy, putting her on a retractable leash can give her the distance she needs while still getting her used to being "on lead."

Even hard-core rural dogs can become happy Metrodogs with a little patience, understanding, and training.

• **Walk her on pavement.** Dogs who like to squat in grass often refuse to do so on concrete. If you can make a habit of walking your dog on your driveway or street for urinating and defecating, then

rewarding her for compliance with a romp on the lawn, she should soon get down to business quickly. (If she does not, please read "Cold Turkey" in the section "From Papers to the Park: Getting Your Pup to Go Outside" on page 107, as those techniques will help you.)

- **Start a crating routine.** If you plan to leave your dog for several hours in her new urban digs, you should start a crating routine now. Even a dog who is relaxed in a rural home may be restless and overstimulated in the city. A preestablished routine will help make the change in environment easier.

- **Training class.** Find a class and go! Most non-Metrodogs see other dogs only occasionally, which can heighten their excitement and/or aggression toward strange dogs. In the city, your dog will face strange dogs daily, and getting her used to that event now will help her be calm later. (Please see page 116, "Finding a Trainer.")

- **Discourage barking.** Noise can be a major neighbor annoyer, so discourage it as soon as you can. Discouraging entails *not* rewarding it. (See "Barking" in the section "Metrodog Problems with Solutions" on page 233 for tips on how to do this effectively.)

A volunteer with the Walter Turken Training for Adoption Program (Brian's pet project) helps train and socialize dogs so they'll make better adopted companions.

SARAH WILSON

Adopting the Older Dog

Every year millions of people open their homes and their lives to deserving dogs. Anyone who questions a dog's ability to feel and express emotion should see the gratitude in an adopted shelter dog's eyes. Once you're home, there is much you can do to help your new companion adapt.

STRUCTURE

His new life begins today. Every interaction is teaching him what his new life is like, and if you indulge his every whim, he'll think that doing so is your purpose. Instead, direct him calmly and kindly. Start formally teaching him new things in low-stress, positive ways. This will also do an override on some old habits, creating new positive ways for him to respond to you, other animals, and the world.

UMBILICAL

Keeping him on leash with you in the apartment will both help bond him to you and prevent any previously learned "bad" behaviors from showing themselves. You'll be right there to praise and reward the right choices as well as calmly prevent or redirect the choices you don't like.

CALM

He's been under a great deal of stress, losing his first home, being in a shelter or foster program, and then coming to you. Whether he shows it or not, he needs rest, routine, and rewards.

TIME

You'll probably see a lot of anxious activity for the first few days. He may not lie down often or, if he does, may get up frequently. He may stick to you like glue or keep to himself. Both are equally normal.

SIGN UP FOR CLASSES

After ten days or so, start some training. Either join a class or have a trainer who uses a positive approach come to your home. This will have multiple benefits, including building the bond, replacing some unhappy experiences with pleasurable ones, and getting to know your dog.

 METRODOG

Sources

No matter where you look for your new companion, there are pros and cons. Following is a quick overview that we hope will inspire you to do some serious research.

Your Metrodog will interact with everyone; it is well worth the time to find a happy, stable dog to be your companion.

CHRISTINE PELLICANO

BREEDERS

Pro. Good breeders raise the pups in their home and handle them daily. Often training has begun, their animals are tested for common health problems, and you get a lifetime of support and advice for free.

Con. Not all breeders are good breeders, and people who aren't won't tell you (or even know) they aren't. Proceed with caution. Good breeders have one or two litters a year, health certifications, written contracts, spay/neuter requirements, and a lifetime return policy—they want their dog back any reason, any time, any age. If this is not what you are hearing, be suspicious. Do your homework, ask for professional referrals, and proceed with caution.

OPEN ADMISSION SHELTERS

Pro. Open admission means these facilities take any dog who ends up on their doorstep. With a steady influx of a wide variety of dogs, euthanasia is necessary.

So taking a dog from one of these facilities is making room for another dog to be there another day.

Con. Because they have no control over the dogs who come in, temperaments can vary widely. It is hard to have a temperament testing policy with the numbers some of these places handle. Great dogs are in there; just take an experienced dog person with you when you look.

You're lucky if you have a facility such as this one near you. They offer training and day care, and all animals are neutered before adoption.

LIMITED ADMISSION SHELTERS

Pro. Normally privately funded, these shelters can pick and choose who joins their ranks. Because the numbers are controlled, temperament testing is easier to administer and keep up with. Often these facilities also have strong volunteer groups that do walking and training.

Con. A dog kept for months (sometimes years) in a shelter can go insane. Some shelters do not temperament test their dogs and, because of "no kill" policies, will adopt out dangerous animals—knowingly or unknowingly. Some limited admis-

METRODOG

sion shelters refuse to take back any animal you adopt from them that bites because, after all, they are "no kill." That is ridiculous. Any animal any shelter adopts out they should take back. Period.

RESCUE GROUPS

Pro. Here are devoted people caring for homeless members of this breed. At its best, rescues make room at local shelters for more animals by taking their breed out, they educate potential owners about the breed's needs and tendencies, and they screen animals to make sure they are safe.

Con. At its worst, a rescue can be a group of dog lovers who don't believe any dog can be dangerous. They don't temperament test, and sometimes they adopt out aggressive dogs and then resist taking those dogs back. Such naiveté is rare, but always ask for testing and return policies.

PET SHOPS

Pro. They are convenient and take credit cards.

Con. Not only will you pay more for a poorly bred, stressed, often sick animal than you would at a top breeder, but you will also be supporting the puppy mill industry. Pet stores will *all* tell you they don't buy from mills. We can promise you one thing: No good breeder would ever sell an animal through a pet store. It would never happen. Good breeders want to know where each of their precious pups ends up and would not sell anonymously to any soul with a credit card. Do not buy anything from a store that sells puppies.

All puppies are cute, but anyone who buys a puppy from a pet store supports horrible abuse of animals. Want to save a dog? Call a rescue!

DIANE LARATTA

CHAPTER 2

The Apartment Puppy
(Seven Weeks to End of Quarantine)

F ew things bring as much joy into your life as a love affair, and a love affair is what you are about to embark on. You will have moments of utter contentment watching your pup sleep draped across your lap, glee as you play with each other with complete abandon, annoyance as you step into that unseen puddle. Not every moment can be good—not every moment of any love affair is—but it will be worth it.

The period you are about to enter is the most demanding, exhausting, amusing, bewildering, fun period of any dog's life. Enjoy! Take pictures. It will all end too soon.

Let's start at the beginning of this process, with setting up your home for your newest arrival.

THE APARTMENT PUPPY 17

Between the stuffed toy and the large
rawhide, this pup is ready to have
a good time in a good way.

Setting Up Your Apartment for Success

"Into everything" aptly describes most pups. Everything is new, from the roll of toilet paper she unrolled down your hall to the pile of magazines she shredded while you were on the phone. Surviving this stage can be simplified by doing a few things ahead of time. Here is how you set up your home for puppy-rearing success (none of this takes the place of personally supervising your puppy):

- Remove all breakables less than three feet from the floor (higher if you have a giant breed).
- Remove all food items less than three feet from the floor and clear off countertops.
- Tie up loose electrical cords and apply an antichew product to all cords within puppy reach. (If you use a spray, lay newspaper under the cord when you spray, as the alcohol base in many of them can damage some finishes.)
- Put wicker and newspaper elsewhere, as this has a seemingly universal appeal for pups.

- Apply wood-safe antichew stuff to rungs and legs of furniture (these appear to be perfect chew toys to the average puppy).
- Close the doors to all rooms, and confine pup to one main room during play or supervised free time. We use the main room that is adjacent to the kitchen. If there is no door (as is true with our home), use a gate. We use something called an "exercise pen" opened across the six-foot entry. An "ex-pen," as it is called, is simply several panels of metal barred squares that can be hooked together to form a movable pen or unhooked to stretch across an opening. When not in use, it folds up and can slide easily under the average bed. You lucky people with studio apartments have no option but to keep your pup with you at all times. This will simplify housebreaking considerably.
- Set up a crate in a busy area of the apartment. The crate is not a place of punishment, it is a containment system. Isolation will only cause your puppy distress. At night, have a crate near your bed. This may mean moving one crate or having two crates at first.
- Get safe, hard-wearing toys. We recommend a plain rope toy, a nylon chew bone, a rubber "Kong" toy (looks like a soft rubber ice-cream cone), and a sterilized bone. Toys that pups generally love but are not as long wearing are a latex, hedgehog-type squeaker (the dogs seem to like the soft spines on it) and artificial-sheepskin toys.

Not every piece of fun has to be purchased. Here the lid off a box delights Lila, a Cavalier King Charles Spaniel pup.

NORMA MOFFET

Countdown to Your Puppy

The day approaches; are you ready?
   Do you have the following:

   A crate and/or baby gate?
   Toys?
   Bowls?
   Food he's used to?
   Odor/stain remover?
   Antichew product?
   Extra paper towels (a few rolls at least)?
   Extra plastic bags?
   A supply of newspaper if you have to paper-train first?
   The name of a good, close veterinarian?
   A trainer or walker all lined up?
   Some nice bottles of wine to appease the neighbors with if there is noise the
      first few nights despite your best efforts?
   Camera and film? (You won't regret any shots you take of your pup. They
      grow so fast, and the weeks easily slip by without record.)

Housebreaking—The First Steps

Metrodogs and their people face some special housebreaking challenges such as
quarantine (please see page 46) and a long trip from apartment to elevator to
lobby to street to an appropriate potty spot.

   Luckily, most dogs want to be clean in the apartment, and most Metrodogs
learn this skill early and well. Following are a few guidelines to make that process
as easy and puddle free as possible, even if you live on the twenty-seventh floor.

METRODOG

WHAT IF YOU CATCH HER IN THE ACT?

You see your dog squatting—what do you do? Startle her with a loud sound (a clap, a "Hey!," or a wall slap will do) and hustle her off to her papers or outside. No yelling, scolding, face rubbing, scruffing, or any other form of punishment. If your puppy knew how to tell you she needed to go (and maybe she did and you didn't know what she meant), she would tell you. Punishment will only make her think that you hate it when you see her go, and that will lead her to going out of sight and/or not wanting to go on lead near you. Both things are bad.

First, your pup needs to be in your sight every moment he is free until he is reliable. Reliability usually arrives somewhere between six and eight months of age. Your companion will probably be clean weeks and months before that, but that success will be due more to your use of routine and prevention than to his full understanding of what is expected.

The puppy must stay in the room you are in. You can close the door, use a gate to block the doorway, or keep him on lead near to you, but near to you he must be. If you plan to leave the room for more than a minute (literally), the pup either comes with you on lead or goes into his safe confinement area. This will not only prevent mistakes from happening without your knowledge, it will keep him safe as well.

Second, watch for signs of impending urination or defecation. These include wandering away from you, sniffing the floor, restlessness, whining, panting, and circling. Certain things frequently bring on a need to go, and they include chewing heavily on a toy, eating, ten minutes or so after a big drink, waking up from a nap, or a rollicking game of anything.

When you see any of these signs or your pup has just done any of the above, take him to the papers or, if you have a safe outdoor area such as a rooftop or garden, go there. ("Safe" means not frequented by other dogs likely to be unvaccinated.) If you do have an outdoor area, carry your pup there and then walk him on lead. Since he will be walked on lead outside in a few weeks, best to make that part of the routine now.

Finally, remember to pick up after your dog meticulously. If you find it disgusting—get over it! You owe it to your building, your neighbors, and all other dog owners. It is also critical that you clean up thoroughly after any accidents indoors.

Proper cleanup is critical to housebreaking success. Here are two, of many, choices.

PROPER CLEANUP

The smell of past mistakes will attract a pup to those same spots, so make sure you use an odor neutralizer/eliminator specially made for the purpose. Homemade concoctions such as vinegar and water will not do the job. And never use a mixture containing ammonia, as it is present in urine and will encourage mistakes.

YOUR OPTIONS

At this point there are three housebreaking possibilities: you are paper training your pup and plan to continue to do so, you are paper training your pup and plan to housebreak her ASAP, or you have access to a safe outdoor area and plan to housebreak immediately. Each of these is handled in slightly different ways.

TIPS FOR TOYS: TOY PUPS ARE DELICATE

Tiny pups can suffer from life-threatening hypoglycemia (low blood sugar) if they don't have access to food frequently. Leave food out for them in their confinement area all the time. These pups can become very sick very quickly. Also, you have little margin of error for normal puppy events like stomach upset. Diarrhea that a larger pup takes in stride can dehydrate and kill a two-pound treasure. Any health questions or troubles? Go to the veterinarian ASAP! Do not "wait and see."

STRAIGHT PAPER TRAINING

Many small breeds can be trained to use papers (or a litter pan). This is a major convenience during foul weather or human illness. This does not mean that your dog becomes apartment bound, simply that you are able to set your outside time around your schedule, not hers.

Here are the basic guidelines for successful paper training:

Set up one set of papers (or two if you live in a large loft/apartment/brownstone). To avoid floor damage, place the papers either in a tray or on a heavy sheet of plastic. Alternatively, use "blue pads," which can be bought in bulk from any medical supply store for much less than the cost of the puppy training pads sold at the pet store. These pads have the advantage of not getting ink on your dog, which can be important if you have either a white dog or a white home.

The ideal paper area is a small, narrow room—often a bathroom fits the bill as well as any place. (If you have no such spot, you can create one using an ex-pen.)

A wire mesh/metal baby gate needs to go across the door so the pup can see out but not get out. Some pups are climbers, so if you can install the gate so that it leans inward slightly, this will make it harder to climb.

Put the papers toward the rear of the room with bedding, food, and water up front. The hope is that your pup will soon learn to leave the bedding area and potty on the papers in the rear.

Your pup will ideally choose to urinate and defecate at the far end of the area, away from her bed, food, and water. This is not always the case; some pups go right up front, then jump up and down in the mess. You can help to refocus your pup by dabbing the clean papers with a bit of urine from the paper toweling after cleanup. The pup will be attracted to the smell of her own urine and hopefully be more on target.

Be sure to clean under the papers daily with an odor neutralizer/eliminator, as this will mop up any urine that might have seeped over. If any smell is left at the edge, your pup may squat with her rear end several inches or more off the papers.

PAPER TRAINING BEFORE HOUSEBREAKING

A common Metrodog situation. If you're doing this, proceed as recommended in "Straight Paper Training" but skip the wild praise for success. You don't want to instill this behavior deeply, since you will be abandoning it ASAP.

Whenever possible, get your pup to safe areas outside. On the weekend, try to take him to the country or a friend's house with a backyard. The more experience he has urinating and defecating outside, the easier it will be to make the transition later. However, plenty of pups don't get weekend road trips but still end up perfectly housebroken.

Once it is safe to get your pup out, proceed with "From Papers to the Park: Getting Your Pup to Go Outside" on page 105.

STRAIGHT HOUSEBREAKING

This is possible only if you have a reasonably safe area near to you and are willing to take the risk. Sarah's Bouvier des Flandres pup insisted (at seven weeks old and at the top of his lungs) that he be taken outside. She relented and carried him out to their quiet side street, then carried him back in for as long as she could manage it.

Is there a roof area on your building? If yes, maybe you can play with your pup

up there on lead if it is safe. Many roofs have low boundary walls and/or are fenced, but keep your pup on lead anyway. If the roof is not fenced, do not use it, because a dropped lead could mean heartbreak. As always, pick up promptly and totally. Many buildings also have a small back area. Watch out for rats, though; their feces carry diseases your puppy can catch.

Maybe your veterinarian knows of other pups in the area. Sometimes one of them has access to a small backyard area that can be used for playful romping. Be creative!

WHEN TO WALK

Pups urinate and defecate a lot. You can expect either or both after waking up from a nap, heavy play, heavy chewing, excitement, eating, or drinking. Each pup has a unique pattern, but in a few weeks you'll know that half an hour after eating, she needs to get outside or to the papers. Keeping track of this during quarantine will make complete house-breaking easier on you both. Noting when she eats, drinks, urinates, and defecates will help you see the patterns more completely.

Sample Schedule

One possible schedule for working folks might be:

Crate overnight next to the bed.
To the papers/outside ASAP in the A.M. Plan to get up early for the next few
    months to give your pup time before you leave.
Hang out with your pup as you do morning routines.
Feed breakfast.
To the papers/outside.

Confined in safe room/area, with crate open, water, and papers.
Midday cleanup, feed, play.
Home, outside if safe, or on lead with you around the apartment.
Dinner.
To papers or outside if safe after eating.
Water is picked up around seven P.M.
Last chance at papers or outside after ten P.M.
Crate next to you at night (yes, even pups being paper-trained).

A sample schedule for people home all day would be the same as the work one, only instead of confining during work hours, keep your pup on leash near you or crated within earshot. If you are home to hear your pup get restless, then short bouts of crating can be helpful. If you are going out for more than a short errand, confine your pup to a safe papered area.

Food and Water

With the exception of toy pups who need food all the time, the more control you have over when food goes into your pup's body, the more predictable it will be when things come out of her body. We feed pups under twelve weeks of age three times a day. We put food down for fifteen minutes, then pick it up. This will teach your pup to eat when the food is available, and our dogs universally eat what is fed when it is fed. If your pup seems to pick at her food consistently, please consult your veterinarian.

Water is given with meals, when the pup is warm, and every few hours in between. A pup needs as much water as she wants throughout the day, and controlling when she gets it should not be confused with controlling how much water she gets. We've seen too many puppies who have been deprived of water to the point where they drink everything in sight. If your pup is thirsty, let her drink. Just realize that if she drinks a great deal, she'll need to urinate several times in the next couple of hours.

Some foods seem to promote heavy water drinking, so if your pup is drinking

up a storm every day, please consider slowly changing over to another brand and see if that makes a difference. If you have concerns, speak to your veterinarian.

TIPS FOR TOYS

"It does seem to take toy breed pups a long time to become reliably housebroken, and it seems to me that many new dog owners sort of expect 'turnkey' dogs: bring 'em home, open 'em up, and they should be perfect by morning. It was truly a full year before I could say with confidence that my newest toy pup (now four years old) was housebroken. And I think a lot of the failures we hear about are really dogs that just haven't been given sufficient time to learn before being given the run of an apartment. Also, a lot of toy breed owners have issues about walking their dogs on lead and just don't take them out frequently or for long enough walks."

—CHRIS PELLICANO, Maltese Rescuer, NYC, NY

SHERRIE WESTIN

Stable, well-reared puppy + sensitive, gentle child + attentive, responsible adult = good times for all.

Homecoming: Making the First Day as Easy as Possible

The name of the game is "minimize stress."

Get as much equipment as you can set up ahead of time. This avoids unnecessary trips and having to leave your pup alone on the first day.

Find out (when possible) what food she's been eating, and lay in a supply. Even if you plan on changing it, keep the food the same for the first two weeks or so. Going to a new home is stressful enough; no need to add more with a food change. (*Hint:* If you don't know the food, mix half well-cooked, long-cooking white rice with the new food. This will help minimize stomach upset.)

Limit visitors. When possible, keep things quiet for the first few days. Let her explore (under close supervision). Stay calm yourself. Now is not the time to rev her up with wild play. Now is the time to watch, help, encourage, redirect, and reward.

Distract rather than correct. Your new pup will pick things up, jump up, attempt to chew, and otherwise be a puppy. When she does these things—distract her. Call her to you happily, offer an interesting toy. If she scampers about too quickly, let her drag a leash on a flat collar so you can get hold of her easily. (Please see "Introducing the Collar and Lead" on page 56.)

Some pups (especially toys) get spooked by people trying to pick them up at first (wouldn't you?), so instead get as small as you can—on the floor, on a chair, squatting—and call her to you. Lure her with a treat or a toy if need be. Then stroke her calmly before scooping her up—one hand under her chest, one under her rear.

Do not lift her up under (or by) her front legs, as this can hurt a pup and cause her to avoid you.

Limit children to your own. Have them sit on the floor when they want to interact. Do not allow them to pick up the pup, because if she squirms out of their eager hands, she can get hurt. Like children, pups can get overtired and wound up. If you see this (sudden wild mouthing and shoe grabbing are typical signs), it's time for a nap.

Expect normal puppy behavior. All pups nip, yip, pee, poop, chew, dig, get stuck behind and under things, annoy the cats, steal food from children's hands, and race around like mad demon dogs once or twice a day. That is perfectly normal puppy behavior. Normal does not mean acceptable, normal means that she isn't retarded, aggressive, or crazy.

CHILD-FILLED HOMES

The more hectic your home, the more important it is for everyone to have a safe place to take a break. Your new canine will need a retreat from your child's attentions and demands. Any retreat your dog makes should be absolutely respected. It is your dog's primary way of saying, "I've had enough for now." If you do not respect your dog's need for a break, you may force him to state his case more forcefully.

The Family Dog

Dogs can add so much to family life. They have been and continue to be the constant companions of children everywhere. The more change happens in the rest of our lives, the more important the unconditional love and predictable presence of a dog can be in a child's life.

Our book *Childproofing Your Dog* is devoted to having a wonderful experience with your kids and your dog together. If we are to give you one hint about making it all work, it is this: Don't allow a child to do to a dog what you would not allow done to a younger child.

No worries here, these two are having great fun.

Taken to heart, this eliminates dog harassment such as chasing, sitting on, pulling ears, hitting with toys, and other things we routinely hear about. It also encourages supervision, the only real way to know exactly what is going on between child and dog.

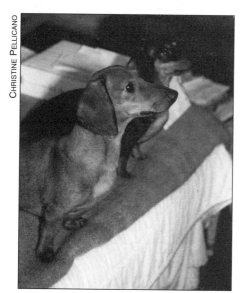

When you have two, train one at a time, and then when they both are doing well (as these two are), start working them together.

Introducing Your New Pup to Other Pets

TO AN OLDER DOG

Ideally, introductions are best done on neutral territory. Maybe a friend would let it happen at her apartment. If not, have both animals on lead and under control or sepa-

LONG LIVE THE KING

Treating your dogs as equals can cause them to fight. In the world of canines, every individual is either in front of or behind everyone else. If you treat your dogs as equals, you are basically saying, "I have no opinion about your order, you guys work it out." To prevent aggression, treat your older dog as number one. Feed him first, greet him first, pet him first, give him treats first, let him out of his crate first . . . you get the idea. Dogs don't mind being second, they only mind not knowing where they stand.

rated by a gate. If you use a crate, you can bring the pup in crated and allow the adult dog to sniff through the gate. If it is a wire crate, covering it and setting it on a chair or in a corner can keep the pup from being surrounded.

As the adult approaches the crate, praise him warmly and set a calm, happy tone. How they interact will give you an idea about how to proceed. If it is all tail wagging, wait for things to calm down a bit and then let them out together. Things should be fine.

If, however, the adult is stiff, with his hair standing up, continue to set a calm, happy tone. Give him some time to relax. Many dogs will get past the initial tension if given a few minutes. If he isn't relaxing, you can play the "you get treats near the crate" game to help him focus on something else, but I would not let the pup out with the adult yet. If possible, use a gate to allow the pup some freedom to explore but enough protection from getting mugged. Any nonaggressive interest from the adult toward the pup should be rewarded.

If the pup screams and tries to hide, ignore this, too. Often this is tension related, and given a few minutes the pup will calm down and his natural curiosity will take over.

It is important that you have confinement areas for both dogs. They can share a crate by having one in while the other is out; otherwise you'll need two crates or a crate and a baby gate. This will allow you to separate the two when things get rowdy, you get tired, or one of them is injured or ill. Perhaps even more important, you'll be able to give one at a time your undivided (and uninterrupted) attention for training or just some private time with you.

Most introductions are harder on the nervous humans than on the dogs, but if you have doubts, here are a few wise words from someone with plenty of experience:

"I do best with the 'separate but together' approach. When I bring in a new one, they live in the same apartment as all the others but are always kept separate, behind baby gates, one crated and one loose. When the new dog first arrives, all the dogs get excited about the presence of the stranger. After two weeks they are all used to each other, and actually putting them together is anticlimactic; they often ignore each other and are unlikely to squabble."

—LINDA TRADER, National Rescue Coordinator,
Boston Terrier Club of America

KITTY LITTER BUFFET

Many dogs love to snack on cat poop. It helps if you keep the cat box spotless, but that won't totally control this. We suggest keeping the box and the dog separated. For a large dog, use a covered box turned toward the wall or a large hook-and-eye latch to prevent the dog from getting into the room that holds the box. If you have a small dog, putting the box in the bathtub or using a baby gate can control canine access. Since this is such an astonishingly disgusting habit, it is well worth applying a little ingenuity to prevent it.

SARAH WILSON

Cats and dogs can become fast friends, especially when they grow up together.

CAT

The secrets to introducing a new dog or pup to a cat is to make sure the cat has good hiding places he can get to easily and keeping the dog under control. "Under control" means on lead so no chasing is possible. Crate training your dog (or using baby gates that the cat can get over but your dog can't) will allow your cat to keep well away from your dog.

A simple game you can play with your new pup/dog is called "cat=treats." Whenever the cat is in view, give your dog treats. If you are generous with this, your dog will soon want the cat to be around, which is a good place to start. (You can play the same game with your cat if he'll take treats, and this will help reinforce that the dog is a good addition to the family.)

As your dog begins to like this game, you can start requiring her to sit calmly before the treat or even lie down. You can walk toward the cat, then back away and call your dog to you, rewarding her with treats and praise when she arrives. This will start building a strong "come" command as well as teach her how to "leave it" when you say so.

Cats frequently take great offense to having a dog in their home. They may hide and/or hiss at the dog for weeks. This is normal, and as long as they get dog-free time (when your dog is crated at night, for example), everything should settle in with time.

THE APARTMENT PUPPY

OTHER PETS

Most other pets will be smaller (birds, rodents, fish) and will require your protection from your new dog more than anything else. The best approach is to limit access to the rooms holding your smaller pets when you can't watch the dog or confine the dog away from those animals using gates or a crate.

Playing the "pet=treats" game with them can have the same calming effect as it does when played near a cat (as described above).

SARAH WILSON

This much intensity and intelligence had better be confined for his own safety and the safety of your home.

ABCs of Confinement

Want the age-old dog training secret to raising a puppy? Okay, here it is: Supervise, supervise, supervise, and when you cannot supervise, confine.

Many new dog owners cringe at the idea of confinement. They envision their dog running free through the apartment, playing with toys, waiting patiently for their beloved and understanding owner to return home for a happy, tail-wagging reunion.

What most new dog owners cannot imagine is the couch pillows (or the couch itself) in various stages of disassembly, a chunk of linoleum ripped up, wallpaper ripped off, a hole in the Sheetrock, the TV remote gnawed (last used by a human snacking on chips and salsa), and a suspicious wet spot on the nicest (lightest,

Responsible breeders would not dream of rearing puppies without careful confinement. This litter is resting in an exercise pen.

most cherished) rug. Worse yet, the rushed trips to the veterinarian followed by frantic surgery after the pup has swallowed something he shouldn't have swallowed.

None of this happens with a well-trained dog. But those well-trained dogs don't grow on trees; they are carefully created through the sensible use of confinement, supervision, and teaching.

CRATES

"What! Put my puppy in a cage?" is what we hear often. Our response is: Would you put your child in a car seat? Your toddler in a playpen? Of course you would, because it is your job to keep the innocent safe.

A crate, properly used, is a wonderful tool for just that purpose. And, like a car seat or a playpen, it can be misused by the adult in charge. Leave a pup in the crate for too long and you invite housebreaking problems, hyperactivity, and stress behaviors. Used sensibly, crates make the world safer for a pup who does not know any better.

A crate can be used when your pup is

- **old enough to control his bladder and bowels.** This varies pup to pup, but don't expect too much too soon. A seven-week-old pup has little or no control over his bladder and bowels. Crating a pup too early can force him to dirty his crate, which can lead to long-term housebreaking problems. Pups can be crated a few hours at a time before four months of age, but not more. If you have to leave your pup all day, either 1) hire a walker to come in once or twice a day, or 2) set your pup up in an area with papers, water, and a crate with the door tied open or removed. The *most important* part of housebreaking a young pup is preventing accidents in his crate. It is the desire to stay clean upon which *all* housebreaking is built. Lose that, and what should have been an easy process will be prolonged (and possibly corrupted).

- **clean in his crate.** Only crate a pup who is clean in the crate. A pup who dirties his crate is either being left in there too long, has worms or a poor, varied diet, has too much absorbent bedding (we recommend none at first), is stressed/upset, or has lost his desire to be clean. Pet store pups can suffer from this last problem. It can usually be resolved with some careful work. (See page 109.)

- **adequately exercised, socialized, and trained.** Sometimes folks can go overboard with the crating. Your pup should not spend the majority of his time in a crate.

Hint: Never put newspapers in a crate. They encourage a pup to use the crate as a bathroom—not what you want. In fact, for all but the boniest pups, do not put any bedding in the crate, as keeping things sparse tends to encourage keeping the crate dry.

Types of Crates

There are numerous types of crates. Our favorite are the plastic crates, as they are, in our experience, safest and most reliable. They last a long time, are hard for the dog to get out of, and clean up well. Their drawback is that they do not fold up, making large ones awkward to move around and hard to store in the city.

Because this dog is crate-trained, he can travel with his owners with ease. This dog is waiting to board a flight at LaGuardia Airport.

Metal crates come in many makes and models. Our primary complaint about many of them is the gap under the door. This is just the right size for your dog to catch her foot in when going in or out. When this happens, the dog's natural reaction is to try to pull herself free, which is frequently impossible (she needs to back up, something she will never think of on her own). This is frightening and painful and can cause real injury.

It is beyond us why the crate manufacturers do not design some solution to this problem. Until they do, blocking that opening with duct tape, cardboard, or a blanket will prevent harm to your pup.

Hint: For your pup's safety, any and all collars should be removed before crating your pup.

Introducing a Crate

A crate is a wonderful training tool for a dog of any age. When possible, introduce the crate over the weekend so there is time for your dog to adapt a bit before you need to put him in for hours on end.

If you have a young pup (under ten weeks old), he can be crated only a couple of hours at a time, so this introduction can be done even more slowly during the time he is confined with a gate.

If the dog is old enough for some crate time, set up the crate in a busy area. If it is a metal crate on a hard floor, put a blanket/bathmat under it to keep the crate from shifting or rattling. Prop open the door or, as with plastic crates, remove it. Then ignore it. Allow the dog to explore it at will. After an hour or so, put in a comfy blanket (which will be removed once the real confinement starts) and toss his toys into it and a few treats as well. Leave a treat or two in front of the crate in plain sight, then ignore it again. Allow the pup to explore at will. Do not attempt to cajole him over and point it out. Both those things tend to make a pup more hesitant.

Once he has checked out the crate for a day or so, start feeding him next to it. If he is relaxed with that, put the food bowl just inside the door. When he eats from that without a problem, move the bowl farther back into the crate. Soon he will be eating inside the crate without problems. Now it is time to put the door back on or unprop it. During meals, close the crate door. Stay right there and open it again before he has a chance to fuss. Be calm and matter-of-fact. After a day or so of this, put him in the crate for naps. Now the barking/fussing may begin.

Game: Love My Crate!

Show your pup a treat, then toss it into the crate. When she is inside eating, step away from the crate. When she comes out of the create, repeat. Once she gets used to this, show her the treat and walk toward the crate, but don't toss one inside. Wait and see if she'll go in on her own. If she does, toss her a treat. If, at any time, she seems reluctant to come out of her crate, toss her another treat. No command is involved, she's just learning that the crate is a pleasant spot.

PREVENTING CRATE DOOR RUSHING

Rushing out of the crate can be prevented by opening the door a small amount but refusing to open it all the way if your pup tries to rush out. Hold it closed, wait for him to stop being pushy, then praise calmly. Now, move to open it slowly again. If he rushes, repeat the procedure. Soon he'll learn that the door opens only when he is calm. (Please, don't try it when he is desperate to go to the bathroom; that isn't fair.)

How to Handle Crate Barking

Start closing the crate door during the day when your pup's normal barking will not unduly disturb neighbors or your own family. Pups bark and fuss until they adjust and realize that quiet behavior is the quickest route to freedom. Following are a few ways you can help your pup to understand this more quickly.

Plan for Success

Start when you have several hours to spend on this. You might want to warn your neighbors that this is going to happen and to thank them, in advance, for their patience. More than one city owner has found that a bottle of wine helps to smooth things over. Choose a time when your pup's bladder is empty and he is tired. Adding a stuffed toy (made for dogs) for companionship can comfort him as well.

Develop Self-Control

A little self-control can help your pup stay calmer in the crate. Some pups are born with it, some need help developing it. Working on self-control exercises such as "leave it" will have gotten your pup well started on the "if I stay calm and control myself, good things will happen" mind-set. (To learn how to start teaching the "leave it" command, see page 80.)

Teach Your Pup to Lie Down

Most pups are calmer when they are lying down. If you've been teaching your puppy to "down" (as described at the end of this chapter), you can use that for crating. Once your pup does a nice down for a food lure outside of the crate, you can start showing her a treat through the gate and lowering it straight down toward the bottom of the gate. Hold it there. In a moment or two she should lie down, at which point reward her with the treat and praise.

If she stays lying down, give her another treat. If she gets up, repeat the lure. Any time you catch her lying down in her crate for the next month or so, give her a treat through the bars (low so she stays down).

Reward Quiet

One of the most effective ways to build calm crate behavior is to reward a calm pup. A small treat through the bars, a couple of warm, calm words, and walk away. Sure, this may start the barking again, but that's okay, as it will give you another chance to reward him when he quiets.

Discourage Noise

Some pups just don't have calm moments. They start crying and forget they can stop. These guys may need some help in creating an opportunity to reward and praise. If your pup's been crying for half an hour without a break, go to a door nearby and give it a flat-handed *whomp*. Many pups will startle into silence for a few seconds. When they do, walk in calmly, give a reward through the bars, praise calmly, and either give your pup another chance to settle or let her out of the crate.

Try never to open the door to a crying puppy because that rewards crying and

 METRODOG

barking with freedom, instilling in her a strong belief that noise will open the crate door. Just the lesson we do *not* want her to learn! Also, if you attempt to placate your pup by talking and empathizing with her, she will think your attention is a reward. The exception to this is a pup who really needs to relieve herself. It won't take you long to learn the difference between complaint and need.

Sit, Then Open the Door

If you've been practicing your pup's sit with a food lure (refer to page 75 for instructions), you can use one to lure him into a sit by placing a treat above his head in a wire crate or at the top of the gate in a plastic crate. Wait. When he sits, drop in the treat and open the door immediately. It may take some time at first, but then he'll catch on and sit like a gentleman whenever you come to let him out.

CONFINEMENT BEHIND A GATE

Gates can be wonderful. We use them a great deal around our home to limit access and to keep puppies in sight at all times. As a tool for confinement, they can present challenges.

The best kind of gate is metal or metal covered with plastic. The plastic mesh/wood baby gates are practically useless, as many pups (even toy breeds) will gnaw their way free in short order.

When installed with a slight inward slant, even a low gate should effectively confine an active pup.

If your pup is large enough, use the vertical bar–type gates sold in many pet supply catalogs, as these are the hardest to climb. If your pup can get his head through these, use a mesh-type gate, but keep in mind that these are quite climbable.

If you have a climber, one trick you can try is resting a shake can (empty, rinsed soda can with twelve pennies inside) on the top of the gate. If the pup starts to wrestle with the gate, the can will tip off and make a noise that should startle the pup. Over time, the pup will associate the sound of the can with his messing with the gate and stop (at least that's the plan; some sound-stable, low-surprise dogs will simply play with the can and then climb the gate). This should be done only when you are home, as you need to be able to reset the can immediately.

Hint: This is *not* a good idea for toy pups, who might be hurt by such an object. However, some sporting breeds, being good sound-tolerant gun dogs, will simply fearlessly pick up the can.

Another trick is to install the gate at a slight angle so the top is leaning inward. This makes it nearly impossible for the pup to climb it.

Last, don't reward jumping and climbing. If, when you go to pick up your pup, he is leaping against the gate (and what pup isn't?), stop. Pick him up only when he's not touching the gate. You can use a treat to lure him off, then pick him up, or you can slap the front of the gate with an open hand to startle him back (and then pick him up). The idea is that he learns that being away from the gate earns freedom. As always, match the method to your pup's temperament (and your own).

TETHERED

Tethering your puppy, which means tying her to something, is the most dangerous option and has only a few safe uses, all of which involve careful supervision.

Tethering should always be done on a flat, nontightening collar and in full view! Never leave any dog tethered while you are gone. A German Shepherd Dog we knew almost lost her leg when she got tangled in the tether and panicked, thereby tightening it steadily. Another dog lost his life tethered to balcony fencing when he leapt over the railing after who knows what and hanged himself.

Tethering is a good way to keep a dog near you and out of trouble, but only under supervision.

FRAP

This phrase, coined by a client years ago, stands for "frenetic random activity period," which is the wild racing around barking crazy session many pups have once or twice a day. FRAPs are normal and generally outgrown if you don't reinforce them. Reinforcement can happen if you attempt to distract the pup with a biscuit or hold her, stroking, to calm her down. (You can use a treat, just get your pup's attention and then have her do a few sits or downs before giving it to her so she learns that listening equals rewards.)

How you choose to handle it will depend on your tolerance that day and your dog's personal FRAP style. If your dog is small and races around quietly, you may just want to sit back and enjoy the show. Such displays of pure joy are rarely seen. But if your Labrador pup takes it as a time to grab your shoe and then leap back, barking, you may want to redirect her efforts.

You have several options, including the following:

Crate your puppy calmly, not as a harsh punishment, but as a way of controlling that energy flow. If she tends to FRAP between 6:20 and 6:30 P.M. (yes, they can be that routine), then why not crate her with a stuffed bone at 6:10?

Exhaust her mind. Self-control and problem solving will tire most pups; so, work on positive tricks or games. Building her response to "Leave it," "Wait," or "Down" can all help. Playing clicker games with her can defuse the behavioral bomb before it detonates in your living room.

Generally, these sessions lessen as your dog matures. And one day you'll notice that some time ago they stopped altogether and you didn't even notice.

Hint: What doesn't work? Getting mad at the pup. She's just doing what comes naturally, she's not being "bad." This is where patience is critical—emotional or angry reactions will only confuse your pup and result in more activity.

THE APARTMENT PUPPY

WHAT IS A CLICKER?

A clicker is a small box that makes a clicking sound when you press it. Combined with food reward, it is used to tell the animal that he's done something you like. Why use a click when praise tells them the same thing? you ask. It is a little bit different. Praise tells your dog you are pleased with him, while the clicker clearly marks the exact behavior you are pleased with. All we can say is, try it. (*Hint:* Start with it in your pocket or wrap your hand in a towel to muffle the sound to avoid stressing sound-sensitive dogs. Once your dog knows that clicks equal food, you can relax.)

Making It through the Night

In a nutshell, keep your puppy with you if you want to sleep (and if you want your neighbors to sleep). Work on confinement manners during the day, sleep at night. There are three ways to accomplish this.

CRATE YOUR PUP NEXT TO THE BED

Here's the best choice. Crate him right next to you so he can hear and smell you close at hand. If you use a wire crate, put newspaper *between* the metal tray and the bottom of the crate. The pup can't get to it, but it will help muffle any rattling as he moves around at night.

If the crate itself is on a hardwood floor, putting a folded towel or blanket underneath can keep it from slipping, rattling, and scratching the floor.

There are many "old wives' tales" around for helping pups sleep, and as it so often turns out, those "old wives" were no fools. Worth trying is a ticking clock

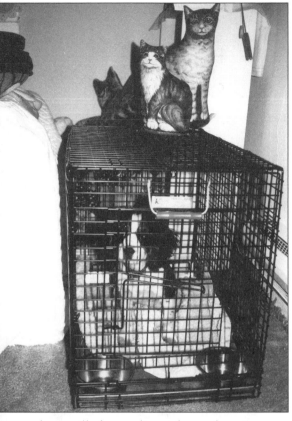

This crate is set up right next to the bed. Notice that the food and water bowls are empty long before we go to sleep.

wrapped in a towel (be sure the alarm is *off*), a hot-water bottle wrapped in a towel, a stuffed, soft, safe dog toy about the size of the pup or a little larger (simulates siblings), a freshly worn sweatshirt, or, for the cold-loving pups, a frozen plastic liter bottle of water. As always, collars come off before crating your pup.

KEEP YOUR PUP ON THE BED WITH YOU

Who gets the wet spot? Actually, many pups will stay clean on a bed; the problem is that they will get *off* the bed. Some toy breed pups (and others) can get hurt jumping off a bed. If they manage to land safely, they will then relieve themselves in your bedroom. In addition, they can't hop back on, so they're left roaming free to get into trouble of all kinds.

TETHER YOUR PUP NEXT TO THE BED

If you choose this, the tether needs to be short so the pup can't move away from the area, pee, and return to sleep, nor can she hop onto the bed or get tangled in anything. When we use this method, we tether the pup to the leg of the bed up near my head, where I can hang an arm over and check the pup in the middle of the night.

SARAH WILSON

Most important, having a puppy is just plain fun, as this dog/owner team demonstrates nicely.

The downsides to this are that the pup can still get tangled and possibly hurt herself without your ever hearing a sound. And it does not prevent chewing—the undersides of your mattress, the corner of your blanket, the leg of your bed (anything within reach is fair game to the average pup). We use this method cautiously, never sleep well when we do it, and much prefer a crate.

Hint: Do not leave your pup loose in your bedroom. This may seem like the easiest answer, but she could hurt herself while you sleep. Things you do not think twice about—the cord to your clock, a pair of panty hose in an open drawer, a stray pin from a shirt—all these things can kill your puppy.

Melodramatic? Not if it's your puppy. A great deal of a young thing's charm is its innocence, and that innocence makes it vulnerable. When you consider if a room is safe, ask yourself, What could she possibly get into? and not, What do I think she'll get into? We promise you, your pup will find things to do that never occurred to you.

Quarantine: Why and for How Long?

In many cities, your veterinarian will tell you not to take your pup outside until he has had all his shots. This has been the common practice for years, because one shot or even two may not give your pup adequate protection from some serious common diseases.

METRODOG

This is because when your puppy suckled from his mother, he received protection from disease in her milk (maternal antibodies). The strength of that protection differs. Sometimes the maternal antibodies fade early (by eight or nine weeks), but more often they hold longer (for twelve weeks or more). While the mother's protection is in your pup's body, his immune system does not respond, and it won't respond until the mother's protection fades away. Once hers is gone, the pup's defenses will kick in.

The problem is that because no one can tell how long the maternal antibodies will last, there may well be a gap between when they fade and the next vaccination. For example, say your pup gets vaccinated at eight weeks, but the mother's protection is still present. Then the maternal antibodies fade between weeks nine and ten. Your pup's next vaccine isn't due until eleven weeks of age, so now your pup has no protection from these diseases.

This is why vets want pups to be quarantined, to protect them during this vulnerable period. How long your veterinarian advises you to quarantine varies from city to city and veterinarian to veterinarian.

Now, this advice is not without controversy.

Trainers and behaviorists point out that the age of quarantine is a critical one for socialization and that a dog is more likely to be killed for a behavior problem than to die of parvo or distemper.

People are now pressing the veterinary community to offer safe alternatives that allow for earlier socialization of dogs. Be sure to discuss safe options with your veterinarian, as she will be aware of any outbreaks of "hot zones" in your area.

SOCIALIZATION

Put simply, socialization means exposing your puppy to the world in safe, not overwhelming, ways. This is critical, because it is in the early months of a pup's life that he learns about people, other dogs, other animals, and the environment in general.

If your pup grows up in your apartment, he thinks that apartment is pretty much the whole world. When you take him for his first walk, he's in for a shock that would be fairly similar to the one you'd receive if you were raised completely indoors until you were ten years old (never saw a photo, watched TV, or read a book about the outside world) and were then taken to Grand Central Terminal.

Socialization is not hard, and the time you spend on it is all worth it. It is not necessary to get your pup out every single day, but exposure to something new several times a week is productive. Even just sitting on the steps of your building (if you have steps) can be a reasonably safe activity, while giving

---

If your pup is small enough to carry, feel free to take her out and about early.

CHRISTINE PELLICANO

SARAH WILSON

Who's having more fun? The baby? The puppy? This is good socialization at work.

 METRODOG

Bracken is a good and careful teacher, and Lila is having a great time learning canine manners. But supervision and knowing your dog are key.

your pup a chance to look around. Here are some more suggestions from individuals who have wrestled with this situation:

"One of my favorite ways to socialize a puppy that is not yet fully vaccinated is to set up 'playdates' the same way you do with a small child who is not yet in school. I choose only dogs I know have been vaccinated, and I avoid dogs who are involved in any organized activity at that time. Obedience classes, agility, and flyball trials are all good places to pick up germs, and it is not worth exposure to the puppy. I also avoid people and dogs who have been in contact with strange animals (or have just been adopted from a shelter or purchased from a pet store) in the last fourteen days."

—Kim Helstein, Quianna Kennels,
Ontario, Canada

"When we take a young pup outside, we are especially vigilant about where we let the puppy toilet. We try to avoid the grassy strips along the pavement because they're highly frequented. We wash off the puppy's feet as soon as we come inside—not a great effort at surgical sterilization, just swabbing with a washcloth.

"You can't overinvest in socialization, and you don't have a lot of time to cash

THE APARTMENT PUPPY   49

in on the 'imprinting' effect with a puppy. Yes, there's a risk of parvo and other nasties, but there's also a risk of having a puppy grow up without benefit of early socialization."

—GEOFF STERN, Charles River Dog Training Club,
Boston, Mass.

"Here is one thing I do to socialize my young pups when I wish to take them many places with me but do not want them walking on the ground or floor and picking up germs. I bought a backpack that has mesh panel across most of the front. I cut a piece of wood to fit the bottom to give it stability and put a towel on the bottom for comfort.

"I wear it turned around so the puppy rides in front on my chest. The puppy in it can see and hear and smell all of the sights and sounds around him. It has a tie string at the top so the pup can't get out. But when they are used to it and will not jump out, I open the top closure and they can stick their head out the top. I can take them safely almost anywhere in this."

—LINDA MCCUE, TaiKesh Tibetan Terriers,
Ottawa, Ontario

"Form minigroup at a friend's home, inside, take turns among friends' homes, add children. Should work well for those who are careful to keep their pups' feet and noses off of grounds where dogs frequent. Even if it's only a few pups involved, the changes into new homes, doing some hands-on touching, sitting for treats, and a short off-leash playtime, the benefit is worth the slight risk, just make sure that everyone has the same feelings about keeping their pups away from possible contaminated areas."

—JENNY CRABTREE, Australian Cattle Dog Rescue
in Ohio

Puppy Kindergarten

Your puppy can be socialized as she learns. Most cities have wonderful training programs available. Look for a small group run in a way that makes sense to you.

Observe some classes. Look for happy people and puppies. The focus should be on fun, as the focus of any kindergarten is on fun. Sure, the pups are learning, but there is no reason to tell them yet (or ever) that learning is anything but a type of play.

YOUR END OF THE DEAL

Playgroups are great, but with them comes risk. Some common things that owners need to both be aware of and accept are that pups may pick up a minor infectious disease such as an eye infection or kennel cough (even when vaccinated against it). They are also more at risk for minor injury, as are children who play at school or on teams. The owner needs to take the occasional "skinned knee," tooth mark, sprain, or broken toenail in stride. Such small matters are to be expected even in the best facilities and are well worth the risk, as long as the facility is well run and professional.

Puppy Playgroups

Ask your local vets, shelters, and trainers if there are any puppy playgroups in the area. This is a free service we offered in New York City that the owners loved. Once people got to know us, they frequently signed up for classes. It served both the community's needs and ours. It also allowed for early identification and intervention on budding behavioral or health problems. A veterinarian, groomer, day care facility, or trainer could all benefit from offering these professionally supervised hours of socialization and fun.

If you have a small breed, please look for a playgroup for small breeds or form

THE APARTMENT PUPPY

your own with a couple of other small-breed owners. The exception to this is some terriers who, regardless of physical size, may do best with larger pups.

At our small dog playgroup in NYC, both owners and pups can relax and have a nice time.

Downtown

The greatest risk for your pup will come from areas that are frequented by large numbers of dogs. Therefore parks, dog runs, grassy strips, and any area where there are strays are the most dangerous spots for pups who are not yet fully vaccinated. Alternatively, areas that are not frequented by many dogs are comparatively safe, though nothing is risk free. For many communities, these comparatively safe locations include business districts and downtown areas.

Wherever you are, steer your pup away from dog feces, as that is a primary way viruses are passed from dog to dog.

SANITY SAVERS: GAMES FOR TIRED OWNERS AND ACTIVE PUPS

Quarantine can seem like some of the longest weeks of your life. When you've been working all day and are exhausted and your pup's been napping all day and is raring to go, conflict is bound to result. How to avoid that? Try any of these activities:

Food Cube

A toy that holds dry food inside. As the pup nudges and noses it around, a pellet will fall out randomly. Some dogs find that mighty entertaining and will play with it for long periods. Worth a try.

Find It!

Have someone hold the pup (or put her on lead and loop the lead over a door-knob). Show her a biscuit or toy. Get her excited about it. Then put it down a couple of yards away, but right where she can see it. Get her and tell her, "Find It!" Go with her to the treat/toy.

Do this a couple of times. Now, put her reward just out of her sight. Repeat as before.

As she comes to understand the game, begin to hide the treat/toy in harder places—first just out of sight, later in places she'll have to really work hard to get to. If she ever seems stumped, happily help her out. Soon she'll hunt high and low when she hears those magic words "Find It!"

Word of advice: Don't teach your pup to dig into the couch or open the cupboards looking for her reward. These "skills" will not be nearly so charming when your pup decides to do them on her own when you're not looking.

Which Hand?

Put a biscuit in one hand and make a fist, leaving the fingers a bit open. Put both hands out in front of you and ask your dog: "Which hand?" Let him sniff both hands, and when he sniffs, licks, or paws the hand with the biscuit in it—open your hand and let him get it.

Dogs catch on to this game fast. Soon you can keep a small treat in a tight fist and your dog will show you quickly that he's not fooled.

QUIET TIME

What crayons and a *Sesame Street* video do for children, these next toys do for puppies. Priceless bearers of an almost guaranteed fifteen minutes of peace and quiet.

Supervised Rawhide

Rawhides are surprisingly controversial in some circles. Some say they have too many toxic chemicals in them. The answer to that charge is to buy bones made in the United States, unbleached bones, or organic rawhides.

Some people say they are dangerous and that dogs can choke on them. (And, in fact, dogs do choke to death on them every year.) The answer to that is supervision and proper-size bones. If your pup can swallow the bone/chip, it is too small. Once the bone or chip is softened by chewing so that it can be swallowed, throw it out. Not sure if it is safe or not? Throw it out. Supervise your dog when he chews, especially if he is a vigorous chewer.

Avoid chews made of tiny bits of rawhides pressed together (often in unnatural colors and shapes), as these are too easily consumed and can cause diarrhea. Also, who knows what dyes and chemicals go into them! Compressed rawhides, several brownish gray layers formed under pressure into bones, rolls, and so on, can make long-lasting chew items.

Stuffed Kong

Take one Kong toy, insert a few biscuits or smear the inside with cream cheese or a bit of peanut butter, and let your dog have at it. Most dogs will work hard to get out every bit of yum.

Stuffed Bone

Same game as with the Kong, works just as well. Either toy can be put in the dishwasher if need be.

Frozen Rope Bone

Take one rope toy. Soak it in water, wring it out, then freeze it. Cool chew for a teething pup.

BEING A ROLE MODEL

Dogs look to the leader to see how to handle a new situation. Your pup will look to you. The rule? Act as you want the dog to act. If you want the pup to accept that noisy bus, you accept it. Keep your breathing even and regular, walk at a relaxed pace, speak in a happy, cheerful tone. Your pup will understand that everything is okay. But if, when your pup leaps in fear, you hold your breath, speak in a worried tone, and stroke him quickly, he will read your concern and add it to his. So model the behavior you want and you will be more likely to get it.

Good Habits: Start Now!

Whether you mean to or not, your pup's education begins the day you bring him home. At seven or eight weeks old, he is a learning machine. Nothing goes unnoticed.

SARAH WILSON

"I may be small, but I'm ready to learn; are you ready to teach?"

If you reach to pet him, he mouths you, then you pet him—he has just been taught to mouth.

If you reach to pet him, he mouths you, you withdraw and ignore him for a few seconds, then try again—he learns that mouthing does not get him attention. Every interaction teaches him something. What do you want him to learn?

It may be necessary to have your pup under physical control while doing some problem solving, so let's start by discussing how to introduce your pup to a lead and collar.

INTRODUCING THE COLLAR AND LEAD

These two commonly used training tools can make your (and your pup's) life easier or more difficult, depending on you. To make things easier, use a wide, flat buckle collar on your pup. You will be in teaching mode for several months at least and will not be using many (if any) corrections. First you teach, then you practice, then you proof or test or challenge your dog. Corrections come after the dog fully understands what is expected.

Many breeders use collars as a way to tell pups apart, and thanks to these, the pups become comfortable in a collar. If this hasn't happened to your pup and it is a new experience, introduce the collar simply by putting it on. You should be able

 **METRODOG**

to slip two fingers between the collar and your pup's neck without much trouble. Too loose and she may get a paw caught in it from scratching it. Too tight and it may irritate her. Expect scratching, maybe a little whining, falling over, or turning around. This is normal. Leave it on until she ignores it, then remove it. Repeat a few times a day, and in a day or two it can be on full-time without a problem.

Traditionally, introducing the lead meant clipping it on and allowing the pup to drag it wherever she went. Unfortunately, this teaches the pup that she can go wherever she wants when on lead. Try another approach, one that teaches something entirely different. Take one hungry pup and one pile of delicious treats, clip on the lead, hook it over something stationary (we hook it on the far-side doorknob and then close the door on the lead), and sit down nearby. Understandably, she will probably fuss since she doesn't know why she can't move about freely. Ignore any upset. Wait for the one moment when she stops fussing and the lead slackens a bit. At that moment, praise her and give her a treat. (If you're using a clicker, click the instant there is slack in the lead.)

WHAT IS A CORRECTION?

Anything your dog doesn't enjoy can be used as a correction. One of the most mild but effective forms of correction is the removal of a reward. Show your pup a treat, she jumps up, you put the treat behind your back, she sits, you give the treat. You've just corrected jumping and rewarded sitting. A typical list of corrections might include removal of treat or toy, stopping praise, stopping petting, ignoring the pup, tethering or removing the pup away from you, verbal disapproval, a sudden, startling sound, a spritz of water from a plant sprayer, a well-timed leash correction. Notice we do not include hitting, yelling, shaking, smacking, yanking. Anger does not belong in teaching.

Why?

Because we want to teach the pup from the very start that pulling on lead is *not* effective. It does *not* get you where you want to go. We want her to learn that not pulling gets the good stuff. If she learns this young and we play walking games with her in the apartment, we may get a pup who backs up when she feels tension rather than lunging forward when we get outside.

Once she is calm when tethered (always with you right next to her), start working on walking. Praise her warmly for walking with you. She will probably balk and jump around, but just stay calm and wait her out. When she stops, call her to you and reward her. By ignoring her upset and rewarding calm behavior, she will soon be walking after you like an old pro.

Here are a few games to play once your pup is used to the lead:

Stop, Then Go

This simple game can have a big impact. Around the apartment or halls, walk with your pup. When the lead gets tight—stop. Simply stop. Say nothing. Wait. When the lead goes a little slack—praise and reward the pup, then start walking again.

The rules are simple: Tight = Stop. Slack = Walk.

We don't expect this to hold up under temptation, but this early habit will become a pup's natural response to leash tension, which will be mighty helpful when he is eighty-five pounds of gangly enthusiasm.

Treat Retreats

This game works well with the "leave it" (see page 80) exercises. Hook your pup up on lead attached to something immobile. Show him a treat (keep a better one in your other hand) and put that not-so-good treat on the floor three or four feet away from your pup.

At first he may show some interest. When he allows slack in the lead, praise him and give the even better treat. Repeat. You can slowly move the not-so-good treat on the floor closer to him, which will increase the temptation. Often, in less

 **METRODOG**

than a week, you'll have a pup who will not leap at food on the ground but will wait, with slack lead, for his reward. Now, wouldn't that be nice?

Follow the Lure

With your pup on lead to your left side (nothing is magic about your left side, just training tradition), show your pup a treat in your left hand. With the pup focused on the treat, take a step or two forward, then, if the pup is still focused on the treat, give him the reward and praise. The game is: Show lure, focus pup, take a step or two, feed, and praise.

This game can be played with equal success with a desired toy. If you keep a special latex squeaky toy set aside for this exercise, you will find most pups eager to play this game.

Either way, the goal is to teach your pup that attention equals reward.

CONTROLLING BARKING

Few canine behaviors cause more urban problems than barking. There are several things you can do with your pup to prevent barking from developing in the first place.

Play Stops When Barking Starts

If, while romping with your pup, she starts to yip in excitement, say nothing. Simply become very calm and very quiet, get up, remove any toy that was involved, and go sit down for a few minutes. During this time, ignore the dog.

After a few minutes, start the game again. Repeat as above. You may spend quite a bit of time starting and stopping at first, but your pup should soon make the connection and attempt to control herself when excited.

Do Not Reward Vocalizing

A reward is anything your dog enjoys. So if you are watching TV and your pup wanders over and whines at you, and you absentmindedly scoop her up and stroke her belly so she doesn't interrupt your favorite show—you have just rewarded her for making noise.

Similar interactions happen when owners are on the phone and the pup is in a crate or behind a gate. What about when she is excited by the door because she knows someone is coming to visit? Just ask yourself: In this situation, is making noise getting my pup what she wants? If the answer is yes, you must turn the tables so that silence gets the goodies, not noise.

LURE? REWARD?

A lure is used to guide the dog into the behavior you want. A reward is given to the dog after he has completed an action. A lure is used to initially teach a behavior, but move to a reward as soon as you possibly can. If you stay with a lure too long, the pup may start performing only when a lure is present. It is your job, as the teacher, to keep expecting more from your student. If your fourth-grade teacher was still giving you gold stars for saying "cat," wouldn't you have become bored long ago?

JUMPING UP

A dog who greets you and others politely with four on the floor will make him more likable to others and less of a hassle for you.

Most of us reward some jumping in puppyhood, but be aware that every time you do so, you make jumping as an adult harder to control.

There are a few ways to deal with puppy jumping:

Ignore

This is the simplest answer. Ignore it. When your pup jumps, do not look at him, speak to him, or touch him. Stand still, look away, and wait. The *instant* he stops

When the pup jumps up,
trainer Toni Kay-Wolff puts the treat
to her nose . . .

. . . guides her off by
lowering the treat down
and away from her . . .

. . . and lures her into a sit.
Good work, you two!

jumping, praise him and give a treat if you so desire.
This will no doubt get him jumping again. Good!
Gives you another chance to educate him. Repeat as
above. Soon he'll get the idea.

Redirect with Food Lure

When ignoring isn't reasonable, try redirecting your pup. Do not stroke her or
speak kindly to her when she jumps (or unkindly to her, either; she is, after all, just
paying you a compliment). Simply reach down and lure (guide) her off as you say,

"Off," then praise her. You can also use a treat/toy to lure her into a sit, then give it to her.

Step On the Lead

Another option is to allow your pup to drag a lead around in the apartment attached to a wide, flat buckle collar. When he comes over to greet you, step on the lead (knee bent, weight over foot on the lead). If he jumps, he will self-correct. As always, ignore the unwanted jumping and wait patiently. When he stops trying to jump—reward him with words, touch, and treats. Try to say, "Off," just as he is taking his feet off of you. If he starts to jump again, ignore him and wait.

While you are teaching your pup these new skills, ask your guests to make things easy and ignore your pup. If you ask them for their help, you may get more cooperation than if you tell them what to do. Also, giving people a chance to participate, by doling out treats when the pup sits, can get people positively involved.

WHAT NOT TO DO

Do not inflict pain or confusion on your puppy for being happy. Skip all the methods that talk about paw squeezing, toe stomping, chest kneeing, and the like.

Will some of those work?

Sometimes, but they also teach your pup that you randomly inflict pain. That out of the blue a person may hurt him for being friendly. Is that a lesson you want him to learn?

MOUNTING PROBLEMS

Pups mount things—each other, stuffed animals, pillows, your leg. Some pups do this when they become excited/stimulated. Others do it because they've learned it gets them all sorts of attention. And a few really ambitious types mount early in life because they plan to rule their world as soon as they are able. Notice that none of these reasons involves the pup being "turned on" by your shin.

This may seem like a slightly amusing problem, but a client of ours is actually being sued by a disgruntled employee who claims that the client's dog "disfigured" her knee. We cannot imagine what she means by this, but it's a strange world these days. Be cautious.

Ways of handling this behavior include the following:

- As with jumping up, if you step on the lead where it touches the ground when the dog/pup is standing, he will correct himself when he attempts to "mount up." Ignore his efforts to jump, then praise him calmly when he stops.
- Try a firm "Off" and physically guiding him off by the collar. Calmness reigns. This is not a big deal, so don't make it one with your reaction.
- Neutering early is a good idea for persistent male pups.
- Increase your work sessions (keep them short, under five minutes, but do them frequently). Then direct your pup away from the mounting and to a more desirable behavior like "down" or "sit."
- Don't play games that get your pup intensely excited.
- Try a spritz of water from a plant mister. This isn't likely to deter a water-loving dog like a Labrador, but it might surprise a toy breed enough that he'll hop off, creating an opportunity for praise.

If your pup persists, don't get into a battle with him. Just calmly put him in his crate for a few minutes. After that, let him out again. If he mounts you or a guest, remove him again. Repeat this as you have tolerance to do so, because eventually he's going to connect mounting with time alone and start cutting back on the behavior.

ACCEPTING HANDLING

A dog who can handle your handling is easier to groom, less stressed at the veterinarian, and more relaxed about home health maintenance like ear cleaning or wound treatment. How do you teach your dog to accept your handling calmly? Here are a few easy things to do on a daily basis:

When your pup is sleepy, run your hands over her body and down her legs;

Begging is easier to start than stop.

touch all her paws. Put your fingers between her paw pads, extend her nail, wiggle the toes, lift the ear flaps, massage her gums, and generally put your fingers anywhere (within reason) that normal grooming and care will require you to touch.

If your puppy resists or is never *that* sleepy, you can use treats. (This game is even easier with a helper.) Take the treat, let your puppy lick at it in your fingers, handle a foot gently, then immediately give her the treat. (If you have an assistant, have him give the treat for you.) So it's show the treat, touch the foot, give the treat, and praise. Repeat on each foot. You can apply the same principle to looking in her ears.

A fun game I heard first at a Donna Duford lecture was this: To get your pup used to having her mouth opened, open her mouth, pop in a treat, and release. Open, treat, release. Do this three or four times a day for a week or so and your dog will be hoping you open her mouth. Fun and effective, and it builds the dog's desire to want to do what you want her to do—perfect!

BEGGING

Preventing begging is pretty simple: Don't feed your dog from the table or your plate.

We know: "He's so cute," "It's just this once," "After all, the morsel already fell on the floor," "It's gristle," or whatever. Fine. If you want him to have it, put it in his bowl after the meal is over. Or go ahead and feed him when you are at the table, just don't get upset later when he sticks a drooling muzzle on your knee, woofs at you for a piece of your dinner, or attempts to take the food off your plate.

"Yeah, I'm chewing your T-shirt . . . and your point is?" If you don't prevent chewing now, you'll be dealing with it for years to come.

DESTRUCTIVE CHEWING

All pups chew. Some pups chew a lot. Any dog can be a rampant chewer, but a few breeds—usually the really athletic ones like retrievers and Siberian Huskies—chew as a favorite hobby. Accepting that chewing is a normal part of being a dog, not a dog being "bad," will help keep the focus on prevention rather than correction.

Stress and/or lack of exercise can increase chewing. So can punishing the dog for it after the fact. Since punishment often is both confusing and scary, your dog's stress level will increase, and so will his . . . you guessed it! Chewing!

So prevention is the name of the game. Either remove the chewable things from your dog or remove your dog from the chewable things. This means putting away shoes, socks, underwear, panty hose, and any other item of clothing that your pup might find seductively stinky. To your pup, to smell you is to love you, so in your absence something with your smell on it (the more the better) is a comfort.

If clothing isn't available, then the TV remote you held last night as you ate dinner, your eyeglasses, your wallet, the seat of your favorite chair—those things will do as well.

We recommend confining your pup away from these items any time you cannot keep your eyes on him.

Redirect him to appropriate chew toys. No, not the old sneaker you have in your closet that you don't care about. The fact you don't care about it will be lost on your pup. All he will learn is "My human likes it when I chew his shoes."

This pup needs chew toys—good solid chew toys. Hard rubber Kongs, nylon bones, sterilized bones, and rope toys all fill that bill. If your dog is not a heavy chewer or you are willing to supervise his playtime, then latex squeaky toys and stuffed toys made for dogs are also big favorites.

If you see your pup eyeing the antique table leg, redirect him to a toy by asking excitedly, "Hey, pup, where's your ball (or bone or squeaky)?" and then going with him to get it. Play with him a few seconds to get him focused on it, then let him be. Over time he should trot off to find his toys when he has the urge to chew.

One hundred percent supervision/confinement/redirection will get you through puppyhood damage free.

SUBMISSIVE URINATION

When you reach toward your pup to pet her, she leaves a tiny (or not so tiny) pool of piddle. Is this a housebreaking problem? Should you correct her? Doesn't she "know better"?

In short, no, no, and no.

Urinating when a human greets her or when a human is upset is a polite puppy signal. It simply says, "I am a small puppy. You are big and strong. I salute you the only way I know how." This behavior is thought to be left over from the first few weeks or so of life. During this time, pups go only when the mother dog licks their rears, consuming the urine. This allows the mother to keep the den area virtually spotless and helps prevent disease and predator-attracting smells.

Most pups will grow out of "submissive urination" if you ignore it. Never scold them for it. If you do, this will guarantee that it will be set in stone. (After all, they are trying to appease you. If you get upset with them, they will try to appease you more.) Some breeds, such as the American Cocker Spaniel and Golden Retrievers, seem to be more prone to this behavior.

What to do:

- Instead of greeting your pup when you come in, ignore her and toss her a biscuit. Anticipating the treat and eating it keeps her out of submissive mode and may help prevent the behavior.
- As this problem is worse when the pup is excited, have guests ignore your pup for the first five to ten minutes until things calm down.

- Have them greet her when sitting (or squatting). Have them reach under her chin to scratch her neck. Don't reach over her head or bend over her. Both gestures have dominant meanings to a pup, who may respond by showing submission—for example, urinating.
- Greet the pup on an easy-to-clean surface. Even an old towel can become a greeting area, absorbing the urine before the pup dances in it gleefully.
- If your pup pees with excitement when you reach to open the crate door, try this. Do not look at or speak to her. Turn to the side when you reach to open the door and move away immediately, allowing the pup to come on out. Immediately toss down a treat or two to give her something else to do.
- If she urinates when you reach to put on the lead, again, give her a treat, then reach underneath her chin to clip on the lead. Do not look at or speak to your pup while you do this. Squat and turn sideways rather than bending over her.
- Last, don't scold or hit your pup in general, as this will frighten her—making submissive displays more likely. This doesn't mean let her do anything she wants, it means teaching her the right stuff and ignoring or calmly dealing with what you don't want. Try to keep negative emotions out of the mix.

FEAR OR SENSITIVE PERIODS

Most pups will show fear at some point. In fact, pups go through fear (or sensitive) periods as they mature. The classic ages for these are around eight and then eleven weeks, but each pup is a bit different; for some, these periods can arrive any time between seven and twelve weeks. These "sensitive periods" can revisit your dog during maturation. Don't be surprised to see them again at around five months and then between seven and nine months. What your pup needs most during these times are support, guidance, and structure.

This looks like a stable dog taking all in stride: The food vendor, the woman with the bags, and the crowd are of no concern.

Dealing with Different Temperaments

You will be a more effective teacher/trainer if you know your dog's temperament tendencies and then deal with them accordingly. Which category fits your dog best?

SENSITIVE

The sensitive dog is a shy, sound-sensitive, visual-sensitive, "takes everything to heart" dog who has large reactions to new things in his environment. Generally these are the dogs who freeze, slink off, cower, and look extremely "upset" when stressed.

The sensitive dog may approach people, but when the human reaches out the dog retreats, urinates submissively, or turns his head away. When people visit he may anxiously approach and retreat while barking.

Other signs of stress include startling, tucking his tail, pulling toward home, shaking, panting rapidly, and climbing your leg. Less obvious signs might be pupil

dilation, closing his mouth, licking his lips, sweating from his paw pads, displaying a tense muzzle with facial wrinkling, ducking behind you, and clinging to the side of the building on a walk.

What Can You Do?

To help this dog, encourage him to explore and be bold by behaving as you want him to behave. Be observant and reward even the smallest sign of exploration, play, happiness, confidence, or even lack of fear. Introduce him to new things regularly, but in small doses that he can handle. Use treats generously to help your dog enjoy new things. Know that he is depending on you to teach him to be safe, secure, directed, and happy in what is a challenging environment for all.

Explore "clicker training," which is a great way to build confident behavior. Look in our resources section for information on this fun way to communicate. Join small, fun training classes. If your pup's fearful reactions are severe, please consider getting the help of a private trainer or behaviorist. Timely intervention can help prevent tendencies from becoming habits.

REACTIVE

When a reactive dog gets stimulated, he may spin, bite the lead, race back and forth, leap up, and grab your clothing or hands. The common human reactions to frustration and pain, such as yelling, slapping, fast movements, and pushing the dog away, all cause these dogs to act out more intensely.

What Can You Do?

Whenever possible, allow the world, rather than you, to correct and control. You need to be a source of reward, calm reassurance, and direction. Relax and model calm behavior for this dog, because the calmer you are, the calmer the dog can become.

Keep his able mind occupied. Structure his day by having him work for everything he enjoys, taking him to class, and exercising him. Give him many ways to succeed and few ways to fail. We've had great success with calm, clear leash and collar work with these dogs. Unable to structure themselves, they seem to benefit from having you take over that job. Luring into position with food can work well, but the food can overly excite some reactives. Try either a different, less exciting food or a different method. Clicker work can focus these dogs. A head halter, introduced slowly, can be helpful, though the reactive may fight it at first. (Please see page 180 for information about head halters.)

Reactives can be astonishing working dogs once you learn how to help them display their innate intelligence.

BOLD

A bold dog pulls you out the door, greets everyone like a long-lost friend, has little fear of other dogs, and generally lets the world know that she has arrived! Her motto would be "Howdy, we've never met, but you're gonna love me!" Things don't startle her much, and she recovers quickly if they do. She lives her life on the far end of the leash, dragging you off to some new adventure.

What Can You Do?

This temperament is both easy and challenging. It is easy because this type of dog is unlikely to build stress about life in the city. She copes well with the urban hustle and bustle. She doesn't mind a few minor changes in schedule and is fine with strangers both human and canine.

But she can be challenging. She will absolutely take over the leadership position if you let her. She may run off to parts unknown to explore. She is likely to look at you when you issue a command with a "So?" look on her face. She needs consistent direction. Use your commands all the time, especially when she least expects it, then be ready to reward immediately when she complies.

INDEPENDENT

He isn't frightened of much. Strangers? He can take 'em or leave 'em. Follow you around the apartment? Why? He knows where you are going. When he obeys a command, you can pet him, but don't be surprised if he wanders away in the middle. When guests come by, he gives a brief sniff, then goes about his business.

What Can You Do?

Make yourself relevant. Have your dog respond to a command to get to anything he desires. This will get his attention. Once he understands the deal—listen to you and all good things come—he will start focusing on you more.

Another option is to put away his food bowl and feed him completely by hand and only in small doses when he listens and responds. Measure out the day's food in the morning; then, if he gives you no response or a slow response, let him see you throw that handful back in the food bag.

Give him brief, sincere bouts of attention—less than ten seconds each—then ignore him. Always try to stop before he withdraws. Leave him wanting more!

STABLE

She startles, but then explores, hangs back for a second, then says hello to a friendly stranger. She's aware of all that goes on around her, but it does not frighten her unduly. She does not build stress about things and is as relaxed at the end of the walk as she was at the beginning.

What Can You Do?

Enjoy! Expose her to new things, have fun, teach her everything, treat her as the partner/companion/buddy that she longs to be. Build on the good behavior, ignore or redirect the less wanted behavior, and she will flower into a terrific companion. The biggest threat to the stable dog is that she is so darn good, you can let her training slide. Don't, she's got too much potential for that.

REWARDS

A reward is anything your dog enjoys. Your pup's list may include (but not be limited to) belly rubs, laughter, treats, ear rubs, praise, tennis balls, rawhide, dinner, curling up on your lap, chasing you around the apartment, an ice cube, gentle stroking, a chunk of apple, a chance to go out the front door . . . be creative. Use anything he enjoys as a way to reward a job well done. The more creative you are, the more interested and focused he will likely be.

Commands Every Metropuppy Should Know

Following is the first stage of command training. At this stage your job is to teach the dog/pup that a certain cue—in this case a word or command—means he should do a specific behavior. This work is done indoors, in a calm environment.

The second stage is described in chapter 3, "Hitting the Streets," and talks about how to build response in more distracting situations, as well as how to physically enforce the command should that be necessary.

Proofing your dog's response so that he responds regardless of what is going on is described in chapter 4, "Inner-City Youth." Then in chapter 5, "Smooth Sailing," more attention is given to some of the behaviors people find most challenging, such as jumping up, pulling on lead, and not coming when called.

Though these stages are put into age-related chapters, all dogs need to go through these training stages regardless of age. So if you've just adopted a gleeful Lab mix from your local shelter (good for you!), start here.

When to Start Training?

Right now, today, no time to waste.

Every time your pup interacts with you, she is learning to be polite and respectful, compliant and responsive, or she is learning to be rude and pushy, intrusive and demanding. Which would you prefer?

Rules to Live By

- Make a list of what you want to see in your adult dog. When you know where you are going, it is much more likely that you will get there.
- Only encourage behavior in your puppy that you want in your adult dog. That cute little game where you roll on the floor while your pup jumps all over you and bites at your face? Picture that with an adult dog. Does it still seem fun?
- If you let it slide when your pup does not respond to your "sit" command, your adult dog is likely to ignore you as well.
- Rude for people is rude for your pup as well. Falling into this category is leaping onto your lap without permission, mouthing your hands, bumping into you "by mistake," growling over food, or "humping" you.

Every puppy should learn a few commands. Not only does this make them easier to live with, it also teaches them how to learn. Once they understand that sounds can actually mean something specific, they will learn more quickly throughout their life.

What you need: a leash, a flat buckle collar, some soft, easy-to-eat treats, a few minutes of free time, a willingness to have some fun, and knowing what to do.

Many wonderful methods are available these days, and we offer you a couple of favorites here. In general, persistence and practice will get you results using almost any method. Please, avoid methods that focus on catching your dog making a "mistake" and punishing him for it. If you aren't spending the majority of your time praising/rewarding the pup, then stop! Find another way.

Keep the sessions short but frequent. Pups can pick things up astonishingly quickly, but keep in mind that it can take hundreds of repetitions for a command/behavior combination to really sink into a pup's mind.

MY PUP DOESN'T LIKE TREATS!

If your pup won't work for treats, try better treats (maybe bits of cheese or plain chicken meat) and try working him before a meal or ignoring him for half an hour before you train. If none of that helps, try a toy or play. See if something else will motivate your pup. If that doesn't help, you can move on to placing your pup into position and praising. Generations of dog trainers have used it, and it will work for you if you keep at it. The real secret of training is sheer persistence.

CHRISTINE PELLICANO

This Bulldog pup is learning early how to sit on command. Doesn't he look relaxed and focused?

SIT

Used at curbs, at doorways, in the elevator, greeting people, and waiting in line, this is an essential command for every Metrodog. It is also a wonderful way to quickly get some control over a rambunctious pup, work her brain when she is bored or restless, and start any dog's education.

Step One

Goal: For the pup to follow a treat with her nose, raise her head, and lower her rump to the ground.

You: Holding treat between fingers so the pup can't grab it, place the food just in front of your dog's nose. Raise the food slowly up and back above the pup's head.

This food is held too high . . .

. . . so the pup jumps up to get it.

By lowering the food back down . . .

. . . the pup sits almost immediately. Good puppy!

Dog: Follows food with her nose, thus lowers her bottom to the floor. Immediately give her the treat and praise her when she does this.

Potential problems: Your pup jumps at food. The most common reason for this is that you are raising the food too high over your pup's head, which causes her to jump up at it. Alternatively, your hand is remaining stationary (or moving too fast, so that your pup can't follow the movement easily).

As for your pup, she may lose focus and miss where the food went. The solution is to move it slower and to reward slight head raises for a few repetitions. Or she may back up instead of sitting. If this happens, work her against a wall or piece of furniture so she can't back up. You can also hold her collar gently to prevent any moving around. Once a pup gets the idea, she'll have no problems.

The pup could also sit up—solution, lower the food so the pup is sitting when she gets the reward. Pup may wrap her front feet around your hand/arm, the solution for which is to lower the food again or to pull the food away and restart.

Step Two

Goal: Dog hears "Sit," sees food raised above head, sits.

You: Now that your pup can be guided into a sit, start saying, "Sit," just before you raise the food up over her head.

Dog: Starts to associate the word "Sit" with the act of sitting.

Potential problem: Your dog doesn't respond to the "sit" command. Most commonly, owners repeat the commands, causing the dog to learn that the command is not "sit," but rather "sitsitsit." Dogs learn exactly what we teach them. If you want your pup to listen and respond on your first command, say the command once.

  **METRODOG**

Toni shows the pup the treat
in her hand . . .

. . . slowly lowers it straight down
toward the ground . . .

. . . then gives the pup the treat,
along with plenty of petting and
praise for a job well done.

DOWN

Down is a safety command, a way to stop your dog. Leash breaks? Down! Dog chases squirrel toward road? Down! Dog thinks about growling at that person? Down! It also keeps your dog out of the way but under control when you are carrying groceries, making dinner, or talking to a friend you run into on the sidewalk.

Step One

Goal: Pup follows food as you lower it to the floor and lies down.

You: Bring the food to the pup's nose, then in a smooth motion lower it to the floor and then pull it away from the pup slowly so he can follow it. This looks something like an "L."

Dog: Follows the food with his nose; as the food moves away along the floor, he lies down.

Potential problems: Your pup stands up. You may be pulling the food out in front of him instead of lowering it straight down between his feet. Try lowering it more slowly. If that fails, then reward him for his best effort before standing up. By doing that a few times, you should be able to ask for more and he will give it happily.

Try resting your free hand gently on his back to prevent standing. Do *not* push down on his shoulders, as this will cause him to push against you and stand up.

Your pup fails to follow the food. If this happens, then the food is either not interesting enough, the pup is not hungry, or you are moving your hand too fast. Try a more enticing treat, working before your pup's meals, or slowing down your motions, respectively.

METRODOG

Step Two

Goal: To link the word "Down" with the action of lying down.

You: Say the command "Down" while you guide the pup into position.

Dog: Begins to associate the spoken "Down" with the action of lying down.

Potential problem: You repeat the command. Don't. Say it once and guide him into it. Be patient. Reward him well with your attention, approval, and praise for compliance. He'll get the hang of it.

DOWN FOR THE NON–FOOD MOTIVATED

If your pup doesn't show any interest in treats or toys, you can still do the work. Start with your pup sitting and you next to him. Pick up his front leg farthest from you and put your hand on his shoulder closest to you. Now, with your hand on that shoulder, ease him away from you. This should settle him into a down position. This is our favorite method. Others include putting one hand on your pup's back and, with your forearm, lifting both front legs up as you ease him down.

Any method you choose, use even pressure, praise him as you do it, and spend lots of time praising and petting him when he is down. Stay calm and keep at it, and he'll get the hang of it. If you two aren't making any progress, seek a professional trainer or a puppy class to give you some hands-on help.

Anyone who can get their bird dog to sit calmly amid a flock of pigeons has a very good "leave it" and all our respect.

SHIRLEY MINATELLI

LEAVE IT

Metrodogs are faced with temptations on almost every walk you take together. From taunting squirrels to sauntering pigeons, from food on the sidewalk to another dog on the street, "leave it" gets hard use in an urban environment. Don't leave home without it.

Step One

Goal: Dog does not grab at food in your hand. (Really, stop laughing, this will work.)

You: Hold food in your open hand. When the pup dives for it, close your hand. Ignore all her efforts to get at the food. The *moment* she stops trying to get the food (and she will, even if it is in sheer frustration), praise her, open your hand, and give her the reward.

  **METRODOG**

Dog: Stops trying to get food in hand. Often the pup will sit in puzzlement. *Praise!* And reward. Pups figure this out quickly.

Potential problem: Your pup does not stop trying to get food. Wait her out. If she is too wild, try teaching this right after a meal so she'll be more full and less desperate. Do not give her food as she snuffles at hand. When she does give up, usually in a minute or less, open your hand and give her that food as well as a really good treat.

Step Two

Goal: Have dog resist diving at food on the floor.

You: Place a bit of not-too-interesting food on the floor. Say, "Leave it." If the pup dives for it, cover it with your hand. When the dog backs off, praise and reward with a really yummy treat.

Dog: Does not dive for the food (or stops herself quickly). Ideally she will sit and look up at you. Good job! Reward and praise!

Potential problem: Your dog gets the food. Oh well, try again. If your dog is just too quick, give yourself more room between her and the treat. Or tie her to something so she can't grab the treat. Once she learns the basic deal of "resisting temptation will get you good things," you can try it with her free again.

OUT

Your pup will, at some point, pick up that you don't want him to have something and that you don't want to pry open his mouth to get it. "Out" (meaning "spit it out") prevents wrestling over some disgusting thing. It also helps prevent possessive aggression by teaching your pup the behavior you want in a positive way.

Step One

Goal: To play the exchange game of "give up that and I'll give you this much better thing."

You: Get your dog interested in a not-too-interesting object like a sock or a non-favored toy. If he'll put it in his mouth—great! If not, when he is focused on it, tell him, "Out," and give him a treat.

Yes, it's basically a "leave it" at this point, but that will change. In fact, it is good to teach this after your pup understands the "leave it" game, as he'll pick up the deal you are offering more quickly.

Dog: Begins to think that "out" equals "treat."

Potential problem: Your dog does not take the treat. If this is the case, either the treat isn't interesting enough, the dog isn't hungry enough, or the object you gave him is *too* interesting. Try doing this before a meal, using a better treat, or offering a less interesting object. Your goal is always to be successful, not to test an untrained dog.

Work at this level for a while until he spits out mildly interesting things willingly. Once he begins to understand the game, try hiding the treat but rewarding him the instant he complies.

It is critical that you do not reward resistance. This is easier to do than you might think. Your dog has the item. You say, "Out." The dog does nothing. You show him the treat. The dog holds on. You show him a better treat, and . . . your dog just learned that if he holds on, you'll produce a better treat. Uh-oh.

COME

If any command is going to save your dog's life, it will be this one. Everything happens faster in the city. If a leash breaks, you have only seconds to call your dog to you before she is in the street—possibly a busy street. If she takes off after a

This dog's leash got dropped and now he's chasing a squirrel. If he heads for the road, can his owner call him back?

squirrel, you have moments to get her back. A dog who responds well to "come" is safer and will have more freedom in her life.

Step One

Goal: To teach your pup that "come" equals *fun!*

You: Several times a day, walk up to your dog, say, "Come," and give her a treat. Any time you have a toy she wants, say, "Come," happily and hand her the toy.

We know, she isn't actually coming yet, so what the heck is *this* about? What you are doing is linking the word with pleasure. That simple. This will pay off big-time later.

Dog: Eats treats. Takes toy.

Potential problem: We can't imagine. You'll have to write us and tell us.

Step Two

Goal: Dog walks several steps to you when she hears "Come."

You: Have treat/toy/dinner in hand, merrily say, "Come," take a couple of steps backward. Your backward steps will entice your dog to move toward you. Good!

Dog: Moves toward you several steps to get treat or toy or dinner bowl.

Potential problems: Your dog is at your feet the whole time. You can't step back because your dog is right there! Good! Perfect! Excellent! Her enthusiasm will serve you well later. Don't worry. This is all part of the grand plan.

Your dog won't move toward you. Hmmm, if you have a young pup who won't approach you when you sound happy, have a qualified trainer/behaviorist come in for a look. It should not be hard to get a pup to approach, the hard part should be to get her to leave you alone.

Step Three

Goal: Pup comes to you and sits.

You: Do as with step two, but this time keep your hands (holding the treat or toy) low in front of you. As you move backward and the pup approaches, keep your hands as low as you can manage—ideally right at the pup's nose level, although that can be hard with tiny pups. Then, as you stop, lift the toy/treat to your waist level. Most pups will sit as their head comes up to watch your hands.

Dog: Comes toward you happily and sits when you stop.

Potential problems: Your dog does not sit. Work on your sit away from excitement. Link "sit" to all things good. Use it many times a day. Then try again.

Your dog jumps up. Ignore her when her paws are on you, and reward her when they aren't. She'll figure it out. Do *not* pet her or praise her when her feet are on you. Consistency on your part will create consistency on her part. Alternatively, you can use a treat to guide her off and into a sit before rewarding her.

CHAPTER 3

Hitting the Streets
(End of Quarantine to Seven Months)

If you are like many new puppy owners, as the end of quarantine nears, so does the end of your patience. Your rapidly growing, active pup, who has larger exercise needs and larger deposits on the papers, is adorable one minute and abominable the next. You're wondering: What have I done?

Not to worry, this is all perfectly normal. Pups quarantined at this age (twelve weeks to twenty, depending on your veterinarian's recommendation) are curious, energetic, mouthy, and bored, bored, bored inside all day. Once your puppy has all the necessary shots and can get outside, this will all get a lot better. We promise.

So the blessed moment has come for your pup to meet the world. This is an exciting and hectic time.

Impossible Behavior or Normal Puppy?

He bites. She barks. He races about with your underwear in his mouth. She gnaws on your wicker. He mauled your table leg. She mauled your ankle. He sleeps belly up, neck to the side, feet in all directions. She likes it tucked behind the toilet. He poops behind the couch. She shreds newspaper. You're at your wits' end. Is this all normal? Will your puppy grow out of this?

Yes, everything described above is perfectly normal puppy behavior. But normal does not mean acceptable, and you can change it. Will the pup outgrow these unwanted hobbies? Not likely. Anything that is great fun will become a habit without some sensible intervention in the form of training, supervision, confinement, and redirection.

TIPS FOR TOYS: TOY TEETH

Toy breeds can have "retained" puppy teeth, meaning the baby tooth (often a canine—one of the long teeth in front) stays put as the adult one grows in. These are easy to see, just lift your pup's lip and see if there are two teeth where there ought to be one. Though normally not painful, it can cause his adult teeth to come in crooked. As a result, the retained baby teeth often need to be pulled. Speak to your veterinarian about the possibility of combining teeth extraction with spaying or neutering.

TEETHING

At around sixteen weeks old, your pup will start to get permanent teeth. This will last until seven months of age, when the last teeth settle firmly into place. Let the chewing begin! During teething it is not unusual for your pup to skip the occasional meal, be a bit lethargic, or even have a slightly soft stool. His breath may

stink, and his gums may bleed. Don't be surprised if his chew toys are bloody; that happens at this age. If, at any point, you have concerns, do not hesitate to call your veterinarian.

If you have a pup whose ears have been standing up, don't be surprised if they drop during this period. If they've been up, they should come back up without a problem. If they weren't up before teething started, you may need to support them artificially for a while. Speak to your veterinarian, breeder, or anyone experienced with your breed for specific help.

Help your pup through this period with frozen rope toys, ice cubes, food that has been soaked, supervised rawhide chewing, and sterilized bones stuffed with something delicious. Be patient with him. Calmly redirect unwanted behavior to behaviors you prefer. He cannot help feeling so uncomfortable. Watch him carefully; if allowed to, he will relieve his pain by chewing on your belongings.

First Week of Walks

When your pup first starts hitting the streets in a serious way, you may see any one of several normal reactions. In order to have things go as smoothly as possible, follow these simple steps:

KEEP FIRST TRIPS BRIEF

Better they be too short than too long. For the first few days, walks under ten minutes are suggested. The exceptions are for extremely stressed dogs (take them in sooner) and bold, relaxed pups (hang outside for longer if you wish). Stressed dogs may pant rapidly, lie down, insist on walking next to a wall, cling to your legs, pull toward the building, leave little sweaty paw prints on the sidewalk, or start shedding madly. These dogs need to be exposed to the city slowly, at a speed they can handle.

RAIN DISDAIN

More than one pup hates the rain. Usually, the thinner the dog's hair, the less he likes being wet and cold. Dobermans, for all their tough reputations, are often weather wimps.

If your pup looks miserable, you must sell him on two things: He must walk in the rain, and it will be fun. Do not stop because he stops. This only rewards stopping and will create a dog who refuses to walk in the rain. Next, be happy (even if you aren't feeling happy), bring special treats, laugh, and act silly—most pups can't stay miserable long in the face of glee.

LET YOUR PUP EXPLORE

Don't worry about him pulling you around to explore or trying to greet everyone he meets. These are good things. Prevent happy assaults by restraint rather than correction. You can continue to play the "stop when the lead is tight" game if you have the time, patience, and inclination to do so.

HAVE FUN

Make the outside a fun place. Give some special treats on walks for the first week or so, and stop and fuss over your pup regularly. It is impossible to praise a pup too much, and a minute or two of petting and warm words from you can give a pup a nice mental break. If she can focus on commands, practice those. Just a few at a time followed by rest or play, whichever your pup seems to need.

STICK TO QUIET AREAS

Don't march a dog new to the city down Fifth Avenue at lunch hour; that can be overwhelming to us humans. As with all training, set him up for success whenever you can, don't "test" him to see what he can handle. There is nothing wrong with

Whee!

just sitting in a quiet area and letting your pup take in the sights. If he becomes stressed, restless, tries to hide, climbs your leg, whines, or moves in a crouched position, you've done too much. Go back inside and let him collect himself. (If he does show those signs, chat happily with him. Be nonchalant. Please don't commiserate with his fear, that will only make it worse.)

STUFF THE PUP

One of the great ways to condition a shy or fearful pup to accept a stressful situation is to make it a pleasant one instead. You can do this by feeding your dog treats she adores in spots she does not adore. Done often, she'll start looking forward to these spots, as they represent an opportunity for really good treats. This is called "counterconditioning" and is an easy approach to take in situations your dog does not enjoy.

GREAT GREETINGS

One of the classic city problems is the pup who drags you down the street, leaping at passing strangers, garnering you everything from an understanding smile to a nasty comment. How do you control this enthusiasm without dampening your pup's friendliness?

When you first take your pup out, don't worry about this. She is just getting used to things, and you don't want to add any type of inhibition at first. Simply prevent contact through restraint or distracting the pup with a happy command, a toy, or a treat.

After your pup is confident on the street (and that may take a few days to a few weeks), you can start shaping a more appropriate greeting.

As with all training, you need to think about what it is you want to achieve before you start. A polite greeting is a good start, but you need to know exactly what you mean by that. Here are a few of the goals I set for this process:

Goal #1: For your pup to keep feet and mouth off of humans when greeting.

Goal #2: For your pup to sit while being greeted.

There are several ways to reach these goals. Here's one way:

Starting indoors, put your pup on lead and collar when a friend or family member is about to enter your home. As they enter, approach the person with your pup, then step on the lead where it touches the floor when your pup is standing.

Done properly, the pup will correct herself when she leaps up at the human. When she is attempting to leap up—become quiet and ignore her. Leaping pups get no attention. When she stops leaping, calmly tell her how smart she is and reach down to stroke her gently. If she leaps, look away and ignore her again. After just a few minutes of this canine version of "red light, green light," your pup will probably start figuring this game out and she'll stop popping up. Goal #1 achieved (at least while you are standing on the lead; true self-control and understanding of what is wanted takes many, many repetitions).

92 METRODOG

On to goal #2. I'm assuming you've practiced "sit" with food rewards away from this situation, so your pup understands what is wanted.

Now, when she stops jumping, direct her to sit, *then* praise and reward. From here on, in practice sessions, she gets the attention and treats only for sitting. When a new situation is presented, she will need more practice and patience before she is reliable again.

If she doesn't catch on quickly, no matter. Every dog learns at his or her own rate. Simply keep doing this for the next few days and she should improve steadily. If no improvement is happening—*stop!* Either the pup has too much slack in the lead or this method is not going to work for her.

Want to speed up her understanding? Practice playing with her by backing away and sounding very excited, then telling her to sit. The instant you say, "Sit," freeze and become silent. When she sits, praise, pet, and/or give her a treat, then begin the game again. This teaches your dog how to listen when distracted and how to calm herself when stimulated. These skills help make a wonderful companion dog. (Besides, it's a lot of fun to play!)

THE SCOOP ON SCOOPING

Picking up poop is a necessary evil. It isn't fair (or sanitary) to ask the rest of the city to step around or tromp through your dog's feces. It is something you will get used to, we promise.

By far the most universal and easiest method is the plastic bag "mitten." Insert your hand into the bag, pick up the poop, pull the bag off your hand, and voilà! Poop is in the bag, hands are clean, no muss, no fuss.

Second choice is newspaper. This is not quite as tidy unless you can teach your dog to allow you to slide it under while he gets into position. Many people do that, and this is indeed an easy method. Slide, wrap, dispose.

Scooping is an international habit. Here is a German machine that dispenses bags made for the purpose.

Picking up poop on the ground with newspaper is dicey. You can get more smear than pickup, and sometimes your fingers break through the paper... enough said.

Whichever method works for you, please pick up religiously.

Being a Leader Worth Following

As your pup matures and now that you are heading outside where off-lead play is soon to follow, it is time to reassess whether or not your pup views you as his leader. Your dog's responsiveness is based on training and on how he perceives you.

Think of the best teacher or coach you have ever had. Chances are excellent that all of them had a few traits in common. A really good teacher is fair. They don't scold you for no reason or test you on material you've never learned. They are fun. They cheered on good effort, shared in your successes, saw the best in you, and brought it out. They had high expectations for you. And those high expectations led them to be firm, meaning clear, focused, and unwavering. Firm is not angry or cruel. If you apply these three traits—fair, fun, firm—to yourself, you, too, can become a leader your dog looks up to, learns from, and follows.

This young pup obviously thinks Toni is a leader worth following.

  METRODOG

CAREFUL WHAT YOU CORRECT

No matter what your intentions are, your dog will link your behavior to what she did in the last few seconds, not what she did in the last few minutes. For example, if she steals a dish towel, and you see her, tell her, "Out," and she spits it out, and then you scold her for taking the towel, you have just unintentionally scolded dish towel–dropping behavior. Next time she will be *less* likely to spit out the dish towel. Instead, if she drops it on command, praise her. That way she'll drop it faster next time.

This smart person is developing a working relationship with her puppy early. Her pup is calm, attentive, and willing. No monster dog here.

HOW TO CREATE A MONSTER DOG

- Give him attention all the time, whether or not he asks for it.
- Don't teach him how to please you, and for heaven's sake, don't practice. Just expect him to know it, then get mad at him when he doesn't.
- Ask nothing of him—no self-restraint, no response, no compliance.
- If you do ask, don't follow through.
- Don't take him anywhere with you, keep his world small.
- Correct him harshly, frighten him, hurt him, teach him you are unreliable and dangerous.
- Work around him constantly—if he's lying down in the hall, step around him; if he's on the couch, sit at the other end; if he's in bed, scrunch in so he doesn't have to move.
- Stroke and soothe him when he shows confusion, fear, or aggression.
- Limit your praise; after all, he "knows" he did right.
- Skip neutering.
- Consider any treats as "bribes."
- Refuse to consider other methods. Spout to everyone that using treats or not using treats, using collars or not using collars, is stupid. Instead of trying something new, allow your dog to fail.
- Get angry at other dogs (and owners) when the older dogs attempt to appropriately discipline your pup.
- Think of your dog as your baby.
- When a correction doesn't work, do it harder.
- Refuse to consider medicating your dog, if recommended.
- Think of any boundary setting as "mean."
- Ignore the behavior you want.
- Hit him because it "worked" on your last dog, or your parents hit you, or you watched your parents hit your dog, or you can't "control yourself."
- Be inconsistent with both your expectations and your reactions.

RUDE HUMAN BEHAVIOR

Humans often behave in ways that frighten dogs. Human behaviors that can spook pups include direct eye contact, long eye contact, walking directly toward, reaching quickly toward, looming over, moving suddenly, and reaching a hand in and then pulling it away. Many of these behaviors would be rude if done to a human stranger, yet we seem to forget ourselves around animals. Fact is that their social systems share some of the same rules: Strangers stand at a distance until introduced, both parties must want interaction for it to proceed, rapid body contact is inappropriate, staring is rude . . . If we thought to follow some of our own rules of conduct when interacting with animals, it would make things easier for the dogs.

Handling Common Fears

When you notice that your normally confident pup hangs back a bit or barks at even familiar objects, she is probably in another fear or sensitive period. During these times, your dog is more aware of any changes or new things in her environment. To bring your pup through these times in one emotional piece, don't hide her away from the world; instead, help her to cope with her reactions. How you handle her fearfulness can mean the difference between a short-term phase and a long-term problem. How would you handle the following?

You and your pup, Daisy, are on the elevator on your way down for a midday walk. The elevator slows, the doors open, and in walks a large, bearded man in some kind of uniform. Your pup growls, and the fur on her back rises up slightly.

You

1. giggle in an embarrassed way and stroke the pup nervously while saying, mostly for the gentleman's benefit, "It's okay, Daisy. He's a nice man." You stroke her to soothe her and to show the man that she is harmless.
2. yank the lead hard and scold the pup, saying, "No, bad Daisy, bad dog!" You won't put up with this behavior for one minute; it ends right here!
3. stay calm and relaxed and step a bit closer to the man, leaving the leash loose. You understand your pup is just reacting to his newness. She will watch you closely for clues about how to handle the situation. You breathe evenly, laugh in a relaxed way, and say something like "Puppies! They've got so much to learn." If the pup stops growling and takes a tiny step closer, you praise her warmly: "Thatta girl, Daisy! Don't be silly. Good girl!" If she retreats, you ignore her. You take out a treat and let the man feed your pup if he will or simply reward her for stepping toward him.

The correct answer is 3. Answer 1. is likely to be mistaken by the dog for praise, making this growling reaction *more* likely in the future. Answer 2. may convince your dog that there really *is* something to worry about, associating the corrections with the *man* and not with her own behavior.

Answer 3. neither rewards her growling nor adds to her worry. Instead, it rewards friendly, confident behavior and ignores the fearful stuff. You also *model* the behavior you want (while demonstrating that there is nothing to worry about) by stepping a bit closer to the "scary" person and praising all confident behaviors. How close you step will depend on how the other person reacts as well as your dog's behavior.

Hint: Do not drag your pup toward the person. Instead, support her every effort to overcome her fear and let her set her own pace. This is the safest (and fastest) route to better behavior.

MY DOG IS TOO SCARED TO EAT

When a dog gets frightened enough, she will refuse treats altogether. If you find this is happening, try moving farther away from the thing/person she fears. Plan ahead. Bring better treats (like cold cuts or cheese), or do this work before meals. Any of these minor changes can create a situation where your dog will be bold enough to accept a treat. Once she's taking treats with ease, her training around fearful things will be considerably easier.

Never drag a frightened pup.

Instead, offer him treats and let him set his own pace for courage.

Dogs can react fearfully to people who are different from what they are used to seeing. These two look unconcerned.

FRIGHTENED OF PEOPLE

Metrodogs encounter many different people each day. If she has seen only one race, sex, or age of human, she will react to anyone different the same way you would react to a towering, purple hairy human on the street. You might feel frightened and try to move away. You might feel aggression rising. Your dog is not so different.

One way to counter this response is to expose your pup to as many different people as possible. Understand that any fear or aggression is probably confusion. In general, if you ignore the pup completely and let her approach in her own time, you'll have better success.

Hint: If you step or sit next to your guest instead of across from him or her, your pup will see that you are not frightened. She will want to be close to you, which will draw her closer to the stranger at the same time.

Game: Say Hello!

This simple game can be played with people your dog knows, and it will help her greet strangers with happy confidence. All you need is someone she likes (such as a family member), a handful of treats, and a hungry dog. Have her on lead with a buckle collar. Say happily, "Say hello," and walk her toward her friend (walk in on a slight curve, not straight at the person, and instruct the target not to look at your pup). When she arrives, have her friend hand her a treat and you move her away.

Command
Approach (praise)
Treat (praise)
Move away (praise)

Moving away allows her to get distance from the person before she has a chance to move away because of fear/stress. No matter how confident she seems, move her away happily after the treat. Later in training, as she grows consistently bolder, you can linger a bit and give another treat or two.

If she is food motivated, she will soon wag her tail when she hears, "Say hello." When she starts looking forward to this, you can have her friends put on hats or coats (anything to change the appearance) and repeat the procedure. Many dogs react to unusual clothing, movement, size, and so on. If that happens, just work on the basic version of "say hello" until the pup is relaxed.

When she merrily "says hello" to friends no matter what they are wearing, move on to less well known people. Continue to move away after she gets her treat.

Once she approaches people happily, you can linger for a second treat before moving away. You can have the person speak to her or touch her (on the chest or under the chin) *before* the treat. Progress slowly. Each tiny step forward is a step in the right direction. Celebrate it, because tiny step by tiny step you will reach your goal.

Hint: If at any time she balks or refuses to move forward, do *not* force her. Instruct your friend to toss the treat to her, or give your pup the treat yourself when she gets as close as she is willing to (but before she hits the brakes). This can be tricky, but keep your goal in mind: rewarding her best effort, not her worst.

FRIGHTENED OF OBJECTS

"Check it out" is almost exactly the same as "say hello," it just means "check out this object." You can either put the treats on the object or, if your dog is really spooked, hand him the treats when he gets as close as he confidently can.

Again, as with "say hello," start with objects your pup does not fear so he can learn the routine without stress. Working with things he knows may seem silly. But it is teaching him the routine, and it is the routine you will fall back on when he is frightened. Later, as he gets more confident, add in new things that he might react to fearfully.

As this Bichon Frise pup grows bolder, her "hiding place" should keep slowly walking away, encouraging her to explore.

Start from Confidence

Start at a place where your dog isn't frightened, then progress in small steps, rewarding frequently and taking breaks often. So if your pup is frightened of the children at the playground, start by sitting on a bench far enough away that he shows no concern whatsoever. Get up and walk casually in the general direction of the playground, stopping frequently to reward him. Periodically go back to the bench and let him relax.

Quit While You're Ahead

This is more easily said than done. Stop when your dog looks happy and relaxed. You're doing things right if your dog never shows any stress.

Reward Abundantly

Heap on the goodies. If the best things in his life happen near this thing he is nervous about, he'll soon start feeling less nervous and more eager. Just don't go overboard with rich foods that can upset his tummy, like liver. Cheese tends to be both appreciated and well tolerated.

Retreat Often

Any time you're working around fear, retreat frequently to a "safe" distance. Spend time there petting and praising. Play a bit if your pup will. Allow her to completely diffuse any tension she may be harboring before you move toward the fearful thing again. This simple process—retreat—can shorten training time significantly.

FRIGHTENED OF OTHER DOGS

Arrange playdates with well-socialized, calm adult dogs or a smaller, calmer pup. The ideal dog will ignore your pup completely, allowing your pup to recover and explore. If possible, visit on neutral turf. Always make sure that all toys, bones, and any food is picked up to avoid triggering any aggression/possessiveness in either animal.

Ignore your pup's reactions entirely and sit down to chat with your guest/friend.

Do this in an easy-to-clean area, as your pup may submissively urinate when she finally greets the other dog. Keeping the adult on lead so she stays in one place can help limit the pup's stress.

Since fear of other dogs can easily flip into aggressiveness toward other dogs, it is important to get her around as many calm dogs as possible. Doggie day care, puppy playgroups, and training classes can all help an anxious pup learn the canine social ropes.

SARAH WILSON

This six-month-old Lab spots another dog. He's unsure; his tail is still partway up, but he is tense.

As the other dog approaches, this pup's tail goes down and the fur along his back comes up. He's becoming frightened . . .

. . . and explodes into barking from fear. Notice the way he holds his body low and how he's ready to retreat.

From Papers to the Park:
Getting Your Pup to Go Outside

Having spent the last weeks using the papers for the bathroom, your pup will often view the outside world as a fabulous place to visit but not as a toilet. This is an aggravating but usually brief period. Our best advice is simply *hang on*—be persistent. This too shall pass, and when it does, you will never have to deal with it again.

The following basics apply to all plans:

First thing in the morning hurry to the designated toilet area and then walk in slow circles like a sailboat on a pond (movement will help get things moving). Say nothing to your little precious, as it might 1) distract her or 2) be mistaken for a fun chatty time and not a mission.

If you are lucky, and she goes, *then* celebrate! Petting, treats, praise, whatever gets that pup happy. Leave no doubt in her mind that this is exactly what you want.

Now, take her for a little stroll. This serves two purposes. First, it is a reward for a job well done. Second, if you take her directly back in, she may associate relieving herself with going home, which could cause her to tighten her sphincters. This is, of course, excellent socialization time. Take her around the block or up a street. Go to different places each time. (A walk won't be possible every time, but do it as often as you can.)

The exception to this hike is the fearful dog. While they need extra socializing, they also need not to be overwhelmed. For them, an adventure into parts unknown is a punishment, not a reward. These dogs should be walked in quiet areas and given lots of cheers and food rewards for all bravery shown. And bravery it is! Just imagine what any modern city would seem like at your pup's size, with no idea what any of the noises or smells meant. It would be terrifying, yet most pups learn to cope with it all within a week or so.

Here are a couple of approaches:

HANDLING WALK-UPS

Going from no real exercise one day to hiking up and down several flights six or more times a day for housebreaking can put a lot of stress on a young pup's body. We suspect that many cases of orthopedic difficulty in pups in walk-ups might be caused by this sudden demand. So start slowly. Let your pup do one hike out for a few days, then allow him another. If you can still carry him safely, do so. Keep him on lead on stairs to prevent rushing and possibly tumbling. This gradual introduction can't hurt, and it might help.

PLAN A—THE GRADUAL METHOD

This is best for owners who are currently working and need to leave their pup alone for long hours. Leave the papers down. It is not fair to remove all options before the puppy understands that outdoors is okay.

Walk the pup outside on schedule but allow her to use the papers as needed between times. Do not comment on the paper use. Focus on getting outside results first thing in the morning and on weekends.

On workdays mornings, walk her first thing before shower, before coffee. Get up quickly, do the minimal, grab pup, outside. Between the time you get up and the time you get the pup outside, ignore her. Greeting her will get her excited, which may result in a wet crate. Even when you go to get her out of her crate, do so calmly and with little conversation. Instead, greet her outside, preferably after she "does her business," as yet more motivation for her to do so.

Once outside, walk back and forth in the bathroom area or, if you are close by and she is a happy, social creature, take her to a dog run. Running around gets things moving for most dogs.

If she does not go, take her inside and keep her on your lap or in her crate. If she (when she) starts whining, panting, circling—take her right outside again. If, despite your best efforts, she has not gone by the time you have to leave, put her on her papers! She cannot hold it all morning, and our goal is always to avoid in-crate mistakes.

On the weekend, be firm! Walk or crate. If you want her out with you, then keep her on your lap (size permitting—of lap or puppy, your choice). Give her exercise outside with long walks. But inside, limit her freedom severely until these few days are past and she understands what is expected.

Usually, once the dam has broken and you have had success a few times, the deed will be done. Try not to be angry if she shows fabulous self-control and holds it admirably until she gets back indoors onto newsprint. She's just being super well trained. Once she gets things straight, you'll have a wonderfully housebroken dog. If you're dealing with this, go to plan B: cold turkey.

PLAN B—COLD TURKEY

This is for folks who are home and have some time. It will take three or four annoying days, so be ready. You take up the papers; you walk your puppy. A lot! If the pup does not go outside, then you crate him and try again in fifteen minutes or an hour, depending on the bladder capacity of your new companion. Your pup gets almost *no* free time in the apartment until this is accomplished. That is okay because he should be exhausted from all his walking anyway.

Be firm! Consistent! On your lap or in the crate! If you leave him on the floor for just a few seconds, he'll probably pee. If possible, enlist the help of a friend for puppy hand-offs. You keep him outside for an hour, your friend takes him around the block while you run inside to take care of what you need to take care of, then out you go again. The creative use of a dog walker is a good plan as well. Hand your pup off to the walker for an hour while you take a break. Just give clear instructions on what to do if your pup urinates or defecates outside, then go in and take a well-deserved break.

For pups trying hard to stay paper-trained—tank that pup up! Tanking up is an activity for a pleasant morning when you have nothing else to do. First thing in the A.M., pack up a book and bring your cell phone, some letters you've been

HURRY UP AND GET BUSY

Bodily functions hold no shame for a dog. They are just one more thing they do every day: sniff, yawn, whine, pant, urinate, defecate. Because there is no shame involved, it is a pretty easy process to get them urinating and defecating on command. Here's what you do:

When you see your pup beginning to urinate, calmly say, "Hurry up" (or whatever cue you select, the words don't matter). When he finishes urinating, praise him and hand out a treat or two. The same pattern with defecation. We use "Get busy" for that.

Say the cue word *as* the pup begins to go. Don't sound too excited or you may distract him from the business at hand.

If you do this for a few weeks, he will soon associate the act of urinating or defecating with the cue words. When it is pouring rain or you're running behind schedule or it's cold and late, being able to tell your dog exactly what you want will make your life much easier.

Hint: This is not a command you can force, so if he doesn't go when you say the words, don't get angry or you will just make compliance less likely. This is a convenience, not an ironclad obedience trick. It is a behavior built through enthusiastic reward. It can work brilliantly for some dogs and less well with others, but since you are witness to the events anyway, why not work on putting them on cue?

meaning to write, magazines, and whatever. Then mix up a large amount of warm water combined with a little wet food or chicken broth for flavor. Let your pup drink—and drink—and drink. You want that belly distended. Then scoop him up and out you go.

Don't expect much to happen for the first hour or so, but as the water processes through, he will urinate. Eventually. Be prepared to sit on a bench for a few hours

 **METRODOG**

if need be. Meet a friend in the park, take photographs, but stay outside and keep moving.

Sometimes a retractable lead will allow your pup to get far enough away from you to be comfortable relieving himself, if he is shy about such things.

When it does happen, celebrate! Praise him, give wonderful treats, have a great time. Get that puppy tail wagging. You want no confusion in his mind about how pleased you are.

Now, sit back down for a bit. One pee is not going to empty him out. The next one will come sooner (hopefully). Have another praise party when it does. Normally, once a pup has gone outside a few times, the light bulb goes off and it is no longer a problem.

For defecation, a less delicate method is applied, a method that is tried and true, to be sure, but not pleasant: suppositories. Purchase an infant suppository from the drugstore (we'd recommend latex gloves as well). Straddle your pup, snug your legs around his body, lift his tail, and do the deed. Speed is your friend, because once he starts struggling in earnest, it's a frustrating game of trying to hit a moving target. He may yip with surprise when you insert it—completely understandable. An old training trick is to do the same thing with the business end of a *paper* match. Dip it in Vaseline, then insert as above. This works for small dogs, for whom even an infant suppository is frighteningly huge. This is for use once or twice, not as a regular habit.

PLAN C—FOR PUPS NOT CLEAN IN THE CRATE

Some pups do not keep their crates clean when pressed. It is critical that the crate stay clean. That takes priority over all else, since all housebreaking is based on keeping the sleeping and eating areas clean. If you lose that, you lose everything.

Use plan A, but take things slow. When you can, walk your pup, and if she doesn't go outside, keep her on your lap or on lead next to you. If you must leave her, then she must have access to papers. On nice weekend days when you have time, tank her up and spend the morning outside. With extra time and patience, this pup will be as clean as any other.

GETTING OUTSIDE DRY

Few things are as embarrassing as your pup squatting in the elevator or lobby. Don't correct him if this happens (he is doing the best he can to make it outside), but prevent it. Here are a few ways:

Carry Out

If your pup is small enough or you are strong enough, carry him outside to his potty spot. After a week or so of this, put him down a few feet from the spot and walk him to it. Then put him down just outside the door of your building and walk him to the spot. Then just inside the door, then a few feet from the door, and so on.

Cover Up

Often, if a pup's genitals are covered, he (or she) will not urinate. For females, use Velcro-tabbed dog panties; for males, use a scarf tied around their waist or purchase a Velcro-tabbed "belly band." Both will prevent most pups from squatting on the way out. Just be sure to take them off promptly when you get outside. Sure, you may feel silly at first, but not nearly as silly as cleaning up a wet spot in the elevator.

Support

Fold a towel and sling it under your pup, or loop your lead under your pup's waist to encourage him to stay standing. Do this gently; if you are rough or intense, you will only intimidate your pup, and that may cause him to go to the bathroom.

Distract

Don't give your pup time to think while waiting for the elevator. Use treats to keep him focused and distracted. If you pause, he may well squat. Same goes in the elevator—distraction and calm movement may help prevent an accident.

METRODOG

This is normally a short-lived stage (thank goodness). By picking a potty spot close to your building (the closest fire hydrant, as it ought to be clear of cars), you can focus your pup on that spot, which should help him understand the task at hand.

SARAH WILSON

Oops! Right in the middle of the sidewalk. No one's perfect. The handler hustles to clean up.

DEVELOPING THE URGE TO CURB

You will avoid so many glares from annoyed sidewalk users that it is worth the week or two to teach your pup to step off the curb to relieve himself. Try from the start to set your pup up for success by walking in a safe area of the street or close to the curb, but don't begin to focus on this until your pup is going outside consistently for at least a couple of weeks.

If he starts to use the sidewalk, hustle him to the curb. Do not correct him or be angry, since he might associate your upset with going to the bathroom. The message we want to send is that it's the location, not the activity, that is at fault. If you are consistent and persistent, he'll get the message and curbing will become second nature.

HOUSEBREAKING—THE NEXT STEPS

Now that you are heading outside consistently, things should move along nicely. Most dogs can be 100 percent clean (with your help) by five months and about 100 percent clean on their own by seven or eight months.

Once your pup is going outside without any hesitation, start using this rhythm: walk, supervised free time, water, then on lead or in crate until the next walk. Compensate for this increase in crate time with short, fun training sessions and longer walks. This is not a complicated formula, but it is an effective one.

PAPER TRAINING—THE NEXT STEPS

The biggest mistake people make in paper training their dogs is not using the crate. Instead of the crate, they put the pup in with the papers, and this causes a couple of problems. As the pup matures, she may start considering that whole room her bed and refuse to dirty it. She will then use the rest of the apartment as her toilet. Second, it does not teach the pup to hold it, nor does it allow you to know when she needs to go.

We recommend that you follow the exact same pattern as regular house-breaking but simply take the dog to her papers instead of outside. Once she learns to hurry up on command on the papers, you can start taking her out of her crate and walking with her back to her papers. When she gets the hang of that, put her down in different parts of the apartment and have her run back to her papers. That teaches her an important skill and gives you a chance to reward her abundantly for doing that.

Hint: If you have a male dog, wad up a couple of sheets of newspaper and put it in the center of his papers. This will give him a spot to hike his leg. Also, taping some plastic to the wall that runs under the papers will prevent any damage should he decide to hike his leg against your walls.

TIPS FOR TOYS: HOUSEBREAKING

Yes, toy breeds can go outside, but why? Considering how dirty they can get (long coats plus low to the ground) and how much they hate foul weather, we suggest you paper-train, then walk for socialization, fun, and exercise. That will give you the best of both worlds: a happy, well-adjusted companion and the luxury to sleep in on the weekends or to stay inside during stormy weather.

KEYS TO HANDLING INQUISITIVE STRANGERS

You're walking your new pup, and just as he spins in for a long-awaited poop, you hear, "Ooooohhhhh, how *cute!* I just *love* puppies!" You don't want to be rude, but you are tired and you know that if your pup is distracted from his task, it could be another ten minutes before he settles down again. What can you do?

Level One—The Delay Move

Smiling, you step in front of the pup and extend a hand toward the stranger. Your message: "Wait just a sec till he is done and then we'll chat." Once your pup completes the mission, you smile again, thank the stranger for waiting, and strike up a conversation.

Some "dog lovers" will simply stay focused on your pup and move to duck around you. Step to the side and block again. Keep smiling, but be clear.

Level Two—Thanks, but No Thanks

If you are walking, smile, don't break stride. You can shrug or say politely, "Not right now." Most people will be fine with that; anyone who isn't was probably not anyone you wanted to stop and talk to anyway.

If you are with a pup who is thinking about relieving herself—finally—do as with level one, but skip the big smile. Say kindly but firmly, "I'm sorry, but this isn't a good time." Yes, you run the risk of insulting the people.

Level Three—Subterfuge

As an alternative to level two, try lying. We're not proud of it, but sometimes you just don't have the patience to explain for the twelfth time what a Tibetan Terrier is or to wait another five minutes while some stranger gets your pup worked into a frenzy.

Anyone who has not raised a pup in the city may find this advice appalling, but for those of us in the trenches, a little lie can keep you from screaming at some poor, well-meaning stranger.

Phrases that stop strangers midstride are "Oh, he's got a tummy bug," and "Oh, he's got a funny skin thing." (Scratch your arm as you say this.) Either one will allow you to smile and say, "Maybe another time."

If you are a dyed-in-the-wool urbanite, you can simply speak the truth: "Ma'am, I have to walk this pup. You're the twelfth person today to stop me, and I don't have the time or energy to talk to you right now." But that takes a lot more chutzpah than the white lies above.

"When I walk my Maltese, I can't get ten feet without being approached by everyone of every age cooing and oohing and stopping us in our tracks so much that you would think I'm walking a giraffe and not a couple of nice-looking toy dogs. It makes training very 'challenging' (that's a finishing-school girl's word for 'a pain in the a——!')."

—CHRISTINE PELLICANO,
Pet Sitter, NYC, NY

Jumping like this is fine for a toy breed pup but would be dangerous for a German Shepherd Dog or Golden Retriever youngster.

City Services

TRAINERS AND BEHAVIORISTS

Most dog owners will need some help along the way. That is normal; we all do—even pet professionals. A fresh view and new ideas can be just the thing to smooth over the rough spots. But do you need a good trainer or a qualified behaviorist?

A good trainer of companion dogs (rather than competition dogs) should be able to help you with the common dog problems: jumping up, chewing, pulling on lead, puppy manners, and housebreaking. (A behaviorist can as well, but these are often harder to find and more expensive than your average trainer.) If the problem is resistant to change (you've tried a trainer, but it hasn't helped), is severe/dangerous

Brian teaching a class in Central Park with all dogs under control and relaxed.

(aggression, separation anxiety, noise phobias), or may require medication, it is time to find a behaviorist.

Finding a Trainer

In a big city, there are as many different types of trainers as there are chefs. Each feels passionately that the methods he uses are the best, most humane, most effective. So how do you select the right one for you and your dog?

Referrals are great, especially professional referrals such as a veterinarian's or a groomer's. But base your final decision on your own assessment, as not every dog professional is an expert in the field of training and behavior, nor can they necessarily separate what sounds good from what is good.

The trainer you want

- **has small classes or does private work.** A dozen dog/human pairs—maximum—and we prefer fewer than eight per class, with an assistant or two. If private, in-home sessions are offered, do that first. Get the basics started in calm, nondistracting circumstances, then join a class when your trainer feels you are ready. The exception to this is young puppies. Get them into a fun, small class ASAP.

- **encourages you to observe a class or two.** Beginners class will not be polished, and that's okay if they look as though they are learning. Try to speak with some of the participants after class. Expect fun *and* results. One without the other is not acceptable. People should be smiling, tails should be wagging, and everyone should be learning.

- **uses a variety of tools.** Try not to be prejudiced about training tools. Some look harmless and can cause harm. Some look dangerous and generally aren't. The single best expert on the training is your *dog*. Trust her! If she enjoys herself, wags her tail, responds better and better—then this method works for her.

If your dog becomes frantic or increasingly distracted, if she becomes stressed and upset, if she gets more submissive rather than less, if she does not respond—stop! It isn't working for you and your companion. Luckily you're in a city, so go find someone who is a better fit. Training is all about service, and not every trainer is suited for every client—no more than every doctor, counselor, or architect.

Talk to the Trainer

Pay attention to how articulate they are. It does little good if they are wonderful with the dogs but awkward or ineffective with people. The trainer's job is to teach you how to handle your dog. Expect more than an ability to handle your dog; that should go without saying.

Fees

What do they charge? If a package, do they refund if you are unhappy? Do they offer any discounts for adopted dogs or seniors?

What corrections do they use in the worst-case scenarios? No corrections is not always realistic, but they need to be fair and used judiciously. Old methods (hanging, scruff shaking, grabbing, shaking, yelling, smacking) are outdated, inhumane, and unnecessary.

Call the Better Business Bureau and local shelters. Have they heard of this trainer? Have there been problems? How were those problems handled?

What about guarantees? All a teacher of any subject can guarantee is that he will try his best. No one can know how much practice time you will put in or how adaptable your dog is to the training. Be wary of anyone who says her training is "guaranteed," as this is often a sign of trouble. You may be getting hustled. "Money back if you aren't satisfied" is fine.

Find someone with good professional referrals, happy recommendations, and no problems with the Better Business Bureau or Bureau of Consumer Affairs. Those are the best "guarantees" you can have.

FINDING A BEHAVIORIST

A behaviorist is someone with a Ph.D. in animal behavior or a veterinarian who is board certified in behavior. Anyone else who calls herself a "behaviorist" is probably an amateur who would like to be taken seriously but doesn't have the education to back it up. Any trainer can certainly say "specializes in behavior problems," but that does not give any of us the right to call ourselves "behaviorists."

A veterinary behaviorist is trained in the science of behavior and can prescribe any necessary medications. At the time of this writing, there are only a few dozen veterinary behaviorists in the United States, but if you have a serious problem that is resistant to change by the methods you have available and/or may cost your dog his life, seek out one of these professionals.

Your veterinarian, or a large local veterinary hospital, should be able to get you pointed in the right direction. Or contact the following:

American College of Veterinary Behaviorists
Dr. Katherine Houpt, Secretary
Dept. of Physiology
College of Veterinary Medicine
Cornell University
Ithaca, NY 14853-6401

Association of American Veterinary Medical Colleges (AAVMC)
1101 Vermont Ave., NW
Suite 710
Washington, D.C. 20005
Phone: 1-202-371-9195
Fax: 1-202-842-0773
Internet: www.aavmc.org

Use both resources to locate professionals near you; they cannot respond to individual problem inquiries. Ask them, "What resources are near me?" rather than "What do I do about . . . ?"

Perfect! Three dogs each and a buddy to watch the "gang" while the other drops off or picks up a dog.

DOG WALKERS

A good dog walker is a wonderful aid in raising an urban puppy or keeping a Metrodog happy. Dog walkers come to your home when you aren't there and take out your dog. With pups too young to go out, a walker may stop by once or twice a day to clean up the papers and feed and play with the pup. Walks are normally half an hour to an hour long. Prices vary from city to city and by service. Someone walking just your dog will charge more than someone walking a large group. There are walkers who know about training and can support the training you are doing. That usually costs more. But how do you choose a good walker? Here are a few things to ask.

Recommendations?

The best walkers are bonded and are recommended by several pet care professionals such as veterinarians, trainers, groomers, and so on.

How Many Dogs Do They Walk at One Time?

Even though you see walkers handling a large pack of dogs with seemingly effortless finesse, walking large groups of dogs (over three or four) is popular because it is convenient and it allows the walker to earn lots more money per hour—not because it is safe.

Think about this. A leash breaks, a dog scoots off. How does the walker move to catch the dog? She may not get to the escapee quickly. This could happen to any walker, but the larger the group, the less responsive the human can be.

We feel comfortable with three dogs at a time. If you have a toy breed, have him walked separately or in a group with other small dogs.

Do They Keep Your Dog on Lead?

It may appeal to your emotions to have someone let your dog run off lead in the park, but don't allow it. Accidents can happen in a second. One client's dog became frightened while off lead and ran all the way home from the park—across several major avenues. Luckily the dog made it okay, but the rule is, the only person who takes your dog off lead is you.

What Happens When They Pick Up Other Dogs?

Two acceptable answers: An assistant watches the dog(s) outside, or the walker brings the dogs in. A large group of dogs being tethered unattended while the walker goes into a building is absolutely unacceptable. Anything could happen, and happen quickly. Only luck prevents disaster. Don't have your dog pay the price when that luck runs out someday.

DOGGIE DAY CARE

Doggie day care is springing up around the United States. Here dogs can spend the day safe and sound, with both human and canine company. They get walked and have play sessions several times a day. Done well, doggie day care helps housebreaking, crating, socialization, and basic manners. It also alleviates working-owner guilt. Done poorly, it can set you up for long-term separation problems or injury to your pup.

A good doggie day care

- **has and uses crates.** They do not leave the pups in playgroups all day. (Nobody—no matter what they tell you—will supervise a group of dogs every minute of every hour. Some use videocameras, which will only give you a record of how your dog was injured, not prevent an injury. Even if the person happens to be looking at the screen as all hell breaks loose, she cannot get there fast enough.)

- **reinforces training.** It is a nice benefit if any time your pup is walked on lead he sits at doorways and is helped to sit if he jumps up. Rewarding the dog for the right behavior takes little (to no) extra time out of anyone's day.

- **removes all training collars.** No dog should be playing with chain or tightening collars on. A dog can get her jaw caught in your dog's collar (or vice versa), and you can have a disaster on your hands in seconds. Professional facilities use their own collars (with quick-release plastic clips) or no collars at all. Even so, we keep heavy-duty bolt cutters on hand just in case.

- **has safe play areas.** Cute equipment looks great, but it is not safe for unsupervised play (or even supervised play, as no one can control the actions of many dogs at the same moment). Flooring should be nonslippery, especially when wet. Slick flooring is easier to mop and clean, but it can be a hazard for young, romping dogs.

- **divides playgroups by size.** Anyone who lets small dogs romp with big ones is playing the odds. If a fight happens, a small dog can pay severely. A facility's job is to protect the animals in their care, not to make life easy for them (by large group play) or to sell dangerous practices to naive owners. Safety first and foremost is the order of the day.

- **supports a realistic schedule.** The ideal day care walks your pup, lets him play, crates him for a few hours; then at noon gives him another walk and more play; and then again, later in the afternoon, puts him through the same routine. This schedule mimics a "real life" home alone, making it possible to get your pup out of day care as he matures.

- **is recommended by other professionals.** These include humane societies, veterinarians, trainers, groomers, or pet sitters. The facility should also have a good record at the Better Business Bureau and the Bureau of Consumer Affairs.

- **has a strong foundation in dog behavior beyond "I really love dogs."** Where have they worked? What is their experience? Does your dog like them?

Indoor Activities

Your dog is growing up. He is smart. He is young. He is probably bored quite a bit of the time. Every day that magnificent brain of his needs to be used in some positive way or he'll set about using it himself. And what ideas do bored puppies come up with?

Unraveling toilet paper.
Digging out laundry and eating the stinky parts.
Nipping human ankles.
Barking at humans until they do *something!*
Ripping up the linoleum/wallpaper/wall-to-wall carpet.
Discovering what's inside a chair.
Leaping at strangers on the street.
Leaping/barking/barging into strange dogs.
Becoming obsessed with trash blowing in the wind.

The list is endless. Energy must go somewhere! So release it yourself through training and play or have it released in less ideal ways and spend your time coping with correcting unwanted behaviors. Changing unwanted habits is always more difficult, time-consuming, and generally annoying than carefully teaching the behaviors you would prefer.

What coldhearted person isn't going to smile at this little dog?

BRIAN KILCOMMONS

MENTAL GYMNASTICS

The number of tricks your dog can learn is almost limitless. A well-seasoned working service dog can know more than a hundred words and commands. If you'd like to learn more tricks and games to play, please check in our resources section.

Hide and Go Seek!

Okay, fun game, but not so easy in most apartments. However, for those of you with kids or those of you with larger living spaces, it's a fun game.

Start by having one person hold the dog while the hider leaves the room and hides, at first in an easy-to-find place like behind a chair or door. Once they are hidden, say to your dog, "Where's [name of hider]?" in an excited voice. Have the hider give a brief call. Then walk with your dog as he hunts for his quarry off lead.

When he finds the hider—celebrate! Good dog!

This will not take your dog long to figure out. Soon he'll be hunting people down by name no matter how well they attempt to hide. Many kids find this endlessly entertaining, and it can help pass some rainy afternoons.

Name That Toy

Dogs are perfectly capable of learning the names of all their toys. Take two toys (say, a ball and a squeaky toy), put them out about six feet apart. Tell your dog

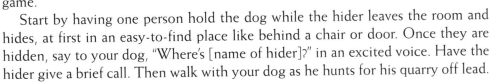

excitedly, "Where's your *ball?*" Walk her over to the ball and play with her for a few seconds. Repeat. If she goes to some non-ball toy, say nothing. Ignore it. Simply praise/reward her when she's right, and she will soon catch on.

Eventually your dog will be able to go get any toy in the apartment by name, and your friends and neighbors will not believe it.

Here Toni and her pupil seize a few moments in a parking garage, while waiting for the attendant, to practice a few sits. Smart time use.

Seize the Moment

Bracken learned to "high five" while I watched TV in the evening. She would sit and stare at me, as she is prone to do. Willing me to do something interesting. So, to amuse us both, I started making a little hand beastie by putting my thumb and fingers together and pretending to bite her nose (complete with dinosaur sounds).

Bracken would watch my hand for a moment or two and then slap it down with her paw. We'd both laugh (I out loud and she with her eyes) while I'd pet her.

Soon she'd slap at my hand more quickly. I decided to make it into a "high five" in our spare time. I started to hold my hand out flat before making the "beastie." Soon she started hitting my outstretched hand with her paw, and a decent "high five" was born.

Now, your dog may never slap at your hand. He may fling himself on his back or spin or pick up a toy. Whatever it is, work with that. See if you can get him to do it consistently, and when you can, put a word on it.

Why?

Because it's fun, and there is too little of that some days. Because it makes your dog think and builds the connection. Because anything he learns teaches him how to learn, and that is of great value.

ORTHOPEDIC PROBLEMS

Different breeds are prone to different problems, so do your research on your dog's breed or mix. Certain symptoms should send you right off to the veterinarian. If your dog (especially toy dog) skips with a back leg up in the air, she may have a subluxating patella (slipping kneecap). If your larger breed gets up by heaving himself up on his front legs first, then pulling his rear up, if he hops upstairs or bunny hops in the rear when he runs, he may have hip problems. Limping in the front can signal a light sprain, panosteitis, or a more serious problem like elbow dysplasia or osteochondritis. Every year brings improvements in treatment, so talk to your veterinarian about options.

Exercise—How Much and What Kind

Exercise is critical to your pup's mental and physical health, but too much or the wrong kind can injure him. Here are a few guidelines:

In general, the larger the breed, the more careful you need to be. Giant breeds who are growing unbelievably quickly can get sprains or twists easily during rough play with other active or powerful dogs. These dogs can be better off during the first year playing by themselves or with one appropriate playmate at a time. The dog run, which looks like such a good time, can be a bad idea. Would you let a first grader play football with junior high kids? No, and it is an equally bad idea to allow a young pup to play off lead with older, bigger, better-coordinated, more experienced animals.

Also, if your pup is hurt as a young dog, he may generalize this bad experience to all dogs and take the offensive in the future. That is how some aggressive dogs are created.

In general, the less hard stopping and turning, the better. Again, be extra cautious with the larger breeds. Toy breeds can play fetch and not risk injury, but a lanky German Shepherd Dog or Great Dane might be at risk. With these larger dogs, we play fetch up slight slopes or wait for the ball to stop rolling before I let the pup go, and we always play on nonslippery surfaces.

No Forced Marching

Yes, long walks are pleasant, and you will have years of them ahead of you. But taking slower, loose-lead walks is a better idea during rapid growth. Some dogs will try too hard to keep up and can stress their young bodies. Instead, start slow and short, then work up to longer distances. Check with your veterinarian and breeder before starting this sort of program.

Biking and running with your dog are terrific forms of exercise, but not until he is full-grown orthopedically, which would be eighteen to twenty-four months depending on the breed. (Medium breeds might be okay at a year; again, consult with your veterinarian.) Grass and earth are easier on a growing dog than concrete, so let him exercise on natural surfaces whenever possible.

Know your breed! A brachiocephalic (short-nosed) breed such as the Bullmastiff, Pug, Boxer, or Lhasa Apso can become overheated quickly. Heat can kill these dogs. Toy breeds, as vivacious as they are, should not be biked. Never mind that it is hard for them to keep up, but even a minor accident could cause them major injury.

KEEP YOUR PUP LEAN

Roly-poly pups may look cute, but this is not always the best for healthy growth. You want your pup lean and strong. Extra weight can put extra pressure on her growing joints. We're not advising that she be ribby, just sleek and streamlined—getting all the nutrition she needs but not extra calories.

Looking down on your pup, you should see a slight waist behind the ribs, and when you look from the side, she should have some tuck-up. Each of these things varies from breed to breed, so talk to people knowledgeable in your breed and to your veterinarian.

FIRST TRIPS TO THE DOG RUN

The first thing to do when you get to the dog run is sit outside. Watch the other dogs play. Is it a rough-and-tumble group or a sedate, sniff-and-trot kind of crowd?

What is your pup doing? Straining at his lead to get in or tucked behind your legs, watching from safety? A bold pup can be brought up to the fence. Chances are the other dogs will come over for a sniff and a general hello. Again, watch your pup. Eager or overwhelmed?

Either way, wait until the pack loses interest, then walk your pup near the fence but still outside. This may stimulate more interest, but what kind? If a dog starts running alongside, barking, or has his tail up and stiff, or is lunging at your pup through the fence, or your gut warns you something isn't right—don't go in.

If your pup is frightened or lagging behind, don't go in. Walking along the outside or observing quietly is plenty. Give your pup plenty of distance from the action until he relaxes.

Another idea is to meet one of his puppy play pals at the run and let them romp together. Same tests before you go in, but if the group inside is basically quiet, let your friends play. Nothing gives one confidence like having a buddy by your side.

Hiring a trainer to come to the dog run the first couple of trips can be a wise investment in your pup's safety and your own sanity. Rule of law: Never throw down food or a coveted toy amid multiple dogs. That's a perfect recipe for a fight, and you don't want your pup to be in the middle.

At first, the pup is polite and a little nervous and holds her tail down. The older dog in the run has his tail up and stiff . . .

. . . but in a second or two, both are more relaxed, with the pup's tail higher and the other dog's lower. The fence guarantees nonviolence.

GAME: TREATS, THEN RETREAT

At a distance where your nervous pup is comfortable, show her a treat. Now, walk with her toward the dog run and stop before she stops. Stop, praise, treats, retreat. (If she stops first, retreat quietly and try again.) Repeat. As she links getting treats with being nearer the dog run, she should be willing to go closer. If she is, great. If she isn't, no matter. Just park yourself on a bench nearby and read the paper. Let her watch and learn.

  METRODOG

ORAL PAPILLOMAS (WARTS)

One year in New York City, warts arrived in the park with a vengeance. Dog owners were finding weird gray, often pea-size growths, usually on their dog's face and inside his mouth, on his tongue and lips. (These are not contagious to humans.) These basically harmless annoyances (unless the dog gets so many that they interfere with eating, which is rare) disappear in a month or two once the immune system mounts a defense. After that, the dog is immune to new outbreaks. But, while immune, the dog can still be a carrier. Always talk to your veterinarian if you have concerns.

DOG RUN RULES FOR PUPS

Dog runs and play areas are wonderful, as long as you apply some safety rules. Some pups of small breeds need to be protected from themselves. They cannot be allowed to play with much larger animals no matter how much they want to romp. They are not aware of the risks they are taking. Some cities offer small-dog runs; seek these out (or create them) in your area.

While most adult dogs will give a young pup "carte blanche," dogs just out of the young juvenile period may come down hard on the younger pups. Older pups nine to twelve months or so are often dishing out the roughest play in the run—not simply because they are young and exuberant, but also because they are protective of their new, tenuous ranking at the bottom of the group and always looking to move up a bit by putting some younger dog below them in line.

This normal, natural behavior needs to be watched. Allowing your pup to be played with roughly can look like great fun, but it increases the chances of injury (with your pup at greatest risk), and it teaches your pup to play this way when he reaches that age.

Here are some typical dog run rules and a run in New York City.

This young Soft-Coated Wheaten takes a break with his owner before heading back into the small-dog run for more play.

A younger pup bellying up to a dog around a year of age is a normal scene, not a cause for concern in most cases.

It is a better plan to have him play with calmer, older dogs, who likely won't add to his energy level or play the canine version of "stuff his head in the toilet and flush."

These adults will start setting clear boundaries when your pup reaches about five months old. They may growl at, pin, or stand over your pup, who may yelp, squeal, freeze in place, or urinate a bit. This is usually both normal and beneficial for dogs who will be doing a lot of group play in the future.

What is not normal is an adult dog who continues to go after the pup even when the pup has submitted (lowered his body, rolled over, tucked his tail). This needs to be stopped immediately but calmly.

WHY NEUTER YOUR MALE DOG?

Do you know what dog bites the most seriously, causing the most damage? Intact male dogs between the ages of one and three years old.

What dogs do more people have trouble neutering for their own emotional reasons? Male dogs!

In general, intact male dogs are for experienced trainers. They often have an intensity, drive, and focus unlike that of either neutered males or females. Assertion and aggression are a natural part of many intact male dogs, and when they react, they react big!

We understand that some people, particularly some men, don't even want to consider this option. It cuts too close to the bone. But men need to take a deep breath and look at the facts.

You will neuter your dog if

- you hate that millions of dogs are killed every year because they have no homes.
- you want your dog to be able to play safely with other dogs (some dogs will always pick on intact males).
- you want your dog to live a long and healthy life.
- you love your wife, children, or partner more than you love your dog's testicles.

Man-made Testicles

For those of you who really can't stand the idea of neutering your male dog, there is an answer: fake testicles. Yes, you can now neuter and have the look of an intact male. If that makes the operation more palatable for you, please ask your veterinarian about that option.

When to Neuter

Here's the deal: Neuter your dog at or before six months of age. There is a trend these days to neutering pups at three to four months. So far, only advantages have been noted: rapid healing, elimination of some cancers, lessening of other disorders. If your veterinarian offers it, consider doing it as early as he or she will.

Neutered males will still lift their leg and bark at the door, but they will be more amenable to your leadership and less dog aggressive (and less often targets of other dogs' aggression) if neutered.

Dogs get fat and lazy if you feed them too much or don't exercise them properly. Neutering won't cause those problems. Our four dogs (from two to ten years old) are all neutered, and each is sleek and athletic. It is the care you give them, not the surgery, that determines your dog's weight.

Hitting the Streets: Obedience

Having done the work described in chapter 2, "The Apartment Puppy," you should now be ready to start building response to your commands in more distracting situations, as well as learning how to calmly physically place your pup into position if that should be necessary.

Keep training sessions short but frequent. Five-minute sessions are plenty. (You can get serious training done during the commercial breaks of your favorite TV shows.) Please learn about the type of temperament your dog/pup has by reviewing "Dealing with Different Temperaments," page 68.

Here, the dog sits before entering the dog run.
Note: The leash is not tight, but the person is
ready if the dog moves forward.

SIT

Having accomplished the basic step of
helping the dog learn to connect the word
"sit" with the action of sitting, you are now
ready for the next stage: learning to sit in
different situations with minor distractions.

Step One

Goal: To learn that sitting brings good
things.

You: Use "sit" before all things your pup enjoys. Going to pet her? Sit. Feed her?
Sit. Open the door for a walk? Sit.

Dog: Dog sits when she hears the first command.

Potential problems: Your dog doesn't sit. Your dog jumps up on you. Look away.
Turn away. Ignore this entirely. When she removes her feet, praise calmly.

Your dog walks off. Play a game with her on leash with buckle collar: If she starts
to walk away, say nothing but back up. When she looks your way, praise! Play!

HOW TO PLACE YOUR PUP INTO A SIT

If your pup does not sit when you say, "Sit," he is *not* being difficult, defiant, stubborn, or willful—he is being a puppy in the early stages of training. So, if your pup stands, staring at you, or starts to walk away, calmly take him by the collar to prevent further forward movement.

Form a "U" with your thumb and middle finger, place that "U" on your dog's back just in front of his hips, and gently squeeze inward and back. The pressure serves as a guide to gently easing him into a sit; it is not wrestling with your pup.

Do *not* lift up with the collar. Though it is tempting and will make your pup sit faster, the problem is that your pup learns that lifting the collar is part of the cue to sit. Then, when the pup is off lead and cannot feel that pressure, he no longer understands to sit. It also stresses some dogs.

Do *not* push down on his back. The idea is to apply some pressure and wait. Most dogs will move away from that pressure into a sit. Good dog!

Alternatively, scoop your dog into the sit. Place one hand on his chest, run your other down his back, over his rear, and gently press in behind his "knees" (stifle area). This is like someone pressing a chair into your knees and causes most dogs to buckle into a sit. Praise!

DOWN

The same exercises as for "sit."

Adding a Hand Signal

This is easy (and will impress both you and your friends). From here on in, arm up, sweep it down, then lure your dog into the down as your hand moves past his

nose. It is one fluid, confident motion: arm up, sweep down, lure, dog downs, reward with treat and praise.

Once your dog has the hang of this, show him the extra-good treat, but don't put it in the hand-signal hand. Give the signal and do the luring motion, just without the lure—then reward. In this way, you can move from luring your dog down to having him down on a signal or command, then rewarding him for it.

IS MORE FORCE BETTER?

Often, if our dogs resist, people think: Oh, if I just used more force, I could "make" him do it. And that may be true, but you could also create resistance. We much prefer to simply stop at the first moment of resistance and wait the dog out. When he resists he's saying "no," and if you respect that small first "no," he won't feel as pressured to go to a larger "No!!" Whether you are placing him into a sit or a down or trimming his toenails, staying calm and neither escalating nor giving up will allow your dog to adjust to the situation as calmly and rapidly as he can. Immediately reward even the smallest effort.

The Enforced Down

A time may come when you ask for a down, the pup looks at you blankly (or stays distracted and unfocused on you), and the treat you are using does not get his attention. If this time comes, we suggest an enforced down.

This down is done *only*

- after a pup has been pretrained with a lure.
- with a wide, flat buckle collar.
- on a slick surface like linoleum, tile, or hardwood.
- when the human is calm and relaxed.

Start the enforced down by applying just a small amount of pressure downward with the lead when you lure the pup into position. Command, downward pressure, lure, pup downs, reward. Repeat. If the pup resists at this point, apply less pressure next time. The goal is for the pup to associate that pressure on his neck with the down.

Once your pup is doing this well, use the downward pressure with the hand motion but no treat in it. Give the treat afterward as a reward.

Last, use the downward pressure by itself and reward afterward. Once your pup is to this stage, you can move to applying the pressure with your foot from a standing position *if* you use slow, even pressure. Do not yank your dog around. The goal is to apply a guiding pressure that the dog responds to by lying down.

If your dog resists for more than a few seconds or struggles, spend more time combining the lure and the pressure together until he understands what the pressure means.

LEAVE IT

You've been practicing "leave it" indoors when your pup is calm and not too hungry. She now understands that, in that environment, waiting patiently has big dividends. Now you are ready to start expanding her understanding.

Goal: Dog does "leave it" in a variety of environments.

You: Once your pup gets good at this, start playing these games outside, in different parts of the apartment, with toys, or in any other way you can imagine. Play only when your pup is both confident and secure; there is no point in attempting to train a highly distracted or fearful pup.

Dog: Learns that self-control leads to good rewards no matter where she is.

BRIAN KILCOMMONS

This pup is diving at some delicious horse manure, a perfect time for "Leave it!"

Out

Now that you're on the street, "out" takes on a whole new significance. It is a command you'll be using often for the next few months as most pups naturally explore the world by putting it in their mouths.

Because you will not always have control over what he picks up, and because some of those things are going to taste pretty darn good to him, we need to add a physical correction into this process about now.

Goal: To have your dog spit out (often disgusting) items on command.

You: You've done the exchange game for a month or more, so your dog is beginning to understand the basics of "out." Now it is time for the next level. The problem with doing only the exchange game is that it can give you a false sense of having trained your dog. Yes, he will spit out an uninteresting thing so he can get a more interesting thing. However, a problem may arise when what he has in his mouth is more interesting to him than what you have in your hand.

Dog: To spit things out readily and on command, even when he doesn't particularly want to! (A head halter can help you control garbage-grabbing behavior on the street, and sometimes prevention is the easiest approach. Please see page 180 for information about head halters.)

Here, we introduce a mild correction, followed by a heaping helping of praise and reward.

One of the best training items for this is a stale bagel. Dogs cannot swallow it whole, it holds up well over several repetitions, and it is only mildly interesting to most dogs.

Have your dog on lead and collar. Have a plate of really good morsels nearby—cheese, chicken meat, hot dog slices. Hand him the bagel, but keep hold of it. Once he has it, tell him firmly, "Out." Look at him calmly, with your body facing his. Do not pull on the bagel.

If he spits it out, move it behind your back or put it away while you *praise!* Celebrate! Reward! Leave no doubt in his mind that he just made the right choice.

If he does not spit it out, give the lead a quick downward or sideways snap. The quick downward motion is followed by immediate slack in the lead. Done well, you'll feel it tighten and then loosen quickly. Your dog should not move at all; if he does, you may be pulling rather than snapping.

This will startle many dogs, who will then open their mouths. If he does, then *praise!* Celebrate! Give him a couple of small treats while you praise. Get that tail wagging! If he does not, please seek professional assistance, as this is a situation that needs to be controlled.

Hint: It is *critical* that you praise and reward your dog when he obeys this command, even if he has just spat out the most disgusting thing. Your goal is to teach him to spit things out promptly, and punishing him after he does will only slow down the response and create unnecessary stress. Once it is in his mouth, all you can do is teach him to drop it. You've already lost the argument about picking it up.

RULES OF CORRECTIONS

When we say correction, we don't mean being harsh. A correction can range anywhere from a serious tone of voice to effective use of an appropriate training tool. It does *not* mean yelling, hitting, frightening, scruffing, or rolling. For example: Your dog starts barking. You firmly say, "Quiet" (the correction): Your goal is both to stop the barking and to create an opportunity to reward silence. If you think of corrections as creating breaks in unwanted behaviors so you can insert some reward, you'll be on the right track.

Corrections, done well, can be useful. The "done well" is the tricky part. Here are a few guidelines we use when teaching our clients about corrections:

• **Corrections are fair.** This means that you have taught your dog the right behavior carefully and over several weeks. Fair also means that you are consistent. You don't allow jumping one day and then correct her for it the next. Also, timing (when you do what you do) is critical in training and must be learned. A well-placed correction arrives when the dog is *thinking about* doing something, not after she is deep into it.

• **Corrections match the situation and the dog.** There is no magic formula in dog training. A sensitive dog may find a serious tone of voice corrective where a bold dog may not even notice. Withholding a treat or toy, putting away his food dish when he fails to sit promptly on command before dinner, issuing a command that goes against his desires (such as "Leave it!" when he dives for a chicken bone on the sidewalk), and a leash correction are a few possibilities. A dog who is revved up, leaping at a squirrel, will need a different type and intensity of correction than a calm dog who is focused on you.

• **Corrections are unemotional.** They are the planned result of a certain action with the goal of creating a new action. The dog moves to jump up, you step on the lead, the dog corrects as she jumps, the dog stops jumping, you praise and reward. Such a correction has *nothing* to do with anger or frustration. It allows the dog to experience a result of her actions—a result that is neither overwhelming nor frightening. If it were either, it would be the wrong choice for that dog and that situation.

• **Corrections are infrequent.** Planned and implemented properly, a correction results in a change in your dog's behavior. If you find yourself using multiple corrections, using them habitually (such as the "sit" by pulling up on the collar habit that is so widespread), or if the behavior you are attempting to correct stays the same or gets worse—stop! You are not being effective. Please change your approach or find someone who can help you.

OFF

You should already have a good start to controlling jumping (see "Jumping Up," page 60), so now it is time to practice real-life situations. Since the front door is the place of universal jumping, we'll start there.

Goal: For your pup to keep four on the floor at the door.

You: Practice sits at the door. With your dog on lead, treats nearby, walk to the door. Reach to open it. If your dog gets excited, stop there. Say, "Off," if he jumps, then have him sit, reward him. Repeat until you can open the door with nobody there and he stays in the sit position.

Then move to knocking on the door yourself (which will get many dogs excited). Work on his sits until he hears a knocking sound and sits immediately.

If you have a buzzer system in your building, use that sound next. Work with that until he can calm himself down enough to listen and respond after the buzz.

By working each of these pieces without any guests actually being there, you can practice calmly and often, getting enough pressure-free repetition that you (and your dog) will be increasingly successful.

Hint: Train *before* you need the command/behavior, not *when* you need it. When you need it is the worst time to train. That would be like trying to teach an elementary class how to read by giving test after test. Who would enjoy that? You'll be astounded how well your dog does with a little practice.

METRODOG

"MAGIC TOOLS"

Everyone wants an easy answer. When you see someone doing what you want to be able to do, it's easy to think it's the tools he uses that make the difference. If only you had a certain type of collar or lead or treat, everything would fall into place. We wish that were true. When watching a trainer you admire, focus your attention on her voice, hands, movements. Copy those, and you will find the magic. It does exist; you can't hold or buy it, but you can learn, feel, and practice it.

COME

Since this is such a critical and difficult command to master, keep doing what you've been doing and add the following:

Come Outside

This begins on lead when walking on the street. As you are walking along, you happily call your dog—"Dog, come!"—then walk backward, praising her. As she comes to you, slide one hand down the lead so that when she arrives, you can prevent her from trotting past you.

Praise her warmly. Have her sit and praise/reward some more. If her tail isn't wagging, work harder on your praise tone and energy until it does.

Repeat this a few times when things are quiet on a walk. She is not ready to be challenged by distractions yet, so set her up to succeed, help her succeed, then praise her for succeeding.

SARAH WILSON

If this woman held the treat against her leg, her pup would learn to come in close and not stop at a distance.

Teach Your Dog to Come Close

Too many dogs have learned the annoying habit of sitting just out of reach when you call them. The four main causes are leaning over when you call (your dog stops under your face), handing treats to him at arm's length (he then stops an arm's length away), walking out to the dog when he stops (he's training you to come), or grabbing his collar when he comes close. This can be prevented (and resolved) using scrumptious treats. When your dog comes to you, hold the treat against your leg. Let him come all the way to you for his reward.

Teach Your Dog to Respond Quickly

Here is a game that Cheryl Hoye, a trainer from Connecticut, showed me, and it can be played by one person with a bunch of treats. Start by tossing a treat away from you (please play this on good-footing, non-slippery surfaces). Just as your pup snatches up that treat, call her excitedly to you, offering another treat. As she races back, cheer her on. Using the treat, lure her close and into a sit. Then reward her with the treat, petting, and praise.

If two people are available, you can call her back and forth between the two of you. The rules: When one person calls, the other takes his hands off the pup, looks

away, and becomes completely passive. The caller praises and claps, encouraging the pup to hustle over. Allow the caller several seconds to praise, play, and give treats before the other person calls happily.

As the pup comes to love this game, you can move positions. When the caller is praising, the second person can move several more feet back or step behind a corner. This adds interest to the game for both you and the pup.

Practice Handling Your Dog's Collar

As your pup licks at the treat in your hand (and that hand is held against your leg, right?), reach down to handle his collar. When you are handling it, give him the treat and let go of the collar. If he gets a treat and praise whenever you touch his collar, he will soon hope for you to do so. Throughout the day, call him, touch his collar, reward, and release.

When you do need to get hold of him, gently take the collar by reaching underneath. Praise and stroke him with your free hand for at least ten seconds before clipping on the lead. This will insert a pleasurable experience between coming all the way to you and being put on lead, which he might think of as not so fun.

NEW COMMANDS

Wait

Any dog who rushes through open doors can be a pain, but a Metrodog can be in more trouble than that. Often in the city you are carrying things in or out of your home. If your pup plows into another dog, or gets in the way of a bicyclist (or just a non–dog lover), you can have a bad situation before you even have the keys out of the lock.

Better to establish a doorway routine such as sit, wait, open door, step out, sit, wait, close the door, lock, go off together.

Step One

Goal: Pup pauses at door. (This game is played only when the pup does not need to urinate or defecate and is relaxed. In fact, playing this just when you get back in the door from a walk is a good plan.)

You: Stand at the door with the pup on lead. Start to open the door. If the pup moves forward (when the pup moves forward), close the door. Say nothing. Be sure to open the door just a bit and close it promptly; *never* close the door on the pup. Repeat.

Dog: Starts to wait to see if this "crazy door" is going to stay open or not.
  Hint: Many pups will start offering you a sit at this point. Praise and reward this. Never miss a chance to reward!

Potential problem: Your pup does not stop rushing the door. Do less tempting things, such as just reaching for the doorknob. Then, when he stays calm, jiggle the knob, then open it a smidgen. Take more time to praise him when he contains himself just a bit. While keeping the pup safe, close the door more briskly. Direct the pup to sit, then praise him when he does.

Place

This is a lovely command for any dog, but it's especially nice for Metrodogs, who usually share smaller living quarters with their humans than their suburban or rural counterparts.
  "Place" means "go there, lie there, and stay there until released." Usually the target is a dog bed, but it could be a crate or a particular corner of a room. If you have a protective/working or herding breed or mix, position the bed so she can see the most heavily used doorways; otherwise she will want to be somewhere else. Usually these dogs hang out where they can see the front door and you at the same time. In lieu of that, they lie in or near the entrance to the room you are occupying.

METRODOG

A dog unconcerned about such matters can have her place in an area away from foot traffic but still with a good view of the goings-on. Don't expect any dog to happily stay in some corner out of sight.

Step One

Goal: For your dog to go to her bed on command and lie down.

You: With your dog on lead with a flat collar, show her a treat. Tell her happily, "Place" (or "Go to bed," or whatever strikes your fancy), and lure her to the bed with the treat. Once she is on the bed, hold the treat in a closed fist on the bed. Since your dog has been doing lured downs for a while now, she should quickly recognize this hand position and flop down. When she does, your hand pops open and she gets the treat. Praise follows.

If you've started from the same spot each time, don't be surprised if you have to do a little refresher course whenever you change locations. That is normal, and your pup will pick it up quickly from the new location with a little support.

Dog: Follows your hand to the bed, gets on, and lies down.

Potential problems: Your dog does not follow your hand. Try training just before meals. Or try a more appealing treat. You might also consider practicing when things are quieter.

Your dog lies down part on and part off the bed. Some dogs like this game so much that they start racing ahead and flinging themselves down half on and half off. Once she understands the basics better, reward her only when she is 100 percent on the bed and she'll soon get it right.

Your dog does not lie down. Practice your lured downs away from the bed. Most dogs will make the jump from a lured down to downing when a treat-filled fist is placed on the floor in front of them.

Your dog gets right back up. Right now that does not matter. As you progress, you'll reward her for longer and longer stays and reposition her if she rises early. But for right now, keep your one task in mind: teaching her to go happily to her bed and lie down there when she hears, "Place!"

MY DOG STOPS AND WON'T WALK

This happens because you stopped when he stopped. By stopping, you rewarded him for stopping, and when you reward something, you see more of it. To fix this, do not stop when he stops. Do not turn and stare at him to see what he's going to do, simply give a quick check to make sure he isn't defecating, cheerily say, "Let's go," and go. When he catches up (and he will) praise him, play, have fun. Teach him that from now on being next to you gets the rewards, not stopping.

Let's Go or Controlled Walking

There are few commands that will make a Metrodog owner's life more pleasant than a good "let's go." "Let's go" simply means your dog walks with you rather than towing you behind him, full steam ahead.

This is a behavior you will build over time. One easy way to get started is simply to reward him when he is next to you and ignore him when he is pulling.

You're walking along, and he happens to look up at you? "Good dog"—praise him, stop and pet him for a moment or two, hand him a treat. Do what works; just let him know that you like it when he looks at you.

You're walking along, and he drags you. You can go with him (which rewards the dragging), you can stop dead and wait (which removes the reward) and then praise him warmly when he stops, or you can turn the other way (removing the reward) and praise him warmly when he catches up. Or you can do some combination of all these things as your time and tolerance allows.

METRODOG

If you focus your energy on trying never to miss an opportunity to reward him for doing something right, you'll be amazed at the impact it will have on his behavior.

BITING THE LEAD

Most pups bite the lead occasionally, but some get persistent about it. Here are a few of your options in handling this:

- Stop playing tug-of-war with your pup, as he may try to start the game when he feels like it—which may be the problem.
- Spray the bottom half of the lead with an antichew product. You may need to repeat this often or try different products till you find the one that works for your pup.
- Give your pup a toy to carry. If he already has something in his mouth, he will leave the lead alone.
- Work on "out" and "leave it," then reward your pup well for responding to those commands.
- Ignore the lead in his mouth and work on "let's go" and "down." Pups are easily distracted, and if you give yours something else to think about, he will drop the lead.
- Stand still and ignore him completely. Normally dogs do this for your response. If you stop and wait, he will often get bored in a minute or so and drop the lead. Praise! Reward! Let him put two and two together.
- Give a lead correction. In this case, take either side of the lead and snap it back toward the back of his mouth with a quick wrist motion. This is done simply to startle, not to get into a fight with your dog. It should be quick, effective, and followed by abundant praise. If it is anything else, please find a trainer to help you change this behavior.

CHAPTER 4

Inner-City Youth
(Eight to Eighteen Months)

He may be big, but he isn't finished growing yet—not mentally or physically. Hormones are coursing through his system, and even neutered animals are experiencing hormonal changes. As an adolescent, new behaviors will emerge any minute: assertiveness, territoriality, independence, aggression, and more. How you handle these changes determines (to a great extent) how your dog will behave with you, your family, friends, and the rest of the world.

If training has not yet been a part of his life, start now. Each day he learns, and what he learns is up to you. Allow him to "do his own thing" and he will learn he's the one who decides what he can and cannot do. Interact with him in a positive way, teach him to work as a team with you at the helm, build on his willingness to please, and you can create a companion of a lifetime and a best friend for many years to come.

What to Expect from Your Adolescent Canine

Adolescence comes at different ages for all dogs; in general the smaller the dog, the sooner it arrives. Expect your Yorkie to be wrestling with these issues at around six months, while your Saint Bernard may be starting somewhere near eleven months of age.

Increases in independence and assertiveness are normal. As your dog approaches adulthood, issues of where the dog is going to fit into the social order become more pressing. Status needs to be defined, and the actions your dog is taking now are efforts at that definition. Dogs thrive on clarity. You'll find that a loving leader/follower relationship makes total sense to your dog.

That sweet pup who hung on your every word now looks at you blankly and walks the other way when you call. When she responds at all, she is slow. If she is naturally assertive, she may become more physical with you, bumping you at doorways, clipping you when she runs by. She might freeze over her toy when you approach. These are signs that she is confused about the order of her universe. Setting clear limits are the actions of a strong, confident leader and do not involve anger or violence. I once read, "Violence occurs when the outcome of an interaction is uncertain." There is much truth in that phrase, and it is well worth pondering next time you feel like having an "argument" with your dog.

Other dogs will start acting differently toward her as well. Dogs who have been allowing your pup free rein behaviorally will often start setting their boundaries. They may snap at her, pin her down, or both. Your pup may squeal in surprise, but a well-socialized adult will rarely injure a pup. (And try to avoid anything *but* well-socialized adult dogs.)

If you think that another dog may be aggressive, put yours on lead, pick her up if you can, put her behind you if she's too large to pick up, then move away. While you're doing this, chat happily with your dog. This may seem unnatural, but it will signal your dog that there is nothing to worry about. That will help minimize any negative association your pup might have with this situation. Do this any time your dog is frightened or confused: Set the tone for her. You may be angry at the

other dog owner, you may be upset, but hold off reacting! Your first job is to make sure your dog gets through this mentally in one piece.

On the upside, your dog will also start developing some ability to focus for longer periods during adolescence. The training you've been working on carefully since puppyhood will really start to gel in these next few months. You'll get a little behavioral preview of your adult companion. If you like what you see, continue what you are doing. If you're not so wild about her behaviors, teach your dog other options today.

SETTING BOUNDARIES

Your life will be easier if you set clear boundaries for your maturing dog. Often, people confuse "being clear" with "being mean." This is not the case. An example of setting a clear boundary: Your dog is not allowed up on the bed. An example of setting a confusing boundary: You're allowed up on my bed except when you are wet, or the sheets are clean, or I have a "friend" over. Learning to set clear, calm, rational boundaries will have an effect many people do not anticipate. The effect is that your dog will be more devoted, more attentive, and more responsive.

Six Steps to a Better-Behaved Dog

Most of us are pressed for time. Never fear! Training needn't take an extra hour or even half hour a day. If you simply put a little snippet of training into all you do with your dog, you'll soon have a wonderfully obedient dog.

The following suggestions improve almost any dog/owner relationship. They calm hyper dogs, embolden cautious dogs, redirect assertive dogs, and nail the lid back down on aggressive dogs. And it is shamelessly simple. Try these easy additions:

Link Obedience to Things Your Dog Enjoys

Next time you feel moved to touch, speak to, throw a toy for, or otherwise do something for your dog, have him do something for you first (such as sit). And any time he is demanding, have him respond to you before you respond to him. Think of it as the canine version of "please." It's simple common courtesy between friends. If he paws you for a pet—"Sit." If he scratches the door to go out— "Come." If he drops his ball in your lap—"Down." Be creative, have fun, but ask for something from him before he gets something from you.

Say Commands Once

Your dog makes a supreme effort to understand you, and your job in return is to make that understanding as easy for her as possible. Keep your commands short and your expectations clear. If the command is "sit," then say, "Sit," and not, "Sit, sit, sit," "Sit down," or any other variation. Language comes so naturally to us that sometimes we call our dogs "dumb" or "slow" when actually we are making it hard for them to learn. Consistency on your part will foster consistency on theirs.

Follow Through Immediately

If you say, "Sit," and then wait for five seconds to see if your dog is going to sit, your dog will wait five seconds before sitting. If you say, "Sit," and immediately place him calmly (or lure him) into the sit position, he will learn to respond immediately. As Becky Bishop of Puppy Manners out in Washington State says, "If you want your dog's behavior to change, change yours."

USE A CALM TONE OF VOICE

Dogs learn best when you are calm. If you become frustrated with your dog—*stop!* Think of new ways to teach her, read books, look at videos, consult your veterinarian, meet with a qualified trainer/behaviorist, take a nap, but don't get mad. You may find that if you keep your voice calm, your emotions will stay calm as well.

REWARD ENTHUSIASTICALLY

Rewards are your dog's paycheck! Heap them on for a job well done. Reward him in ways he enjoys. Take all the emotions and caring you have for this wonderful animal and deliver them to him in a joyful package when he gets it right. If he sits on the first command at the door, praise and open the door for him. If he downs happily, toss him his toy (or a treat or a smile) while you cheer him on. One rule is, if you have to enforce the command, then the door does not open, the toy does not get thrown, and you remain quiet. Wait a few seconds, then try again. When he responds quickly, praise and reward.

SET YOURSELF UP FOR SUCCESS

Work in the apartment, a fenced area, or on lead when you are starting out. If you cannot get hold of your pup (calmly) to enforce the command (followed calmly by praise), then responding to you becomes strictly optional. This may mean leaving a leash on your dog when you are home.

Reading Canine Body Language

Body language is a dog's main mode of communication. They read it fluently. Using body language, dogs usually know within seconds if they will get along with or battle a new dog. They appease their leaders, woo their mates, and intimidate their foes with body language. The better you understand what they are saying, the better you can predict and control behaviors. Take the following quiz and see how well you do.

The yellow Lab is confident, tail up, ears up. The chocolate Lab is frightened, crouching, tail down, hackles up, urinating.

As the yellow tries for a better sniff, the chocolate prevents it with a tight tail tuck and tucking his rear. His hackles are still up.

The yellow lab, typical of an adolescent dog, makes an unnecessary (but normal) point, which the younger chocolate accepts.

A pup (tail and ears low) and a budding adolescent (tail midheight, ears up, slight hackling) greet an adult (head, ears, and tail up, stiff).

THE TALE OF TAILS

As goes your dog's tail, so goes your dog. If your dog's tail is up and the tail of the dog he is greeting is down, your dog is the dominant one. If it's the other way around, he is the submissive one. If both tails are up, it is undecided who's who and a fight may be seconds away. A tucked tail is attached to a frightened dog. A tail with a low, easy wag belongs to the relaxed. Straight up and stiff signals tension! Once you know how to read them, you can predict what is likely to happen.

A wagging tail means the dog is friendly?

1. Of course, everyone knows that.
2. Not always; depends on situation and what the tail is doing.

Answer: 2. With a tail held lower than or even with the dog's spine, wagging in big arcs is usually friendly; wagging can also mean tension or excitement. A tail held above the level of the spine is excitement. A tail held straight up, stiff, and wagging rapidly in small movements is a sign of stimulation, tension, and, in many cases, a precursor to aggression.

A dog approaches your pup, head up, tail up, moving very slowly. He is probably

1. tense.
2. predatory.
3. making friends.
4. nervous.

Answer: 1., 2., and 4. This dog could be tense, with an assertive edge to him. He might be stalking your dog, especially if your dog is small. Chat happily to your dog as you walk on past. This dog may be just fine once he greets other dogs, but you can't tell by looking, and there is no reason to take the risk. You should always ask the owner if his dog "likes" other dogs (and not in an eats-them-for-breakfast way, either).

Your ten-month-old male pup does not lift his leg. Is he a sissy?

1. Yes. Total sissy, possibly incurably so.
2. No. Perfectly normal behavior for his age.

Answer: 2. Perfectly normal. Leg lifting is done to mark territory, and some wonderful, stable, reliable family dogs don't start lifting until over a year of age. Some never do. Some will squat sometimes and lift others. Who cares? He can still be a terrific watchdog.

Generally, the earlier your dog leg lifts, the more of a handful he is likely to be. A pup lifting before six months of age should be neutered pronto and seen by a trainer, since he may have assertive and aggressive tendencies you need to learn to handle and direct before they become problems.

Even some females hike their legs, and a few of either sex will hike both legs, doing a handstand to urinate up higher (usually this is a short dog). The higher the mark, the bigger the dog, the more impressive the act.

A strange dog comes up to your pup, who falls on her back, urinating. Your dog is

1. insane.
2. polite.
3. not housebroken.
4. normal.

METRODOG

Answer: 2. or 4. Both rolling on the back and urinating before an older/higher-ranked adult dog are normal puppy behaviors. Some pups never do this. Others grow out of it. A rare few keep it as a lifetime habit.

In general, sensitive and/or reactive pups are more prone to this display. Pups may also do this when they greet people—known or unknown—or when you are upset or they are frightened or intimidated.

Your young dog sees a bag on the sidewalk. He slows down, lowers his body, and, reaching as far forward as he can with his nose, moves within a few feet of the bag, then scoots away. He is

1. nuts—it's just a bag.
2. frightened.
3. brain damaged.

Answer: 2. For whatever reason, he did not identify that bag as an object he recognized. Imagine if, while walking down the street, you saw something large and unknown right ahead of you. Would you slow down? Would you cautiously check it out? Would you be ready to run? Sure. We're not so different from our dogs in our reactions.

Your dog sits next to you, then nose nudges you, then paws you, then woofs. Your best guess is she's saying:

1. "I love you so much."
2. "Excuse me, could I have your attention?"
3. "Yo! How can I get some service around here?"

Answer: 3. Basically, he's giving you a command. And when you don't "obey" it, he "raises his voice" by becoming more pushy and assertive. If he is rewarded for being pushy and assertive, expect to see more of both. Over time, teaching your dog to treat you this way (and that is exactly what you are doing) can lead to aggression.

STICK IN ROOF OF MOUTH

Your dog is playing happily when suddenly he puts his head down, opens his mouth, and paws intensely at his muzzle. Is he choking? Was he stung by a bee? Maybe, but the chances are good he has a stick wedged across the roof of his mouth. Wrap his upper lips around his teeth to discourage him from biting down, open his mouth, and sweep the roof of his mouth with a finger. If it's up there, you will feel it. Most can be easily and instantly removed. If not, get to your veterinarian, but don't fret too much. Your dog is unhappy, but not dangerously hurt.

SARAH WILSON

Because he is well trained, this Labrador gets to enjoy some quiet time in the park with his family.

This wise gentleman keeps his squirrel-crazed dog on lead.

SARAH WILSON

 METRODOG

Proper Social Etiquette

ELEVATOR ISSUES

Have your dog sit next to you toward the rear of the elevator. The ideal spot is in a corner, with your dog between you and the elevator wall. This limits the amount of leaping at others your dog can do and is the safest place for your dog should another dog come aboard.

Use treats to reward the dog for keeping in place if this helps him focus. As he learns the routine, be sure to give the food less frequently and for the best behavior. For example: An advanced dog might get a treat only when someone enters the car or for the wait as the door opens, while beginning dogs might get treats every thirty seconds or so, as long as they are sitting.

Teach your dog to "wait," allowing you a moment to scope out what lies beyond the open doors before exiting. More than one dogfight has started because dogs met head to head as one dragged his owner onto the elevator and the other was dragging hers off.

Because this is a small space and some people allow their dogs to drag them in, some dogs may become defensive and/or combative in an elevator. Handle this by

- **neutering your dog, especially if he is a he.** Other dogs react to intact males more assertively. His life (and consequently yours) will be much easier if he is neutered.
- **doing a short obedience session before you leave your apartment and while waiting for the elevator.** This is calming and will put your dog in a "you lead, I follow" mind-set.
- **using a head halter.** This will also give you better control over your dog's head and mouth, which can be a real plus in a tight space.
- **keeping your dog sitting, in the corner. The lead should be short but not tight** (not slack, but the clip of the lead should still be hanging down). This will give you good control.

- **rewarding your dog freely for staying seated.** A sitting dog can't get into too much trouble, so concentrate on that. Be sure to praise him for holding position. Try not to hold your breath when a new dog or person gets into the car; that will simply signal your dog that you, too, are scared.

If you are nervous or are having a hard time getting your dog under control, please seek professional assistance. Do not delay. Aggression rarely stays at the level it is at—it tends to increase unless you actively take positive steps to change it.

Here Sarah's charge has gotten tangled. She's just waiting him out, encouraging him with her voice.

In a few seconds, he's figured it out and they are on their way, with one more Metrodog obstacle conquered.

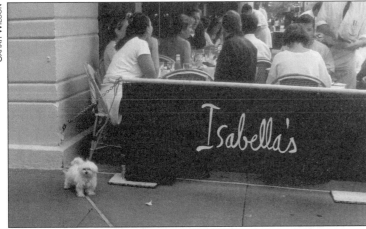

Creative and devoted Metrodog owners find ways to bring their dogs with them. Here a little Maltese walks the Board of Health's fine line.

ON THE STREET

There are amazing numbers of people, objects, and events a Metrodog needs to learn how to handle on a basic walk. Parking meters, for example. She needs to stay next to you when you walk by and not go around the far side, getting you both tangled.

If this happens, the solution is fairly straightforward. Wait. Let her figure out how to get herself untangled. If, after a minute or so, she is still stuck, guide her around it. Do not untangle her yourself. If you do, then the responsibility for resolving the situation falls on your shoulders and you'll be untangling her for years to come.

When you're out and about, remember that just because your dog is friendly doesn't guarantee everyone else's is as happy and outgoing. Always ask before you allow your dog to greet another dog. If you cannot control your dog adequately to prevent unwanted interactions, you need to work harder on "wait," "leave it," and "let's go."

Dog handling is complex. If you are not progressing as quickly as you would like, seek out professional assistance. If you're not sure how to get the response you want, there is no way you will be able to teach your dog. We're all novices at the beginning. Don't fret, get some help. A good professional will teach you how to teach your dog.

This woman is oblivious to the look the man her dog just cut off is giving her. Stay aware. People have right of way.

Retractable Leashes

Wonderful ways for a dog to get some exercise and to work on obedience commands such as "leave it," "come," and "stay," retractable leads need to be used where there is room—not on city sidewalks.

Few things annoy us as much as walking one of our charges on lead only to hear a dog on a retractable lead rushing toward us, the leash making a sound like giant fishing line being yanked out at record speed, with the owner trailing behind, inevitably yelling, "He's friendly, he's friendly!"

So what? Our dog may or may not be. He may be frightened of strange dogs, may be recovering from some illness. Unless you're greeting old friends, it is socially inappropriate for dogs or people to charge at each other. With both species, a charging stranger creates a defensive/aggressive situation.

All retractable leads come with a locking mechanism so you can control the length of the lead—use it! Always ask someone whether your dog can visit before making contact. It is safer for everyone and just plain good manners.

METRODOG

MUTE SWANS

Mute swans, native to Europe and Asia, are thriving in North America. Unlike other varieties, these swans are serious parents who defend their young aggressively, and they can kill dogs (and have), either by dragging small dogs off the shore or attacking swimming dogs and drowning them. So in the spring, steer clear of any swans you see, and don't swim your dogs in ponds with swans who might be nesting or raising young. If you see an unusually large swan coming right at you, simply call your dog and leave the area. Please do not harass the bird for simply defending what it holds dear.

PARK

City parks belong to all city residents, though they can seem, early on a workday morning, to be the sole property of joggers and dog owners. It is not uncommon to enter a city park at six A.M. and see dozens of dogs romping around small groups of people huddled over coffee cups, chatting casually. That social aspect can be as important for the people as it is for the dogs.

Of course, there are risks, such as picnic relics like chicken bones, broken glass, obnoxious or unstable people (rare), obnoxious or unstable dogs (also rare), disgusting edible items (not rare), and disease-carrying rats. But the fun is worth the risks. You learn quickly where to go and where to avoid. In general, stay out in the open, both for your own safety and for your dog's (rat poison can be spread in brushy areas).

Many dog owners choose to break the law and allow their dogs off lead. Safety first, please—safety for your dog and for other park users such as bicyclists, picnickers, and families with small children. Keep your dog on lead if there are kids playing soccer or a family enjoying a meal nearby, as you just know he'll stampede over. It is dog owners who create a lot of the bad blood in their communities, by letting love of their animals blind them to other people's feelings and needs.

SARAH WILSON

We don't know if this is legal;
we do know the dog
was having a blast!

Bodies of Water

Special caution needs to be taken around bodies of water in urban parks. Though some of these can be great fun for dogs, you need to watch for several hazards. Glass is a big one. For some reason people seem to get no end of pleasure tossing bottles into water. Over time this can lead to a bottom littered with broken glass. Cut feet can be a nasty result.

Pollution is another obvious risk. Has the Parks Department put anything in the water to control algae? Has there been runoff from poison or herbicides that have been spread? The good rule is, if you won't swim in it, don't let your dog swim in it—not only for his health, but for yours and that of your family. If he swims and then comes back home, some of that water will get on your hands, and eventually you will ingest it. And this brings me to the last risk: parasites. Specifically the nasty little protozoa called Giardia. This bug takes a week or two to get going, but when it does, you and/or your dog will have one of the worst cases of diarrhea accompanied by flulike symptoms that you can imagine. While this is easily controllable with medication, it will give you horrible insight into the term "sick as a dog."

Since neither dog is standing over the other and both are moving, we can guess this is just "jaw jousting," a favorite canine pastime.

Small dogs can react fearfully to larger dogs and become aggressive. All three smaller dogs look tense here.

Mounting is assertive/aggressive behavior. The terrier would be correct to spin and snap. It is the dog on top who's "asking for it."

DOG RUNS

Dog runs are wonderful ways for cities to transform low-use areas into valuable resources. One city had a playground in a wooded area. Looked lovely on paper, but ended up being an area for muggers to hang out. By turning some land near the playground into a fenced dog run, foot (and paw) traffic went up and the muggers went away. It was a win/win situation for everyone involved.

Dog runs also lessen the number of dogs running off lead, give dog lovers a place to hang out and have some fun, and leave more of the rest of the park for others. Legally or illegally, dog owners will come to the park to let their dogs off lead to play. So cities can either give people a place to do that legally or spend enforcement dollars and manpower ticketing otherwise law-abiding people. An informational booklet, *Establishing a Dog Park in Your Community*, is available through the American Kennel Club Canine Legislation Department (1-919-233-3720 or through www.akc.org).

Each dog run has it own ambience and system. In general, here are a few rules. If it is a small run, such as those in New York City, be aware of the other dogs in it when you arrive. If you have a large, rambunctious Labrador/Bulldozer cross, ask if the lone dog in the run, a Miniature Poodle with a "just from the groomer hairdo," wants to play before letting your hard hitter off the leash.

Watch the body language of the animals your dog is playing with. If your dog repeatedly attempts to put his paws on the other dog's shoulders, lays his head over the other dog's back, mounts another dog, or continuously blocks the other dog's path, he's picking a fight. He is not "playing," and if you do not intervene to stop this, the other dog is well within his rights to clean your dog's clock.

Do not excuse your dog's aggression. If your dog consistently is involved in fights, regardless of who you think "started" it, then the dog run may not be the right place for your dog.

Many dogs develop strong friendships and equally strong dislikes. Both can influence your dog's opinion of all other dogs of that breed or those looks. Being aware of these preferences can help you anticipate problems before they bloom into a spat.

METRODOG

Dogfights

Some dogs never fight, and other dogs almost always want to, but for the most part, dogs avoid fighting when they can. Breed (or mix), temperament, age, gender, and neutering status can all contribute to fighting, though for every generality there are exceptions.

Generally speaking, bold and reactive dogs probably start more fights. Shy dogs try to avoid the fight but will fight if frightened and cornered. Independent dogs tend to avoid the fights but, if pressed, will defend themselves. And those delightful stable dogs will avoid a fight to the best of their ability.

Usually, male dogs fight more, and intact male dogs fight the most often. Intact male dogs certainly get challenged the most by other dogs, but don't count out the females. They may not fight as often, but they can fight more fiercely and can develop individual dislikes that are hard (okay, impossible) to change. (Please see "Dealing with Different Temperaments," on page 68, to determine which category your dog falls into.)

How to Anticipate a Dogfight—Most of the Time

Some fights happen in seconds, but most of the time you can see it coming if you know what to look for.

- Two dogs approach each other slowly and stiffly, tails up, head and ears up. (No one is submitting, so a fight is necessary to ensure that one dog does. There are no "equals" in dogdom.)
- One dog (usually a young dog) continually puts his head or front paws on another dog's shoulders or attempts to hump the other dog. Owners commonly mistake this as "playing"—it is not.
- Two dogs lunge for an object (toy, bone, food) at the same time.
- A dog runs by fast and "by mistake" clips another dog on his way by. The dog who was clipped will often try to even the score the next time that dog comes within reach. Dogs do not bump into each other (or you) "by accident." It is

an assertive move to see if they can do it. *If* they can, you are below them in the universal order of things.

- A dog (often adolescent) rushes into your dog's space. Your dog reacts (as she should), the rusher takes offense, and a fight is on. The rusher's owner often blames you, but if a human were to run at her and stop six inches away, she'd probably react badly to that as well. In this area we have similar social rules.
- A supremely confident dog or one who enjoys a good fight may give little or no warning before firing. The former may stiffen but will rarely growl. The latter can wag his tail and look happy right up to the instant he responds aggressively; after all, since he likes a fight, he *is* happy.

Defusing a Potential Fight

If you see your dog interacting tensely with another dog, you may have a fight brewing. Dragging your dog away may actually start a fight. So, what do you do?

- **Sound relaxed.** If you sound tense or anxious, this may trigger a fight. Try humming or singing something happy. This can help.
- **Keep moving.** If your dog is loose in a dog run, try heading for the gate. This will draw many dogs away from a situation.
- **Give a command.** Saying "Come" or "Leave it" may give your dog the out he needs to slip away. Praise him warmly if he heads in your direction.
- **If on lead, do not pull up.** Instead, apply pressure down toward the ground and back. For some reason, this sometimes can allow you to get your dog out without causing aggression. No promises, though.

How to Break Up a Dogfight

Suddenly your dog is in a fight. You want this to stop right now—what do you do? First of all, be careful. This is a primary bite situation, and you can get really hurt. The good news (if there is any) is that most fights are over and done with quickly. In general, the more noise, the less real danger. But even a short fight can seem long. So what do you do?

METRODOG

Here's what you do *not* do. You do *not* reach in for a collar. When dogs are in the midst of a fight, they may bite any moving thing they see, without realizing that moving thing is your hand. Also, grabbing the collar means reaching toward a dominance hot button (the back of the neck) and creating a recipe for wounds as well as escalating aggression.

Another instinct you'll have that will get you bitten is to stick your leg in between the two dogs. While that may work, it may not be worth the injury that often results.

The first level of safe intervention is a loud noise: Call your dog to you, get on him verbally, and see what happens. Come on intense and serious, not high-pitched and hysterical. Some dogs will fold, others will intensify their aggression if they hear their person is upset. But it's probably worth a try.

Second level is to put something between them that isn't flesh. A garbage can or lid, backpack, or some other handy object can be put between them without too much risk to your life and limb.

DOG BITES

If you get bitten, see a doctor. Dog bites are usually puncture wounds, and puncture wounds need to be kept open and clean while they heal from the bottom up. This means that in many cases even deep wounds will not be stitched up for fear of creating a pocket for infection. Soaking your wound several times a day in a Betadine solution, as hot as you can stand, is good basic protocol, but it should not replace medical attention. Serious bites can be largely avoided by learning more about dog behavior and training.

If you must, grab a hind leg(s) and/or the base of the tail as close to the body as you can. The farther away from the body you grab, the bigger the risk of injury to your dog. Once you have a good grip, lift up and *back up. Continue backing up.* Backing up will help keep the end with teeth as far away from you as possible.

If the dog is small, be careful picking him up because he's not himself in the middle of a fight and may bite you. Hold him away from you and move him to a quiet area to calm him down. Do not attempt to interact with him as normal until you see by his actions that he is calmed down.

What if your dog is not the aggressor? Fine question. You need to disengage the main aggressor from the fight. More than once I have hauled away some other dog because I knew I could verbally control my own. But handling someone else's dog in the middle of a fight is a big risk—you may get injured by the dog and/or bellowed at by the owner, whose dog was no doubt "just playing" or some such nonsense.

In the best of all worlds, the other owner is involved and you both haul your dogs away at the same time. You may need to direct the other owner as to what to do. Most fights are just squabbles, but if things get serious, you'll know a few of your options.

TIPS FOR TOYS: SAFETY

Toy breeds (any dog under fifteen pounds) are at greater risk of both intentional and inadvertent injury than larger animals. If you exercise your small dog in a park area, be watchful of what dogs are around you. Pay attention to their body language. Even a normally nice dog can get overly stimulated by the quick actions, rapid-fire barking, and petite, somewhat preylike stature of a small dog.

We aren't comfortable with small breeds playing with larger breeds, because things can shift astonishingly quickly and the risk to the small dog is extreme.

Better to play with other smaller dogs or romp with you alone. New York City provides a few runs just for small dogs, and they are frequently busier than the runs for larger dogs.

This chocolate Lab is getting treats for being near this toddler, building a positive association as he nibbles.

Safe Interactions: Metrodogs and Kids

No other dogs have as many diverse, un-planned, and sometimes overwhelming inter-actions with children as the Metrodog. One pup we know developed a lifetime phobia of children when he, at an impressionable age of five months, and his owner rounded a corner, only to be swarmed by a mass of giggling, squealing, delighted kindergartners. (This might not have been as traumatic for the pup if the owner had been able to scoop him up and, laughing, move him to a calmer place. Your reaction during this type of occurrence is critical to how your dog will remember it.)

Some breeds (and individuals in all breeds) can be drawn to children. This is especially true if the breeder had children in the home. In any event, there are a number of things you can do to help your pup accept children:

PREVENT SCARY INTERACTIONS

One day in the park, I was chatting with a friend and did not see a toddler heading toward my Australian Shepherd pup. What I saw next was the toddler hopping toward Caras like a kangaroo. The child was giggling, but Caras was in fast retreat, with the child hopping after. No harm was meant, but harm was done. It took me years to get Caras over his distrust of toddlers.

Things that could have prevented this:

- If I was going to chat, I could have called my pup to me and put him on lead.
- When I saw this was about to happen, I could have gotten my pup's attention with my voice, a treat, or a toy and moved away happy.
- Once it was happening, I could have gotten Caras, then asked the toddler's parent if the child would like to give some treats to my pup. If I had praised and cheered him on during these treats, I might have prevented this long-term problem.

If Caras had already had many positive interactions under his belt, this single negative one would probably not have made such a big impact.

BUILD POSITIVE ASSOCIATIONS

Even if you don't have many children in your life, you need to help your pup accept children. Get a pocketful of treats. Go to a local playground. Sit at a distance and, any time your dog looks toward the children, reward and praise. If your dog doesn't seem to notice the kids, move a bit closer.

Two young dogs are earning treats outside a busy urban playground. This is a great way to teach a pup to love the sound of children.

  METRODOG

Watch for signs of stress, such as panting, trying to move away, whining, or trying to get under a bench or onto your lap. If you see those signs, move your dog farther away or quit for the day.

If your dog growls at children or seems terrified (hiding, shaking, and so forth), please seek professional help so this does not become a lifetime phobia. If your puppy is not comfortable with children, she can easily grow into an adult who cannot be trusted around children if steps are not taken to change her reactions. Fear does not generally "go away" on its own. It must be actively changed with thoughtful re-education.

As your dog becomes used to children nearby, move closer to the fencing. (Almost every urban playground is fenced.) Any time a kid runs past—praise

SARAH WILSON

This Dane is nervous. The owner is near the stranger, and the lead is slack, good! The stranger is kneeling and not reaching out, good!

your pup, back away, and encourage her to move and romp, give treats. Do this for a few seconds, then step back to the fence and be silent. Repeat.

Soon your pup will be hoping a child will run by, and that is a fine start to having a puppy who is safe around kids. Hopefully this goes without saying, but don't allow children to hug or kiss your dog on the face. This can force your dog to react with aggression if she is frightened.

Preventing scary interactions is a two-way street. You also need to be considerate of the children. If you know your dog barks at kids (or worse), keep her in control 100 percent of the time. A head halter is a good tool for these dogs. (Please see page 180 for information about head halters.) Giving these dogs exercise early in the morning or late at night can limit unplanned dog/child interactions. Romping in fenced-in areas or on a long-line/retractable leash are other ways of keeping everyone safe.

Eighteen-Month-Old Weenies

Somewhere around eighteen months of age, might be fifteen months, might be twenty, your dog may enter yet another sensitive period. All of a sudden, your friendly German Shepherd Dog may be looking anxiously (or maybe barking) at the man in the odd hat or your Labrador might be unsure of the sign banging in the wind at the corner store—the corner store he's walked by for months.

Given time, this too shall pass. Most of the time it passes in a matter of weeks, but sometimes it can really try your patience, seeming to linger for a month or longer. Proper reaction on your part can lessen the length of this event, just as improper handling can cause it to linger.

If your dog shows insecurity, become the picture of confidence and relaxation. If he balks at something, laugh while you march on past it. "Silly pup, this is just a —— that you've seen a million times!" Praise happily. Courage comes in small steps.

This assumes the dog is hesitant, not panicked. If he is beside himself with fear, then you might want to cross the street and give him room. But while you do it, keep an upbeat and happy manner. Distance and movement are the general antidotes to fear. A dog who is terrified at six feet away from something may be quite relaxed at sixteen feet. Take a truly fearful dog to a distance where he feels comfortable. Give him some other things to do, like "let's go" or "come." Asserting your leadership here in a calm, benevolent way will reassure your dog that you are in control and that he does not need to worry. It also prevents him from focusing on the feared object nonstop.

It does not help for you to become concerned and worried with your dog. Stroking him and soothing him in praise tones while he is showing fear will support that fear, it does not help him relax. Stroke him when he is behaving confidently and you'll make better progress.

Fear is one of the more difficult canine problems to work with on your own. Keep the basic rules that you need to act confidently, support your dog's bold (or at least normal) behavior, and ignore or redirect his unwanted/fearful/neurotic behavior, and you can help your dog through this stage without creating long-term problems for yourself.

METRODOG

OPINIONS ABOUT TRAINING EQUIPMENT

"I could never use . . . [insert any piece of equipment]" is a common statement. And no matter what your preference and prejudices, there are people who are successful and humane with *all* of the tools out today. There are also people who fail or abuse with those same tools. The truth? Equipment will not make you a more experienced trainer. It will not make you kinder or meaner. Use it well and you will succeed. Use it poorly and you will have trouble.

Training Equipment: The Good and the Bad

Different dogs can need different pieces of equipment to succeed. We waited to discuss these tools, as most pups can be worked quite well on a wide, flat buckle collar. As with all training, there are exceptions to this. A large, powerful pup may do better on a head halter or a small prong. A pup with a sensitive trachea may need a harness.

We urge you to get hands-on instruction about the use of any training tool before you use it on your dog. Knowing how to use a tool effectively can make training easier on both ends of the lead.

FLAT—BUCKLE

"Wider is better" applies to flat collars. The smaller the dog, the more potentially delicate the throat and the wider the collar needs to be proportionally.

Best Match

Any dog, but specifically puppies under seven months old and physically sensitive dogs.

Limitations

Often ineffective for corrections, especially when the corrections are done by people learning the skill. Because the collar is ineffective, people can become frustrated, leading to the use of more force (both more often and harder), or the dog learns that all this tugging means nothing and comes to ignore it completely.

Bracken models a chain/fabric version of the martingale.

FLAT—MARTINGALE

This collar can tighten only so far before stopping. It can be found in chain or fabric or a combination of both. It was designed for sight hounds, whose thick, muscular necks and narrow, streamlined skulls made a buckle collar too easy to slip off. These sensitive dogs were not happy on slip collars, so the martingale was born. A middle ground between the two, these collars do not slip off.

Best Match

Thick-necked, narrow-headed dogs. Dogs experienced at slipping collars. This is also a lovely general training collar. The fabric ones are nice on pups and sensitive dogs, the chain/fabric hybrids work for sensitive to stable dogs, and the chain ones can work on most dogs.

These collars work effectively with less-than-perfect timing and won't strangle your dog endlessly if he pulls.

Limitations

For some touch-insensitive (possibly some reactive) dogs, these collars will not be effective if you're using corrections.

SLIP COLLAR (ALSO CALLED A "CHOKE")

These collars have been around for about as long as people have been training dogs. Found everywhere, these are probably the most frequently misused dog-training tool ever invented.

These collars are usually sold without instruction, and people expect the collar to train the dog. What ends up happening is that dogs drag their owners around while being choked by a collar that never loosens because it was put on improperly, used improperly, or both.

Effective use (in skilled hands) requires hands-on training, well-developed timing, and an ability to rate the dog's reaction and change the corrections to match—all skills that no novice will, by definition, have.

Best Match

Instead of matching these to dogs, let us match them to a situation. Best used with a trainer who will combine praise, play, and treats to teach and support the wanted behavior while demonstrating how and when to use this tool effectively.

Limitations

First and foremost, they do not belong on puppies.

As above, the skills needed for effective use must be learned. This is not a tool you can take off the shelf and use successfully without training. And as frequently happens, people who don't have success tend to blame the dog, yank harder and more often. This is never the road to good communication, and if you find yourself on it, please change tools, get hands-on help, or both.

Any time you find yourself blaming the dog, realize that is just another way to say, "I don't know how to change this situation." When we don't know what to do (or we feel we're ineffective), we tend to blame. The more you learn about how to be an effective teacher for your dog, the less you will find yourself blaming the dog.

There is always more to learn. If you've tried everything you know, that doesn't mean you've tried everything there is to try. Keep looking for help, reading, surfing the Net. Try new things. In most cases, something is out there that can help.

CHRISTINE PELLICANO

This dog is wearing a prong, but he's apparently thinking about the next treat he's going to earn.

PRONG COLLAR (ALSO CALLED A "PINCH")

Few tools are as controversial as this one. It looks like some sort of instrument of evil, and people can dislike it passionately without ever learning anything about it. This is a collar that must be used with a larger, backup slip collar (clip the lead to both at the same time). This way, if the prong opens suddenly, your dog will still be safe and with you.

Best Match

Any situation where the dog's power outmatches the human's. This can mean a large dog/smaller female owner combo or a touch-insensitive dog combined with a sensitive person or a dog who has been trained to ignore collar pressure (say, a rescue who was tied out for years). To this list I would add frustrated owners who are at the end of their rope and need to see some results right now to be willing to keep the dog.

These can be excellent collars for dogs with sensitive tracheas who are bothered by anything else around their neck but are not successful on a harness or head halter.

Limitations

Some dogs are overwhelmed by these collars—sensitive dogs of all sizes can fall into this category. Also, some dogs, notably some terriers and herding breeds, can flip stimulation plus discomfort into aggression, though this happens much less in our experience than some seem to say.

This is not the tool to use if you tend to lose your temper. Just be honest with yourself. If frustration gets the best of you, learn about the methods that can be done off lead—like clicker work. If you don't have a lead in your hand, you'll be much less likely to do things you'll regret later. Also, by focusing all the training energy on what can be rewarded (instead of hunting for what can be corrected), you'll find yourself less frustrated anyway.

There are no perfect teachers, just humans doing the best we can. We all have different skills and tendencies. The trick is to know what they are and select methods to match our strengths and not to play into our weaknesses.

INNER-CITY YOUTH   **179**

SARAH WILSON

Bracken modeling a head halter. She can open her mouth, pant, carry a toy. It is not a muzzle.

SHIRLEY MINATELLI

Good training and a head halter allow this young boy to control this massive Dogue de Bordeaux.

HEAD HALTER

This tool fits on a dog's head as a halter fits on a horse. There are a variety of such halters, and new, "improved" versions are being created all the time. Head halters must be used with a larger, backup slip collar (clip the lead to both at the same time). This way, if the halter slips off, your dog will still be safe and with you.

  **METRODOG**

Best Match

Dogs with a nose (don't laugh; we defy you to fit one of these on some Pekingese or Shih Tzu we've met). Dogs who lunge at anything, aggressive dogs, or dogs who pick up garbage off the street are excellent candidates. Halters can be near instant management tools, offering quick relief from some annoying habits.

Some trainers use these exclusively, feeling they are more humane than any collar. Many dogs will adapt to these if introduced slowly and positively. If you simply put one on and try to go for a walk, you may see major canine protest, such as bucking, pawing, face rubbing (on the ground and on you), and resistance. A little reaction is probably a normal part of the process, but it can largely be avoided by a slower, positive introduction to the tool.

Limitations

Don't use if you lose your temper easily. Yanking on a head halter can cause injury. Also, don't use with a long line or a retractable lead, as hitting the end of that at a run can seriously hurt your dog.

Some people find that while a dog responds well with the halter on, with the halter off the dog is much less reliable. That is a training rather than an equipment issue. Finally, because it can be mistaken for a muzzle, some people simply don't care for them.

NO-PULL HARNESS

This rig fits like a harness but tightens under the dog's armpits when the dog pulls. When the dog stops pulling, the harness loosens. Some versions come with padding that protects the dog's armpits from irritation.

Best Match

We've heard of people with sensitive dogs and some Nordic dogs (Huskies, Mala-mutes) who claim good results with this tool. Since the dog causes the tightening or loosening, it seems that people find it easy to use. Also, it's a gentle choice for dogs with tracheal sensitivity or toys with collapsing trachea problems. A trainer we know says she's had good results with this, calming some excitable dogs. We have not used this tool a great deal, so all we can do is report others' comments.

Limitations

Some dogs just don't care about the tightening action. Others learn to ignore it. It does not control the dog's head, so if garbage eating or lunging is a problem, we'd recommend another choice.

The padding has been added to some versions because the cord under the armpit can irritate the skin there. It seems certain to mat long-coated dogs in the pit area, but some trimming should prevent that.

ELECTRIC COLLARS

Some people are tempted to use these to "fix" recall problems in the park or "correct" dog aggression on the street. Properly used (at low levels on behaviors the dog understands extremely well and in a trainer's hands), these can be effective tools. But because the potential for misuse is so high and the results of misuse so potentially traumatic for the dog, these are not tools for novice hands. (For a discussion of electric bark collars please see "Bark Collars," page 235.)

Best Match

Should be used by professional trainers who are experienced, understand the dog, and have complete control over their own temper. Everyone else should steer clear.

Limitations

The pure power of this equipment is immense, and you can take a dog apart mentally if you use it incorrectly. Always test a collar on your own leg to make sure it is working properly. If you aren't willing to do that, do not strap it on your dog.

LEASHES

Leashes are made in virtually every color, length, or fabric. Which will work best for you? That's a matter of preference and training technique. Regardless of the specifics of use, a general truth is that the lead is a tool, it should *not* be your primary means of control. Control needs to come from your relationship, your actions, and your dog's understanding. When it is based on those things, it is irrelevant whether your dog is on or off lead, because she is always in connection with you (or almost always). How do you know if you are using your lead, instead of your relationship and training, to control your dog? Simple. When she is off leash, she does not respond. When that happens, you know you've got work to do.

BRIAN KILCOMMONS

Stepping on the lead, shown here, is a great way to control your dog when you want to chat or you can't pay complete attention.

Length

Our preference is for a four-foot leash, especially in the city. This gives enough length for bathroom duties but also prevents the dog from getting easily tangled. Shorter leads tend to promote pulling, while longer leads can be hard to handle.

Clips

Look for small, strong clips. Large clips may look impressive, but they can smack your dog in the face if you mishandle the lead. They can also hold any sort of tightening collar (martingale, prong, or slip) slightly tight at all times. This will put the dog in a constant state of mild correction, which eventually teaches him to ignore those mild ones.

Material

Leather is our hands-down favorite. Good quality is rarely found in stores, so you may have to hunt mail-order or on-line resources. (A favorite of ours is J and J Dog Supplies, 1-800-642-2050 or jandjdog.com). Leather is strong and gentle on your hands and has some natural give to it. We use three-eighths-inch wide for almost everything, half-inch wide for really big/hard-pulling dogs, and quarter-inch wide for toy breeds.

Cotton is usually easy to find and a good second choice to leather. It can be hard to find a four-foot cotton lead.

Nylon is by far the most common. It is strong, long lasting, and comes in a variety of colors. It also can burn your hands if your dog pulls suddenly and it has no give.

Chain, most commonly used by people who have leash chewers, is hard on the hands, can take out a tooth if it gets caught in the links, and has no give to it.

Retractable leads are great in the open area of a park or on a woodland hike because they allow your dog some freedom to explore while leaving you some control. They are also useful training tools for practicing "stay" and "come" out-

side. They do not belong on the sidewalk, where they can pose a hazard to other sidewalk users.

SARAH WILSON

Drink a cup of coffee, holding on to your dog, in a crowded street fair? Impressive! Enviable! Achievable!

Training for the Inner-City Youth

By now the basic work is behind you, and you two are becoming a real team. Your dog understands you, and you understand him (most of the time). You know that you need to put your time into training to see the results you want, and he can count on you to be fair and positive.

This next level of training is all about building on what you have already done, so don't skip any steps. Go back and do the work described earlier, and then when you are ready for this stage, it will all fall into place smoothly (or more smoothly than if you didn't do the basic work). Please be sure to look up the type of temperament your dog has and the best ways to approach it ("Dealing with Different Temperaments," page 68).

ADVANCED SIT

Goal: Dog sits on command even when you are not looking at him or facing him.

You: When you have your dog's attention, say, "Sit," while you look at the ceiling. (You can also do this facing away from him into a mirror or reflective surface like an oven door.) Because body language is a dog's mother tongue, they often use our physical cues to learn what we want. By changing/removing those cues, we slowly teach the dog that the words are what we need him to respond to, not our eye contact or posture.

This will be helpful later on when he is chasing a squirrel or watching some other dog step into the elevator with you and will not be looking at you when you need him to respond. So don't wait for eye contact to issue a command. It is your dog's job to listen and respond, not yours to contort your body in an attempt to get his attention. We've also seen plenty of dogs who learned that their owners would not command without eye contact and consequently refused to look at their owner if they thought a command might be coming their way.

Dog: Sits no matter which way either of you is facing.

Potential problem: Your dog does not sit. Usually this happens because he no longer recognizes the command in a new situation. Again, he is not being difficult. Simply place him calmly and reward/praise as if he were starting the command all over again (because in a way he is). Soon he will catch on.

ADVANCED DOWN

If you've done the work outlined in the previous two chapters, your dog is now downing from a stand, responding to your hand signal and/or verbal command.

The next step is to teach him how to down from movement. The reason for this is that often your dog is in the most danger when he is moving—fast. He yanks the leash from your hands to chase a squirrel. His collar slips off as he pounces at some paper blowing by in the street. He and a buddy get playing and take off across the park. Once I was standing in Prospect Park in Brooklyn and did not

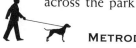

notice my dog playing a major game of chase with a friend's dog—a game headed right toward the road. Kesl, my Bouvier, downed on command about one hundred feet away. His play buddy did not and got hit. Luckily that dog was okay, but the story shows that a moving down should be a part of every dog's education.

There are really two parts to teaching a good moving down. One is getting some distance, and the other is teaching your dog how to down when he is moving, since up until now he has downed only from a stationary position.

THE CRAZY PERSON GAME

Here's a fun game I learned at a Sue Sternberg seminar. The goal is to teach your dog that no matter how crazy a person acts, if she (your dog) sits, she'll get a treat. Start slowly and build as your dog catches on.

- Start with your dog sitting.
- Reward.
- Maybe flap one arm like a bird.
- If she stays sitting, reward.
- If she gets up, have her sit, then repeat until she stays put.
- Now reward.
- Next try lifting your foot out to the side or offering her a treat and withdrawing it or jumping up and down like a pogo stick . . . go ahead and laugh. Having fun is good for you.
- Every time your dog figures out to stay seated, you praise and reward.
- Every time she gets up, you have her sit again without a reward.

You'll be astonished how quickly your dog learns that no matter how crazy you act, if she stays sitting, she gets a reward.

Hint: Crazy does not mean scary. No effort to frighten or intimidate your dog is called for. Your goal is to build her confidence in you, not challenge it.

Here a young Labrador and his owner start work on distance.

Good dog! Notice the person steps toward her pup to reward him in position.

DISTANCE DOWN

After weeks and months of lying down at your feet, many dogs come to think that is where "down" is; they have no idea that "down" can mean lie down across the room.

To test this theory, simply command "down" when he is across the room. If he trots over to you and then downs, you know that's what he thinks "down" means.

One way to address this is to tether your dog on a buckle collar to a doorknob, fence, signpost, whatever. Attach another lead to another collar. Step a few feet away and command, "Down."

Either reach in and guide your dog into a down with the second lead and reward or give the hand signal and wait a few seconds. Many dogs will fuss for a few seconds, trying to get to you, then down. Praise and reward as if it were his idea in the first place. (Don't let this waiting become a habit, though. Once he starts to respond to the hand signal, reward only a quick response. Ignore those slower ones or, if you really want to make your point, show him the treat he could have had but don't let him have it.)

Practice this repeatedly. Add more distance when your dog shows he can down comfortably at the distance he is at now. It usually doesn't take dogs too long to understand this change in the down rules, and they'll be downing from across the room in no time.

Potential problems: Your dog does not down. Do more work close to him. When he is nearly 100 percent reliable up close, step back a foot and try. Increase your distance foot by foot, going farther away only when he is responsive at the current distance. Going slow in this sort of exercise can actually mean you progress faster.

Odd, but true.

Your dog attempts to crawl toward you. This is an important sign that he is anxious or confused. Work a bit closer to him. Go back and praise him calmly, give treats often. Make "stay" a pleasant exercise with no stress attached. When he feels secure, the crawling should stop.

DOWN WHEN MOVING

Just as with distance, your dog may honestly believe that he can lie down only from a standstill, since that is the only time he has had to lie down on command.

Put him on lead, and work in a quiet area where you have some room. (A hall is often perfect.) Start walking with your dog next to you. Give the command "Down," take the lead near the clip, and, thumb pointing to the ground, apply even, guiding pressure forward and downward at the same time, following his forward motion into a down. No yanking! (This is a method Brian learned from the legendary British trainer Barbara Woodhouse, and it works as well today as it did decades back.)

You can also walk backward with your dog coming toward you. Give the command and step toward your dog. Put a treat to his nose, then move it back toward his chest and down. As he tucks in his nose to follow, he will fold back into the down position.

Use one method, use the other, combine—match your training to your dog. As long as he gets the idea, the exact approach you elect to use is not too important.

Potential problem: Your dog resists leash pressure. You may be strong-arming him rather than using a guiding pressure. Any sudden or intense force leads to a dog being surprised or freezing up. This is *not* stubbornness, but an understandable reaction to what feels more like an attack than training. The solution to this is to change what you are doing. Use even, guiding pressure, not yanking or sudden, intense force.

If you are using steady, even pressure and the dog still is having a hard time, you can 1) go back and do more work luring him into a down while applying some leash pressure, or 2) simply wait him out. Often dogs who have good pretraining may brace for a second and then, if you wait calmly, ease into a down. Immediate praise and release will make it clear that he made a good choice.

OFF OF FURNITURE

So far, we've focused our work on "off" meaning "off that human." As this can be a period of testing limits, it is a fine time to start work on another version of "off," meaning "off that couch" or bed or kitchen table.

  **METRODOG**

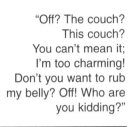

"Off? The couch? This couch? You can't mean it; I'm too charming! Don't you want to rub my belly? Off! Who are you kidding?"

Potential problems: Your dog won't get off. Whether because she freezes in place or says "nope" altogether, handle the problem the same way: Leave a leash on her and guide her off. The moment her feet hit the floor—*Good dog!* How smart! How intuitive!" (Hey, you know it was inevitable, but let her think it was her idea.) Dogs are usually more than happy to take the credit in such matters, and your warm praise will make compliance more likely next time.

Your dog growls at you. Time to call a professional. But until then, how the heck do you get her off the couch? If a lead is on and if she allows you to touch the lead, you can guide her off, then praise.

Why praise if she was growling two minutes ago? Because she was growling on the couch, but when she got off the couch, she was responding to you, and response to you is rewarded. Dogs do not have a concept of "before." So if she growls and you tell her, "Off," and she gets off, and then you scold her, she thinks she's being scolded for getting off, since that is the last thing she did before the scolding started.

As a last-ditch maneuver to get a growling dog off the couch, try ringing the doorbell or buzzer (few dogs can resist flying toward the door when they hear that). Then go read our section "Dominant Dogs," page 247).

Your dog jumps on and off rapidly. Silly and excited, she's just being a goof. Leaving a lead on her can help. Directing her to another behavior, such as a come, sit, or down, can stop the on again/off again leaping.

PLACE—CONTINUED

Now that your dog knows to go to his bed and lie down, it is time to introduce having him stay there. This is most easily accomplished simply by rewarding him frequently when he's on the bed. At first, do this every few seconds, then, as he stays with more ease, reward him every minute or so. If he gets up from "place," just guide him back (leave a lead on him) and guide him into the down and step away. Say nothing. This will make your point nicely.

Be sure to continue to give him a clear release from the command, such as "Okay" or "All done," so that he waits for your cue and doesn't start getting up on his own because he is confused.

NEW COMMANDS

Move

In cramped quarters like studio apartments, dogs can get seriously underfoot. "Move" is both a sanity saver and a pure physical necessity. From the dog training point of view, it is also important as a mental exercise.

In the world of dogs, the lower-ranked group members move out of the way or move around the members above them. So when you step around your dog, guess where that puts you in his mind? To the back of the pack.

Goal: Your dog gets up and moves out of your way when he sees you coming or when you tell him, "Move."

  **METRODOG**

You: "Move" is easy to teach. When your dog is in your way, simply shuffle through him. If he does not move, shuffle with energy! Shuffle rather than walk because you don't want to kick him, you want to nudge him, and because you don't want to lose your balance.

Dog: He moves out of your way, and praise him!

Potential problems: Your dog does not move. Some dogs get confused and freeze in place. If this happens, leave a leash on him and guide him out of the way, praising. Or have a housemate guide him. He's confused and has locked on to the wrong answer. Once he knows what you want, he'll be more than ready to do it.

Your dog growls at you. Call a qualified trainer or behaviorist. Neuter him tomorrow, if not sooner. Read the section "Dominant Dogs" on page 247. Avoid confronting your dog or "showing him who's boss," as this often escalates the aggression. Instead, take control by working him every time you can and ignoring him the rest of the time. That works better (and is easier and safer for everyone) than confrontation.

Stay

As long as we're at it, we might as well teach a solid stay. Since you already have a good "wait" and "place," "stay" should not be too difficult.

While "wait" means "pause for a second or two before we do something else" and "place" means "go to your bed and lie down," "stay" means "stay right where I left you, just as I left you, until I get back."

Stay has a beginning, a middle, and an end. The beginning is the command "stay," the middle is your dog staying, and the end is you releasing your dog from the stay. Now, most of my career I've used a verbal release such as "Okay" to signal my dog. But Becky Bishop of Puppy Manners out in Washington State shared her method on our GreatPets.com message boards, and I think it is an improvement. She uses a physical cue to signal "all done." She uses a double shoulder tap—just a finger tap, tap on the dog's shoulders.

BRIAN KILCOMMONS

Making good use of a retractable lead, the man gives the "stay" hand signal and says, "Stay," at the same moment, as he's stepping away.

What I like about this is that it is clear to the dog. She won't get released by accident, which is a problem with the "okay." Your dog can be staying, you can be chatting with a friend, you wave her off and say, "Okay, we'll talk later . . . ," and your dog is up.

It also requires the human to return to the dog. This is another advantage because it prevents us from ruining a good stay by calling our dogs. If you plan to call your dog, use a "wait." Calling your dog from a stay only teaches her to get up when you are a certain distance from her—not the training goal!

Here's how you start:

METRODOG

This part could not be easier. Have your dog sit, say, "Stay," keep your palm out toward her (think "stop" signal), wait a second or two, then reach in, tap her twice on the shoulder, and step away. Praise! Repeat.

Your only goal right now is to have her sit, stay, and be released. Over and over again. Once she is successful at this several dozen times, simply delay your return for a few seconds. Step back, tap, tap, and praise. Be sure she gets up and moves after your tap on her shoulder.

If you would like to use treats, give her small treats for sitting quietly. When you release her, praise but no treats. Soon she'll figure out that sitting earns her treats.

If she gets up, replace her into the sit and repeat. Stay calm, but be persistent. If need be, keep her on lead with the lead held above her head. *No* tension. It is there simply to remind her to not move forward if she gets up. The word here is "remind," not strangle or pull her off the ground. If your dog gets up, use the lead and collar to prevent forward movement. This makes getting up nonrewarding, which will improve her stays.

Let's Go

Controlled walking is an ongoing exercise and a tough one to do consistently, since you can't avoid walking your dog. People with fenced yards can limit leash time to training time and make the dog's experience on lead 100 percent consistent. But the Metrodog must get from point A to point B.

Here are a few games you can play to help control pulling:

Pulling comes naturally, it's training your dog not to that takes time.

• **Stop and go.** If you stop (when the lead is tight) and go (when the lead is slack), you can teach the dog to give slack when you stop. However, if your dog has been pulling successfully for any length of time, this method will probably be incredibly frustrating but not incredibly helpful. The fact is, few of us Metrodog owners have the time or the inclination to stop every few steps on our way to the park before work. And if you are not absolutely consistent, you can cause a bigger problem than the one you had before.

• **Follow the leader.** This version has you changing speeds or directions as a means of educating your dog about why he should pay attention to you (you're unpredictable). This combines warm praise with well-placed, well-timed leash corrections.

As this allows you to make progress toward your goal of an errand or the dog run, it can be effective. It still can be tough to manage numerous turns on crowded streets, and some people feel conspicuous working this way. If you want to train your dog in the city, you'll have to get over the conspicuous part, no way around it.

This, too, is a method that requires hands-on instruction to manage properly, and done improperly, it will be ineffective at best and really upsetting/unkind to your dog at worst.

THE WALK AND STOP

Is every walk a journey of a thousand leg lifts? Do you ponder how your dog could possibly have one more drop of urine in him? You're not alone, and the good news is, you can change it. At the start of your walk, allow your dog to urinate on two or three things close to home, then after that, walk. Don't stop when he tries to stop. Stay happy, but keep going. This will soon teach your dog to empty his bladder right at the start. This will help lessen dog-to-dog aggression as well, since he will no longer be claiming every inch of the walk as his territory. (Exactly what he's doing when he hikes his leg multiple times.)

CHAPTER 5

Smooth Sailing
(Nineteen Months to Seven Years Plus/Minus)

Ah, adulthood.

A time when behaviors, both good and bad, have become habit. If you've worked hard for the last year and a half, all your efforts start paying huge dividends. People stop you on the street to comment on what a well-behaved dog you have (as if they grow on trees). You know each other intimately, your smallest actions tell your dog what is about to happen, and a look on his face can relay to you his stress, joy, or need to go out.

If you have not worked hard with your pup, or if you've adopted your dog as an adult (good for you), you have some work to do, but it is never too late to train. If you've put off training thinking he will grow out of his problems, only to discover he's grown into them—seek help now. The sooner you teach your new companion what you want, the easier it will be for all involved.

Too much time is wasted on reacting to what we don't want versus teaching what we do want. You can depend on training to make life better if you focus on building the behavior you want. Avoid getting focused on what you don't want; that just cycles into frustration and confusion—often at both ends of the lead.

(By the way, nineteen months and seven years are randomly chosen dates. Few breeds have finished their physical growth at nineteen months, but the age was chosen because the "worst" of the adolescent behavioral phases have come and gone by then, and if you've ridden those out, then things are settling down some. Breeds that are slow maturing may not be done growing in one way or another until four or five. At the other end of the spectrum is seven years. Some giant or short-lived dogs are knocking on the door of old age at five, while smaller/long-lived animals are still in their prime. Seven seemed a fine compromise.)

Health Care

DIET AND NUTRITION

If you want to start a lively discussion in the dog park, ask people what they feed their dogs.

There are people who feed only foods made from "human grade" ingredients; others prepare their dog's food at home; and a few will state, "What is all the fuss about? My dog has eaten brand X for years and seems fine!"

There is a range of high-quality foods on the market today, better than any processed foods ever available to dogs. Educate yourself about the food available; spending a little more on a bag of food may save you money in fewer trips to the veterinarian for skin, coat, and ear problems. That isn't true for every dog, but many dogs are reaping the health benefits of some stiff competition and educated consumerism in the dog food industry.

DENTAL CARE

Dogs who do a lot of chewing of hard items like nylon and real bones generally have cleaner teeth. The downside is that your dog may crack her teeth doing that

chewing. This does not happen to all dogs, but it is happening. Dogs that cannot safely chew hard items (or just aren't big chewers) will need regular dental care, just like the rest of us.

Dogs do get cavities. Not as often as we sugar eaters, but they get them, and when they do, those cavities tend to be at or below the gum line, making them hard to detect. If your dog seems to be having a hard time chewing her food, is drooling more than usual, or is pawing at her mouth, you need to take her to the veterinarian.

Tartar and plaque buildup is the most common (seemingly universal) tooth problem. Your veterinarian will determine the appropriate course of action. This may include tartar removal under sedation or anesthesia, brushing or cleaning of your dog's teeth regularly, supplying safe, hard chew toys, or changing to a dry food diet. Regardless of how you and your veterinarian decide to approach dental care, it is something to consider as your dog enters adulthood.

It doesn't count as exercise if you do all the work.

Beyond Exercise

Boredom is a major problem for most of today's companion dogs, and city dogs are no exception. Often home all day alone, then given an all-too-brief walk in the evening, our adult dogs sometimes don't get the stimulation (mental and physical) or the time in connection with you that they need to be contented.

One answer to this common situation is a dog sport/event. Warning, though: Some of these hobbies are downright addictive!

DOG SPORTS/EVENTS—WHAT THEY ARE AND HOW TO FIND THEM

There has never been such good plain fun to be had with your dog as now. Long-established sports (such as agility) have been spreading like wildfire, and newer sports (such as freestyle obedience) are gaining ground. If you have access to the

Internet, you can find many options at www.dog-play.com. In the meantime, here are a few of the sports/events you can train for within city limits:

This Doberman Pinscher is on a piece of agility equipment called the dog walk. Looks like fun, doesn't it?

Agility

Agility, running obstacle courses of jumps, tunnels, seesaws, tables, and things to climb or weave through, is near to addictive. By far the most popular sport ever to be introduced, agility trials are now shown on more than one cable channel. Several groups run versions of agility, and many welcome mixed breeds in competition. For more information, contact the following:

American Kennel Club (AKC)
5580 Centerview Dr.
Raleigh, NC 27606-3390
Phone: 1-919-233-9767
Fax: 1-919-233-3627
Internet: www.akc.org
E-mail: info@akc.org

Agility Association of Canada (AAC)
957 Seymour Blvd.
North Vancouver, BC V7J 2J7
Canada
Phone: 1-604-230-4225
E-mail: coronet@portal.ca

Australian Shepherd Club of America (ASCA)
6091 East State Highway 21
Bryan, TX 77803-9652
Phone: 1-409-778-1082
Internet: www.asca.org

North American Dog Agility Council (NADAC)
HCR 2, Box 277
St. Maries, ID 83861
Phone: 1-208-689-3803
Internet: www.nadac.com

United States Dog Agility Association (USDAA)
P.O. Box 850995
Richardson, TX 75085-0955
Phone: 1-972-231-9700
Internet: www.usdaa.com

Canine Good Citizen Test

Done under the auspices of the American Kennel Club (AKC), the Canine Good Citizen (CGC) test evaluates your dog and your control in a variety of everyday situations, such as greeting a person walking another dog, allowing handling, and basic manners. The CGC should become the standard for behavior of companion dogs in this country and is a fun goal to train toward. For more information contact the American Kennel Club (please see previous reference).

METRODOG

Competitive Obedience

This tests your dog's response to commands, from something as basic as sitting on command right up to retrieving something you touched from a pile of identical-looking items. For those who love it, this is an engrossing, fun sport. Several organizations offer competition obedience, and a few invite mixed breeds to compete. For more information, contact the American Kennel Club (see above) or one of the following sponsors:

American Mixed Breed Association (AMBOR)
179 Niblick Rd., #113
Paso Robles, CA 93446
Phone/Fax: 1-805-226-9275
E-mail: Ambor@Amborusa.org

Australian Shepherd Club of America (see earlier reference)

Canadian Kennel Club
100-89 Skyway Ave.
Etobicoke, Ontario M9W 6R4
Canada
Phone: 1-416-675-5511
Fax: 1-416-675-6506

United Kennel Club
100 East Kilgore Rd.
Kalamazoo, MI 49001
Phone: 1-616-343-9020
Internet: www.ukcdogs.com

Freestyle Obedience

Often called "dancing with dogs," this is obedience and tricks set to music. The goal is to create a flowing, flawless team exhibiting enthusiasm and joy in the work. People (and dogs) go all out, with costumes and complex choreography. Because of the sheer fun of it, this sport is growing quickly.

Canine Freestyle Federation
Carl Tennille, CFF Treasurer
4207 Minton Dr.
Fairfax, VA 22032
Internet: www.canine-freestyle.org

Flyball

If watching your dog race over a series of jumps, hit a special box that pops a tennis ball out, then race back to you while your teammates cheer him on wildly sounds like fun, contact the following organization:

North American Flyball Association, Inc.
1400 W. Devon Ave., #512
Chicago, IL 60660
Internet: www.flyball.org

Flying Disk (Frisbee)

It's a bird, it's a plane, it's a flying disk dog! This is great fun for the small/medium-size canine athlete who has more energy than calm. Competition ranges from retrieves over distances to freestyle routines that can include vaulting off the human many feet into the air. Can't help but be fun! Involves injury risk, so approach this sensibly and accept your dog's limits.

National Capital Air Canines
2830 Meadow Lane
Falls Church, VA 22042
Phone: 1-703-532-0709
Internet: www.discdog.com

Pet Therapy

If your dog genuinely loves people and you're interested in public service, you may find pet therapy work rewarding. Here, dog/handler teams go in to work with various populations in need. This ranges from straightforward visitation (such as in nursing homes) to assisting with physical and/or speech therapy.

Therapy dogs cause miracles every day. People who haven't spoken in weeks or months will speak to the dog. A child with cancer laughs. A spinal injury patient struggles and succeeds in holding a brush so she can groom the dog. The list goes on and on, but not every dog is a good choice for this work, and testing is involved before permission to participate is granted. For more information on this important work, please contact one of these groups:

Delta Society Pet Partners Programs
289 Perimeter Rd. East
Renton, WA 98055
E-mail: info@deltasociety.org

Therapy Dogs Incorporated
P.O. Box 5868
Cheyenne, WY 82003
Phone: 1-877-843-7364 (1-877-THERDOG)

Therapy Dogs International, Inc.
88 Bartley Rd.
Flanders, NJ 07836
Phone: 1-973-252-9800

RUNNING WITH YOUR DOG

Many people combine their exercise with their dogs and take their companion running with them. Here are a few rules:

- Check with your veterinarian before you start.
- Start slowly, adding a bit of distance each week.
- Carry water.
- Jog in the cool part of the day, especially in the summer. (This is extra important for short-nosed breeds like Boxers, who can get in serious distress quickly if overheated.)
- Keep your dog on lead.
- Use a collar or head halter that gives you control.
- Bring gauze and tape in case of a footpad cut. Those are real bleeders.

SARAH WILSON

After a morning jog, this Brittany will be all set for a quiet day at home.

WHEN DO I STOP CRATING?

We start experimenting with leaving a young dog loose at about a year of age (depending on the dog). This will be for only a few minutes while we run to the mailbox or some such short errand. Most dogs, especially active, oral breeds like retrievers, aren't ready to be on their own for hours on end until their second birthday has come and gone. Some dogs can handle a normal day but will need crating again for schedule changes. Start in small increments to see how your dog handles it. If there are problems, go back to the crate without a worry. Every dog has his own speed for such things.

Home Alone Success

For many dogs, hours spent at home waiting for you to return is an inevitable part of their day. There are things you can do to make this easier for your dog:

EXERCISE

All dogs need exercise for their health, stress release, and mental stimulation. Young dogs need a great deal of exercise, often more than one trip to the dog run a day, and that should have been part of your consideration when getting the dog you did. How long a dog is considered "young" varies from dog to dog. Some giant breeds start settling down before the age of two, and some sporting and terrier breeds are still leaping about as they approach a decade.

WORK FOR A LIVING

Mental stimulation and clarity about their family (pack) structure are two things all dogs need, but dogs left for long hours need more of both. Making them work for a living handles each requirement nicely.

No matter what you plan to do with or for your dog, she must do something for you first. Sit for praise, wait before getting in your elevator, sit before unclipping her lead at the dog run, wait at curbs, down for dinner—you get the idea. The side benefit of this is that you are also getting in tons of training time and you will end up, in a matter of months, with a pretty well-trained dog.

Hint: Guessing doesn't count, meaning if your dog sees the dinner bowl and lies down, that is not enough. She needs to listen and respond. So if she downs, call her to you or teach her how to sit from the down position. Either way, it will serve the purpose.

CALM COMINGS AND GOINGS

This advice hasn't changed in over a decade: Leave your dog as you would leave a significant other whom you've been with for many years. You don't rush to your boyfriend of five years, cling to him, and say in an anxious voice as you leave for work: "Now, be a good boy, okay? Mommy will be right back, okay? Be good for Mommy, okay?" The guy would (we hope) think you were nuts. The usual parting of "Okay, see you later. I should be home five-thirtyish" is a much better guide to how to behave: matter-of-fact, as if it happens every day, because, normally, it does.

Since dogs do not understand the meanings of words, all an emotionally charged leaving will do is create a lot of emotional energy with nowhere to go. And since most of the damage done to homes by dogs is done in the first hour after leaving, leaving the dog emotionally charged is a recipe for trouble.

By the same token, no matter what you come home to, stay calm. Better yet, ignore your dog for the first five minutes or so, then greet her calmly. This should prevent her from becoming unduly anxious prior to your arrival home.

METRODOG

FAKE YOUR DOG OUT

Many things signal dogs that you're leaving. You pick up keys, get your coat, change shoes, go to the door—all these things tell your dog that you are on your way.

Help him stay calm by teaching him that these things do not always mean departure. Pick up your keys whenever you pass them and put them back down. Go to the front door, then walk away. Pick up your coat or bag, put it down. Do this casually, just as a part of your day, and soon your dog will hardly notice. The calmer he is when you leave, the less likely he is to become seriously anxious after you leave.

CHRISTINE PELLICANO

Three well-adjusted friends out for a midday walk. Who says dogs can't smile?

MIDDAY WALK

If it is possible, arranging for a midday walk can give your dog a nice mental break to his long hours alone as well as allow him to go to the bathroom, which has to be nice. While many dogs can and do cope for a whole day without a break, if you can arrange a consistent midday walk, please do.

DON'T LEAVE YOUR DOG AGAIN AT NIGHT

Dogs get used to their routine, but that does not mean they can handle changes to that routine. Even a dog who copes well with being alone all day will often fall apart completely if you come home and then go out again.

Try to socialize on the weekends, but if you must go out after work, drop your dog off at a friend's apartment for the evening or hire a pet sitter to hang out in your absence. This will seem a strange concept to many, but it is about the only way for your dog to have the company he craves and allow you the time to do what you need to do.

Dogs are intelligent and need mental stimulation. Going for a walk in the park with the family can help balance long hours alone.

WHEN CRATING BECOMES CRUEL

Long-term, many-hours-a-day crating can increase restlessness, jumping, chewing, barking, and more. These very behaviors can land the dog back in the crate, creating a vicious, unproductive, inhumane cycle. Dogs who are crated all day need *serious* daily exercise—not a walk down the block, but *at least* thirty to sixty minutes of hard play and training. A break midday with a walker makes the day easier for your dog both mentally and physically. Fortunately, there are pet sitters, walkers, day care, playgroups, training classes, and the beloved dog run. It is possible to put together a schedule that is fair using these services. If you cannot offer your dog a reasonable life, this may not be the right time for a dog.

 METRODOG

Moderate Confinement

While we are big fans of crates for housebreaking and heavy chewing, we don't use them for long-term confinement if they can be avoided. The crate is a small space, and asking a dog to stay there for a full workday, day in and day out, year in and year out, is mind numbing for some and stress producing for others. If you need to use this option, buy a roomier crate once the dog is housebroken. Ideally, enclosing him in the kitchen or a bathroom is a better option if he'll stay behind a gate while you're gone.

If your dog isn't a barker, a bed with a view like this can provide all-day interest and stimulation.

Make the Crate/Bed "Home"

It is important that your dog's crate/bed be seen as an inviting, pleasant place for her. Encourage her to use it for her naps. Put a worn, unlaundered T-shirt or old sweatshirt in with her, as your smell will be comforting. Store toys in there. Give her all her treats in there. Any time you think of it, tell her to "go to bed" (or "kennel up" or "crate" or whatever), walk with her over to it, use a treat to guide her in, have her lie down, give her the treat, and praise her as she eats it. Do this and you will find your dog seeking out her bed/crate at other times for a nap. Any time you see that, praise her and give a treat if you like.

Never haul your dog off the bed or out of the crate to do something unpleasant. Doing so will make that spot "unsafe" and undo all your good work.

A dog on her bed or in her crate is off-limits to children as well. Dogs (like parents) need to take the occasional break without harassment or interruption.

MAINTAIN SIMILAR SCHEDULE

The more things stay the same, the better your dog will cope. So on vacations and weekends, keep his schedule as consistent as possible.

If you give him 100 percent of your time on Sunday and then leave him on Monday, you will create tension and stress. By all means, do give extra time on Sunday, just do it at approximately the same times you would take him out normally and limit your attention during the times he would be alone. That way he will be able to take changes in your schedule in stride.

SOMETHING SPECIAL

The majority of stress about being left (and hence destruction) happens in the first half hour after you leave. Therefore anything we can do to help with that transition time period will help the dog.

I would suggest using Kongs and food cubes (toys that dispense food when the dog plays with them). These items are food puzzles that redirect your dog's basic instincts to hunt.

Your dog should be eating all meals from his Kong (and I mean *all*). There is no law that says a dog must eat from a dish. That is a human social hang-up. Canines were hunters before we domesticated them.

I soak my dog's kibble in water until it is mushy and then pack the Kong (you can freeze it overnight).

To make the game more interesting, you can use several food-filled Kongs and hide them throughout the apartment, so he has to look for them. (You will need to teach your dog to find them so he understands the game.)

The food cube requires a bit more energy to remove the food and is great for dry kibble.

My dogs are so happy to get their food toys that as soon as I start to get them ready, they run to their crates to wait! I give them about five minutes before I leave and then go out the door unceremoniously.

If the dog is very stressed, it may take a day or two to get him to "play." But hunger is a good motivator, so after a missed meal or two he may give in. Once he gets the idea, he'll have fun. Try teaching him the game when you are at home first, perhaps over a weekend.

—compiled by Elizabeth R. Cepero,
St. Hubert's Dog Training School,
Madison, New Jersey

The boss's dog—
he looks like he owns the place!

Taking Your Dog to Work

Increasingly, where building policy and insurance allow, people are able to take their dogs to work with them. This can be a great addition to the workplace if you remember one thing: No one thinks your dog is as cute as you do. And if you're the boss, that goes double. People may say they love your dog, and they may mean it in a non–dog lover kind of way. They mean, "Gee, what a cute dog." They don't mean what we dog nuts mean: "Gee, I don't care about hair all over my clothing or the drool marks on my pant leg." Here are just a few suggestions that may help, from some people who should know:

1. The dog must know and *obey* all basic obedience commands. Stays are especially important.

2. Bathing the dog about every two weeks will help to prevent those with allergies from becoming ill around your dog.

3. Walk the dog regularly; every four hours works well with most dogs.

4. Establish clear guidelines with co-workers as to what you will and will not allow to take place with your dog. Is petting okay? How about treat giving?

5. Every dog needs some down time. Can you take a few breaks during which you spend time with your dog either working on obedience or just cuddling? How about some quiet time in a willing co-worker's office?

—JUDY SAGAL, Owner/Handler/Trainer, Catahoula Service Dog

Who can resist this adorable face? People who don't like dogs, that's who! Keep dogs at work under control. (But isn't she cute?)

CHRISTINE PELLICANO

"If you can, and want to, *please* be sure that your dog *wants* to as well—and can handle it! As a Delta Pet Partner and Pet Partner Evaluator [see 'Pet Therapy,' page 207], I strongly urge folks who want to take their dogs to the workplace to make sure that the dog's behavior is under control—for example, if your dog is going to woof at people coming into your office, will it stop when you tell it to?

"If possible, do a dry run on a Saturday or after work hours to familiarize the dog with the surroundings and different floor surfaces. . . . Some dogs have difficulty getting used to ultra-shiny dark floors, or automatic doors, or elevators (and so on). It is better to work out these glitches with your full concentration focused on the dog than to have to deal with them on a workday."

—CHRIS HILL

In general, the less anyone else is aware of your animal, the more your animal will be accepted (or tolerated). So don't allow your dog to trot around unsupervised unless you own the company and don't have to care what anyone else really thinks. But if you are the boss, we'd advise against that casual approach anyway, because a disgruntled employee can make some claim against you. ("Your dog bit me, knocked me over, tripped me . . .")

It is great fun and a privilege to have your best buddy with you. Guard that privilege fiercely through thoughtful supervision, grooming, and training of your dog and you will be paving the way for other people to be allowed the same privilege.

Dogs and Taxicabs

Cabs are one of the best ways to get around town, if you can get one to stop when you have a dog. Here are a few rules of the road if you plan to mix cabs with canines:

• **Dogs stay off seats.** They can sit in the footwell, on your lap, in a carrier, or on a towel that you brought with you. They do not clamber all over, leaving nose marks on the windows and paw prints on the interior. Keeping your dog under control makes it more likely that a cabbie will stop for you (and other pet owners) in the future.

- **Only housebroken dogs ride in cabs.** If your pup is not housebroken, he stays in a carrier or on your lap. Make sure your dog is "empty" before riding in any cab.

- **Carry plastic bags, paper towels, and premoistened towelettes.** If your dog vomits or has an accident, you apologize and clean up the mess as if the backseat were an heirloom couch. Leave the vehicle cleaner than when you got in and tip the cabbie big—big enough for him to forgive you.

- **Your dog is under control.** If your dog is not well trained, don't ride. If you must ride with a less-than-controlled animal, have him on a head halter or training collar. If you can't handle your dog, bring along a friend who can, or hire one of the growing number of "pet taxis" to transport your rambunctious dog.

- **Groom your dog.** Odor free and well brushed is all we ask for cab-riding dogs. The next rider may have an allergy to animals, so again, it is a courtesy to the cabbie and the other riders.

BUSES AND SUBWAYS

Small dogs in carriers are allowed on many forms of public transportation. Since others may or may not realize you have an animal, it is important for you to protect yours from accidental bumping or being stepped on. Keep your dog in the carrier, and keep the carrier either on your lap, behind your feet, or below the seat. Also, don't allow strangers to put their fingers in the carrier to "say hello." Many small dogs can be nervous on a noisy subway or bus and may feel cornered in a small carrier. Aggression is possible. Best to let people compliment him from afar.

HAILING CABS

It can be hard to hail a cab in some cities even on a good day; add a large dog to the picture and it can become nearly impossible. Here are a few tricks to getting a cabbie to stop:

- **Be discreet.** If your dog is small, buy a soft carrier that looks like a shoulder bag. Carry it like a shoulder bag, and the cabbie may not even know you have a dog.

  When hailing a cab with my ninety-five-pound Bouvier, I try my best to make him look small and cute. No mean feat for a beast that is regularly mistaken for a bear. A colorful bandanna and downing him slightly behind me minimized the look and demonstrated my control over the dog.

- **Dog, what dog?** Another tack is to tuck your dog between two parked cars in a sitting or down position while you hail the cab. When it stops, get in quick and get your dog in the footwell ASAP. Smile brightly and ignore the looks. Give your destination with confidence. Some cabbies will still throw you out, but others, seeing that the dog is well mannered and that you are pleasant, will accept the fare.

- **Money talks (sometimes).** It's not called a bribe, it's called a tip. A big tip. Such a tip can be discussed ahead of time if the cabbie seems unsure about taking you.

- **And when you're told no?** Smile and thank him. Why? Because a cabbie doesn't expect you to do that. He expects a fight, and any good dog trainer will tell you that meeting aggression with aggression creates only more aggression.

  It's his cab, respect his wishes. If you're nice, even in parting, he may think about it later. Or he may not. Either way, *you* won't be thinking about it later, and that's the important part.

Christine Pellicano

If this Lab spooks, this metal box will crash over (even with a chain)! The pole next to it would have been a better choice.

Christine Pellicano

Tied high, this dog can't get tangled or tangle others, nor can it reach the road. This is one way to do it safely.

Tethering Near Store

Many city dwellers tether their dogs as they dash in for a quick errand. This is always a little risky, because someone could steal your dog quite quickly or, if your dog got loose, he might get into trouble. But if you judge it to be safe, keep the following in mind:

- Keep him in sight. If you can't, don't tether.
- Tie him so he can't get into the street. Someone parking a car or zipping into a space may not see your dog standing there.
- Tie him so he can't trip up pedestrians or get tangled.
- Tie him to something solid. More than one person I know has tied their dog to the portable metal signs some stores stand out on the sidewalks, only to have the dog bolt and take off with the sign dragging behind, terrifying the dog. Always have ID on your dog.
- Make sure the collar cannot be slipped off.
- Do not tether a toy breed, because you never know what large, off-lead dog might come around the corner.
- If your dog can't wait quietly, don't tether him until his stays are solid and silent.

In-Store Manners

Fortunately, there are still places you can bring your companion. But they are few, and seemingly fewer every year. We need to protect our rights to visit such establishments (some department stores, banks, hardware stores, and small video rental places allow well-behaved dogs) by acting responsibly and anticipating potential problems.

One of our clients called to say that her young terrier had bitten someone. The story went that the dog was with his walker and they were in a small coffee shop.

The walker was focused on buying a cup of coffee when she heard the dog growl. She corrected the dog. The man the dog growled at stepped closer to "say hello," and the dog bit him. How many things went wrong here?

First, the walker is paid to walk; why wasn't she walking? She should take care of her personal needs between walks. This is unprofessional behavior.

Second, the dog was in a small, tight space with no room to retreat. When cornered, many dogs who ordinarily would not think about aggression can bite.

The walker did not look to see what the problem was, and she made it worse through correction. This little terrier simply got more tense when he was corrected, especially with no direction or praise following. Assume your dog is reacting to something, and find out what it is. If the walker had seen the man coming, she could have stepped between the dog and the stranger, left the coffee shop, directed the dog to down, or used a treat to distract the dog and focus him on her. Any of those things might have served to avoid the bite. It is the human's job to prevent and protect. This walker did not do her job.

If this walker had followed the guidelines we lay out below, she could have avoided putting her client and her dog at risk of a legal action.

It is a rare thing these days, when a dog is allowed access. Protect all our rights by making sure the store has no regrets.

SHIRLEY MINATELLI

METRODOG

KEEP YOUR DOG NEAR

The closer your dog is to you, the less trouble she can get into. Four-foot leads are about right for most dogs. When you are doing something, "park" your dog at your feet in a down. A dog can't be *that* problematic when lying down.

GIVE YOURSELF AN OUT

Always make sure you have someplace to move if you and your dog start feeling cornered, because feeling cornered will escalate your dog's fear and aggression. Any time you even think she might be getting tense, give a happy "Let's go" and go! Trust your instincts. Better to move away than ignore those feelings and have a problem.

INTERVENE ON YOUR DOG'S BEHALF

People in the city can be bizarre. More than once some young woman rushed at a pup in our care, making high-pitched squeals (the woman, not the dog), fully prepared to invade this pup's space in the most intrusive and frightening way.

When we see this coming (normally we hear it first), we stand up tall, step between the woman and the dog, and say firmly, "Excuse me? I'm sure you don't want to frighten the pup, right?"

If needed, step between her and your dog again. She may end up offended. That's okay. Better she is offended than your pup is frightened and learns both that strangers can be scary and that you can't be relied on to prevent the scary thing.

WATCH YOUR DOG!

It never ceases to amaze me when I see a pool of urine in a store or hotel. What were the owners doing while their dog was peeing? There is *no* excuse for this! If your dog isn't housebroken or hikes his leg, don't bring him with you or don't set him down (if he's a toy). Alternatively, use a belly band or panties to control urine output. If your dog does mark, clean it up. Walking away as if nothing happened only makes it worse for all of us.

BE CONSIDERATE OF OTHERS' FEAR

As hard as it is for us dog lovers to understand, there are people out there, many people, who are deeply afraid of dogs. They should not have to face a deep fear in Macy's any more than I expect to have to walk past a fifteen-pound spider on a leash.

If you see someone tense up and step back, simply move your dog out of their path, smile, and put the dog in a down calmly. I usually say something like "I've got him" while I hold his leash or "I won't let him come any closer"—two things that I hope are somewhat reassuring.

It is not your job (unless you are specifically asked) to reform these people by offering to introduce them to your dog or by saying, "He's friendly." Again, it would be something like someone telling me their large pet spider was friendly. I don't care if the thing won a Nobel Peace Prize, I don't want to meet it, touch it, or interact with it in any way.

Dealing with the Mentally Troubled

I was walking a young Rottweiler one day, a delightful, trusting young dog who was more tail wag than suspicion. As we rounded a corner, a large man wearing a floppy hat and a cape leapt forward at the dog. The man spun and made bizarre noises, and the Rott's eyes got as big as saucers.

Woofing, hackles up, he announced his confusion and fear. I laughed and started to work him, give him something else to focus on, set the tone of "This is not something to worry about." And after a minute or so, he relaxed. He watched the man spin and hoot, then looked at me and wagged his stump of a tail. We continued our walk, no harm done.

TRUST YOUR DOG

Your dog has a nose thousands of times better than ours. It probably isn't simply stronger than ours but no doubt has entirely different abilities. It would be like saying that color is thousands of times better than black and white. That statement doesn't give you the whole picture.

Dogs are now being trained to alert their human of oncoming seizures, heart attacks. They sniff out cancers and are used in arson detection, so is it any surprise that they have insight into some people beyond anything we can imagine?

They can certainly detect drug and alcohol use, conditions of cleanliness, adrenaline, and, logic would suspect, chemical imbalances (or differences) in general. So, they have opinions about people we meet, sometimes strong opinions. If our normally friendly dog stays away from or actively dislikes a stranger, we tend to believe the dog. Some people will consider that silly; we think it is silly not to.

Dogs Off Leash on Sidewalks

There was this huge Saint Bernard who walked off lead in our Upper West Side neighborhood in Manhattan. One time I rounded the corner with our three on lead and this two-hundred-plus-pound male trotted toward us with his tail up and over his back. I was frightened.

As luck would have it, nothing happened, but that was just luck. If one of my dogs had picked up on my fear or had concerns of his own and fired, I feel sure to this day the Saint would have responded in kind and there would have been nothing I or the owner could have done to stop it.

An accident takes only seconds but can last forever. Do not do this!

Walking a dog off leash in the city is illegal, dangerous for your dog, and inconsiderate of others. Sure, your dog is fine on the sidewalk, knows not to go in the street, and is generally just like Lassie.

So?

Your dog is not the only thing happening in a big city. Imagine a bicycle shoots by, startling your dog, who leaps sideways into the street, or the troubled homeless man I spoke about before leapt out at your dog, who fled a few feet sideways as a result? What if, in so doing, your dog not only got hurt by the bus pulling into the stop, but people got hurt on the bus?

What about the fellow city dwellers who are frightened of your dog? Or the child who was bitten who now has to contend with your dog loose on the street?

Walking your dog off lead is fine until it isn't, and the line between the two is half a second wide. There are places in the city to give your dog some freedom, but the sidewalk isn't one of them. Everyone, on lead! That's safer for you, safer for your dog, and safer for the rest of us as well.

If your dog is on lead and is approached by a loose dog, stay relaxed. If your dog is small and you feel there is a risk, pick him up. For larger dogs, keep the leash loose and chat happily. If you get tense or tighten that lead, you signal your dog that there is a problem. You can cause aggression this way. After the dogs have had a good sniff, use "leave it" and "let's go" to move your dog along.

Barbara Lewis of Listen Up Pup in Blanchard, Oklahoma, shared this good idea

METRODOG

in our *Good Owners, Great Pets* newsletter: "For my students that walk dogs in an area with a loose dog problem, I recommend they carry an umbrella—one that automatically opens. The sudden opening of the umbrella usually discourages most dogs, and it also gives you something to 'hide' behind." What a good idea!

Other dog owners use pepper spray (though no dog lover likes it) or one of those plastic lemons filled with juice. In all our years in New York City, we've never had to use either, but we have moved a dog behind us and spoken forcefully to a dog coming our way. Fortunately that has always been enough.

Metrodog Problems with Solutions

The stress, close confines, and constant stimulation of city life can cause Metrodogs to exhibit certain behavioral problems. Here are the most common problems and possible solutions:

Too Much Energy

The bane of some Metrodog owners is the energetic dog. The good news is that while physical exercise is important to your dog's overall well-being, when you can't exercise her physically, exercising her mentally will do nicely.

Engage that brain! Use a clicker to teach tricks that involve patience and self-control. That doesn't mean they have to be serious, though. A biscuit balancing on the end of your dog's nose will focus your dog completely. Teaching her to wait until you're okay for the flip and grab will tire almost any dog. Same with "find it," "name that toy," playing dead, place, stay, wait, or leave it. Discover creative ways to use your dog's self-control, and you will not only have a dog who knows tons of tricks, you will also have a dog who is happy to rest afterward.

Couch Hopping

Dogs like soft places that are heavy with your scent. Your favorite chair is ideal, and your side of the bed or a corner of the couch will work just as well. Some bony and/or thin-coated dogs want and need a soft, warm sleeping spot, and you will need to supply it with a comfortable dog bed of his own if you hope to win the war on furniture rights.

Most other dogs can be more easily influenced to stay earthbound with a combination of prevention, making the couch less appealing, and making some other spot more appealing. (If you have trouble getting your dog off the couch or bed, please see "Off of Furniture," page 190.)

One person's problem is another's delight. Scotch is welcome on the couch for evening cuddle time.

Prevention

Gate off or close the door to the room. If you can't, flip up the cushions, put chairs on the couch, or confine your dog away from the couch.

Make the Couch Less Appealing

Dr. Soraya Juarbe-Diaz shared a good idea: Use a plastic floor runner, with bumps on the back, upside down on the couch. This allows your dog to self-correct if he hops up.

You can also use a handheld ultrasonic unit or a spray bottle of water to correct your dog if you see him up on the couch. *Be discreet!* If he associates the correction with your seeing him, he will simply get off when you come in. If he associates the correction with being on the couch, then he will be less likely to get on the couch.

Make Another Spot More Appealing

Set your dog up on a deliciously soft, wonderful bed (can be anything from an old blanket to a new bed that matches the decor) and reward her whenever she is in it. Several times a day tell her, "Bed," then walk her over to it. When she gets there, reward her with petting, praise, and a mildly interesting treat. (A biscuit is a good choice. This will take her a minute to eat and will not excite her so much that she immediately gets off the bed.)

Store her toys on her bed. Go over to her when she is in her bed and fuss quietly over her. She'll soon develop a nice, warm feeling about the bed and seek it out for naps (at least some of the time).

KEEP OFF/KEEP AWAY PRODUCTS

Keeping your dog out and off of places and things he would like to be investigating can be more than a challenge. If your dog is rewarded for his efforts—finds a bagel on the counter or a soft spot on the cream-colored couch—then he will do it again.

And if he gets scolded by you when you see him do these things, he will be inspired not to be seen. This does not make him "sneaky," it just makes him normal. Following are several products that might help.

ELECTRIC PADS
Commonly known as "scat mats," these give off a mild electrical stimulation when your dog touches them. They can be laid across doorways, on furniture, or over counters to deter your dog.

Limitations
These are easy for a dog to see, so some will work around them and others will stay away as long as the mats are present.

SOUND-BASED DETERRENTS
These make high-pitched or ultrasonic sounds when your dog hops up on the couch (jiggles the equipment) or enters a room (comes within range).

Limitations
Some sensitive dogs may respond to these. Others may respond for a while, then get used to the sound. And since nothing truly unpleasant accompanies the noise, they can adapt over time.

BARRIERS
Denying access by using a gate or closing the door is a tried-and-true method of keeping your dog from doing what he wants to do.

Limitations
Few. There are gates to go across almost any opening. Hassle would be a limitation, especially if you have children, as doors and gates will be left open.

INDOOR ELECTRONIC UNITS
The Invisible Fence Company has an indoor unit that plugs directly into the wall. If your dog enters the area while wearing an Invisible Fence collar, he will first hear a warning tone and then, if he does not retreat, receive a shock. Some people find this helpful around trash cans or to keep a dog out of the kitchen entirely.

Limitations
After careful introduction to this system (without any shock), in which the dog is taught what to do when he hears the warning tone, most dogs (and cats) will respond properly. Some people are uncomfortable with the use of shock.

SEPARATION PROBLEMS

When left alone all day, some dogs develop separation problems from mild distress to major home wrecking. There are steps all of us can take to help our dogs handle being alone better, and these are covered in "Home Alone Success," page 209. If the ideas outlined there do not work with your dog, we suggest you find a veterinary behaviorist to help you, as this can be a difficult problem to get under control.

For extreme cases—heavy chewing, door scratching, barking, salivation, and so on—consider a combined approach of behavioral management (as previously described) and medication to help your dog handle his fear. If medication is available and can help, why not?

BUT I *LOVE* HIM SO MUCH!

Too often love is confused with indulgence. If we give the dog everything she wants, she will respect and obey us—right? No. If you indulge your dog, you get a dog who expects to be indulged. Love never spoiled anything or anyone, but lack of boundaries, constant indulgence, and low expectations certainly have. If you really love her, then you will see her as the intelligent, capable, normal creature she is. If you cannot, then you may be fulfilling your needs, not the dog's, and that isn't love—no matter what you want to call it.

DEMANDING BEHAVIOR

Your dog is so cute. When you are on the phone, he comes up and paws you for a pat. Isn't that darling? Doesn't he love you so much?

Wrong.

Adored? You bet! Spoiled, not at all. Could your dog do a sit-stay on a bench with a hat on?

What the dog is basically communicating is "Hey, why aren't you paying attention to me? Give me attention right now!"

Respond to that sort of high demand repeatedly and you are well on your way to training your dog that you exist to serve him. And what starts out as a series of seemingly charming moments can end up by creating a bossy, demanding, possibly aggressive dog.

We often tell our clients to insert a command such as sit, down, or come anywhere they might have a young child say "please." That basically means that before you do anything for the dog, the dog does something for you.

He whines. You ignore it or you have him down and then reward him with your attention.

He paws you. You ignore it or you have him sit or down or back away or leave the room before you reward him with your attention.

He throws a toy in your lap. You have him sit before you throw it (if he's sit-

METRODOG

ting already, you have him down or come or give a paw or something) or you take the toy and put it away or you ignore it.

NASTY NEIGHBORS

One mysterious case of nuisance barking was solved by the use of a sound-activated tape recorder. Turned out that some neighbors that disliked dogs were making sounds out in the hallway to get the dog to bark, then were complaining about the noise. This sort of weird human behavior is odd, but if something just doesn't add up in your situation, it is best to investigate all the possibilities.

BARKING

Barking probably causes more tension between dog owners and their neighbors than any other dog problem. The causes of barking? Multiple. They include boredom, breed trait, anxiety, upset, loneliness, territorial defense, entertainment, and demands for attention. There are as many ways to control barking as there are causes. Here are some general rules:

For barking while you are home:

Redirect

If your dog starts barking at a sound in the hall, first praise him: "Good dog!" After all, part of his job is alerting you. Then redirect him to another behavior, such as come. Once he arrives, have him down and praise/reward him.

If he does not comply with commands, then work on those when things are

This small dog's barking echoes in this hall, and that's a problem. This Maltese is frightened—legs stiff, head thrown back, rear lowered.

calmer to get him to the level of understanding that he'll need to respond in that distracting circumstance.

If you need to, leave a lead on him when you are home so you can get him and insist (calmly) that he come, then reward. As he gets better at it, reward him only for his best efforts so his response will continue to improve.

If he continues to bark, try a rapid-fire series of commands. Few dogs can hold two thoughts in their head at once, and responding to multiple commands usually asserts your leadership calmly and distracts them effectively.

If this doesn't work, you might consider a head halter so you can control that mouth, try a spritz from a water bottle, or use a no-bark collar to help back up your training.

Reward

When a behavior is annoying, it is easy to forget the reward part of training. In the case of barking, when the dog finally quiets down, many people are so relieved that they forget to tell the dog that quiet is what they wanted.

If we are confident the relationship between human and dog is good, then we advise the shameless use of whatever amuses your dog. Some dogs will work well for attention, others for treats, a few more for toys. All of that is fine as long as they are getting the message that listening and responding to you is the best option.

For barking while you are not home:

Confine

If your dog tends to bark at sounds in the hall, then confining her in a bedroom or a crate in the bedroom may keep her far enough away to not hear every little thing. Leaving a radio or TV on low can also help muffle outside sounds.

Engage

Bored dogs tend to be more alert. The more you can do when you are home to keep that mind busy, the more likely your dog is to sleep when you are away. Making him "work for a living," teaching him tricks, using commands that require self-control, all help tire him out mentally as well as reinforce your leadership.

Occupy

Giving your dog things to do while you are away can also help. (Please see the advice in "Home Alone Success" for tips.)

Bark Collars

Bark collars, which activate when the dog barks and are preprogrammed, can be useful in some situations. When purchasing equipment like this, do not skimp. Get the best you can afford, especially with the electronic units. Lower-quality collars have been known to be set off by noises unrelated to the dog or even by other electronic items such as garage door openers or TV remotes.

There are a variety of no-bark collars to select from; here are three general types:

• **Sound based.** These collars emit a sound (high-pitched or ultrasonic) when the dog barks. While these collars may work with sound-sensitive dogs, with other dogs the novelty of the sound can eventually wear off. Often the dog hears it repeatedly and nothing really happens. You might say this sort of collar cries "wolf."

• **Scent based.** This collar squirts a strong citronella scent when the dog barks. This has been found to be quite effective with many dogs. Some clever animals do learn to shift the collar off to one side, but this is a collar that is well worth trying if other approaches are ineffective.

• **Shock based.** Of the three, this collar packs the most punch. There are variations of this tool, and if you go this way, look for the ones that give your dog a set amount of time to bark, then start at a low level of stimulation, increasing as he continues to bark. Once your dog is quiet, the collar resets back to start. These may be called "bark diminishers."

When these work, they are quite effective, but when a dog has a vocal reaction (say, yipping in surprise), a cycle of yipping and correction can be started that greatly upsets the dog. Because of this, these collars should be used only when other approaches have failed, not as the first response to a problem. Also, they should be introduced when you are home so you can see how your dog responds.

NOT COMING WHEN CALLED

One of the most common problems, and it is usually all our fault. What happens? We don't practice enough when we have control before trying it when we don't, and we tend to use the command when other really interesting things are happening. To resolve this problem in the long run, please see instructions on teaching the "come" command starting in chapter 2. However, if you have a dog who won't come when called right now, don't let him off lead. Simple and effective. If your dog ever does fail to come to you, try doing the following:

Run in the Opposite Direction

If your dog is running north, you go south at your top rate of speed. Whoop with glee, clap your hands, sound as if you're having a great time! Dogs hate to miss out on any fun, and many will stampede after you with delight. (Chasing after your dog has the effect of telling him, "Yup, I'm right behind you!" and most will take off thinking you are supporting the adventure.)

Play with Another Dog

Playing with another dog will bring many dogs racing back to your side. If it doesn't, we suspect you've got some relationship work to do with your dog.

Get Fascinated with Something on the Ground

Squat, pick up a bit of stick, and start poking around. Don't look up. Make all sorts of "hmm, how interesting" sounds. This will attract many dogs and is especially good with dogs who come close and then leap away. If your dog does come close, reach up from underneath and get the collar. Don't try a sudden lunge; if it doesn't work, he'll be even more leery of coming to you than he was before.

Dogs Lunging and Barking at Your Dog

You see the dog dragging his owner toward you. This animal's tail is up, maybe his hackles are raised, and he does not look friendly. What do you do?

• **Stay relaxed.** No need to tell your dog you are anxious.

• **Move away.** Step off between some parked cars, cross the street, or put something between you like a garbage can or tree.

• **Turn away.** As much as possible, turn and look away from the other dog. Don't expose yourself to a rear onslaught, but avoiding a face-to-face confrontation can keep things calmer.

• **Occupy your dog.** Work on commands or use a treat to distract him. If that doesn't work, simply prevent him from lunging toward the strange dog.

• **Continue on happily.** As soon as that dog is past, move on, sounding happy. The sooner you set a new tone of fun, the quicker your dog will recover from his own stress about the other dog.

Managing a large, excited dog isn't easy. Get professional help
if these two photos look at all familiar.

YOUR DOG LUNGING AND BARKING AT OTHER DOGS/PEOPLE

First, get some hands-on help. There is no way for us to know if your dog is lunging and barking an enthusiastic hello or a canine curse, so we err on the side of caution and say, Get professional assistance. Until this person arrives, do the following:

• **Use a head halter.** This tool will allow you to better control the unwanted behavior, which should allow you much more opportunity to reward your dog for the behaviors you prefer.

• **Get distance.** If a dog is coming your way (or a person you know he'll fire at), cross the street, step around a parked car, interrupt your dog's view of the oncoming animal/person.

• **Reward nonaggression.** Abundantly reward all nonaggression. Treats galore, praise, and petting can all help your dog stay relaxed.

• **Make him work.** Don't focus on him lunging, focus on him not paying attention. The more demanding you are in those circumstances—the more you change directions, give different commands, make him think—the more attention he will have to pay to you. The goal is to make the dog choose to watch you instead of watch the other dog. To be successful, you must work at a distance where you can achieve this and not keep moving in too close, where the dog becomes overstimulated and fires aggressively.

Done well, quick, well-placed collar corrections combined with praise and food reward can be effective, but because this skill is hard to master we refer you to a training professional for help.

LEG LIFTING

A dog who lifts his leg on your couch is making a clear canine statement: This couch is mine! Leg lifting has nothing to do with housebreaking, and a dog can go for a nice romp in the park, come home, and hike on your closet door. To get some control over this, try the following:

- **Neuter him ASAP.** This problem will not go away without that surgery.

- **Keep him on lead.** Close supervision is key to prevention, and prevention is key to retraining.

- **Crate him.** It is hard to consider yourself king of all you survey when crated. This is both a preventative step and part of an attitudinal adjustment.

- **Down.** Teach it, use it, expect it. At least a dozen downs a day will help refocus him.

- **Cover up.** Purchasing a premade belly band or tying a scarf around your dog's waist will prevent outflow and allow you both to relax a bit.

- **Get him into class!** This dog needs more to think about. Class will not only be interesting, it will also put you in the leader position. Start classes, keep going to classes. He obviously needs the work.

- **Clean up all his marks** with an odor neutralizer from the pet supply store. If you aren't sure where he's been, borrow (from your veterinarian) or buy a black light. Urine lights right up under black light. Just be prepared: This may be a much bigger problem than you realized.

HOUSEBREAKING PROBLEMS

Most true housebreaking problems can be resolved through confinement, supervision, and rewarding for going in the right spot. The information in the first few chapters on housebreaking will resolve most problems if the advice is followed carefully. One exception to that is if your dog suddenly starts to pee all over your

apartment or has loose stools. Any sudden onset of housebreaking problems like this warrants an immediate trip to the veterinarian, as it may be a sign of an infection, parasites, or other condition.

If your dog urinates when he greets you or others, you have a submissive urination problem. Please see "Submissive Urination," page 66.

If he hikes his leg on things or people, you have a leg lifting problem, which is discussed in the section before this one.

If he dirties his crate, please see the section in chapter 2, "The Apartment Puppy," that discusses that. The solutions there should work for a dog of any age.

This may seem obvious to some, but do not get angry at your dog if he is sick. Diarrhea and vomiting are no more comfortable for your dog than they are for you. Getting mad at him for something he can't control just adds more misery to a dog who already doesn't feel well.

TIPS FOR TOYS

"It has been my personal experience with my own dogs and that of pet sitting new toy breed puppies or newly acquired adults being 'recycled': When the owners are open to really training a dog and putting in the exhausting time and the tough love that is needed in the beginning, those toys have taken to housebreaking readily. As long as the owners keep to a schedule feeding/playing/water/walking *and* keep the dog confined either crated or in a small area with a puppy gate, a small breed can 'get it' perfectly."

—CHRISTINE PELLICANO,
Pet Sitter, NYC, NY

Even calm dogs like Norman can develop fears as they age.
No one is quite sure why this happens.

ADULT-ONSET PHOBIAS

For some reason, not yet fully understood at the time of this writing, some dogs develop phobias as they mature. Occasionally there is a clear start point for these, but more often they seem to develop slowly over time. Your pup who played cheerfully during a thunderstorm is now a dog who, at the age of six, hovers by your legs, panting and restless, as thunder claps.

Did she pick up our own anxiety over time? If we sound or act worried, even on the subtle level of breathing more rapidly or shallowly during a time of stress, our dogs may begin to mimic us. In doing so, they may come to fear the storms only because we do.

Did we reward her in little ways? Did your dog learn, over time, to interpret your "comforting" as praise for phobic behavior? Maybe when the thunder claps, your dog leans against you, and you absentmindedly stroke her. You tell her, "It's okay. It's just a storm." Your goal: To reassure her. Actual effect: You reward leg leaning.

Is it a totally separate issue? Nothing to do with environment, but related instead to some chemical change brought on by the aging process? Having your veterinarian run a full thyroid panel is a good idea with late-onset fears and aggression. Low thyroid levels can lead to unpleasant behavioral change. Fortunately, daily medication can get you your old dog back.

No one knows yet, but for whatever reason, this can and does occur. Resolving it can be difficult, however. This is definitely the realm of the veterinary behaviorist, someone who can combine sensible behavioral protocols with needed medications. These medications can be a huge boon and well worth trying for these stubborn and upsetting behaviors. But if a veterinary behaviorist is not close at hand, here are a few things you can try:

Thunderstorms/Loud Noises

Fear caused by sound is a tough behavior to change. Mild cases shake, hide, or seek constant contact. (Sarah's normally aloof Australian Shepherd, Caras, tries to lie on her head.) Severe cases (thankfully rare) can claw/chew through doors in an effort to escape. Yes, there are tapes you can buy and play. In our experience, these don't fool many dogs, but they certainly are worth a try. Here are a few other things that can help:

• **Act as you want the dog to act.** If you want your dog to be happy, be giddy yourself. As the thunder rolls in, toss a favorite toy around, pretend you are having the *best* time. For some mildly stressed dogs, this may be enough of a distraction from the anxiety.

If you have more than one dog, start playing with the other and ignore the fearful dog completely. Toss your other dog treats, play games. If your fearful dog shows any curiosity, toss him a treat casually, then keep playing. Few dogs can stand to miss out on family fun.

• **Herbal and nutritional supplements.** Some people have good luck with melatonin or herbs such as chamomile, valerian, or hops. Others swear by Bach Flower Rescue Remedy. Please look in our resources section for information sources. Don't mix these with medications prescribed by your veterinarian unless directed to do so.

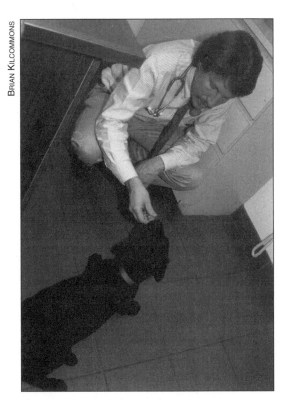

Having your veterinarian give your dog treats from an early age can help prevent fears from developing.

FEAR OF CERTAIN PLACES

Your dog can develop a deep dislike for the veterinarian's office (and sometimes the groomer's shop) over time, because despite how nice all the humans involved are, your dog has been hurt in those places. Injections and getting cuticles nicked during nail trimming are painful, and some dogs take those things to heart.

  METRODOG

In many cases, this can all be turned around, but that starts with the correct relationship between you and your dog. If your dog thinks of himself as the one who has to make the decisions, then nothing you do or say will impact much on his behavior. If you want to help a fearful dog, rule number one is to be the leader. Be the leader at home for at least several weeks before expecting him to trust you enough to risk listening to you when he is frightened. (The "Six Steps to a Better-Behaved Dog" protocol on page 151 is a good way to get yourself back in the driver's seat.)

Now add in commands, because it is your ability to direct your dog's behavior (and cheer on his efforts) that will help you when he is frightened.

Keep his mind occupied in the waiting room and exam room. Work on obedience training, play with him, set a happy tone (even if he looks miserable).

Bring along extra-special food rewards, and use those to reward response. If he'll take the food, have your groomer or veterinarian reward him.

Keep your voice and hand movement moderate. When we are nervous we tend to pet harder and faster, and we speak faster as well. All those things cue the dog that we are not happy, and that will make him unhappy, too. So work hard at acting as if you don't have a care in the world.

Certainly consider using a head halter, but if your dog is still anxious, don't hesitate to muzzle him. Everyone will handle him in a more relaxed manner and praise him more if they aren't worried about being bitten. Even with the muzzle on, continue to praise him happily. There is no reason for you to commiserate with his situation when muzzled; that won't help him.

"GOOD DOG" AGGRESSION:
UNDERSTANDING LATE-DEVELOPING AGGRESSION

"It just started," said the upset voice over the phone lines. "He's always been such a good dog. All of a sudden, out of the blue, he's growling at me!" Although this can be a surprise, the signs have probably been building up for years. Aggression happens in only a tiny percentage of any dog's life, but it is directly affected by how you handle him the rest of the time.

Classically this is a very nice dog, easy to live with. In fact, this dog fits into his family without a yip. And that is exactly the problem. This dog is so easy to live with that the owners hardly ever have to give him a command. The dog simply cruises through the day, doing what he pleases, getting little, if any, direction.

This attitude of "If no one else is in charge here, I guess I am" develops slowly. It starts with the dog ignoring commands he used to respond to reliably. But the owner doesn't really care; after all, he's such a good dog. Then the dog refuses a few commands altogether: He won't lie down, he doesn't come when called, he stays put on the couch when told to move. But the owner doesn't really care. Why should he? The dog is no problem. From here it is a short mental hop for the dog to try a low growl by a food bowl. So far the owner has been 100 percent obedient, serving the dog like a well-trained butler; why not make a bid for leadership?

The owner is shocked! Where did this come from?

The good news is that if this aggression is caught in its early stages, it is very likely to be quickly brought under control. This is not a dog who especially wants leadership; it was thrust upon him. Chances are good he'll hand it right back to you if you give a few clear signs of wanting it.

Here's how to get it back (or prevent this from happening altogether if you think it is coming your way):

1. **Use commands.** Use them a lot. Use them constantly. A dozen downs a day is a good goal, along with a dozen sits, a few waits, and a couple of others as well.

2. **Eat first, make him wait.** In a dog's world the first in status eats first. An easy adjustment is for you to eat before your dog. If he objects, then you know—bingo!—that's part of the problem!

3. **Furniture privileges are revoked.** Any increase in height is seen by a dog as an increase in status. Since that's the case, he can sit on the floor.

4. **No training treats for a while.** Let's get things straightened out first. If you have a dog who'll work only for treats, then he's not trained as much as he's trained you. Treats are a wonderful tool and incentive, but they shouldn't be the sole reason the dog complies.

5. **Increase exercise.** As we've said before: A tired dog is a good dog.

METRODOG

ANTHROPOMORPHIZING

This is a big word for treating a dog like a person. This is considered a dirty word in many dog behavior circles. We say, Go ahead, but if you are going to do it, *really* do it. Follow it all the way through. Would you let a child slam against you several times a day at full speed? Would you smile patiently when a spouse pawed you for attention, demanding hugs *every* time you were on the phone? If a good friend pulled a knife and brandished it in your direction, would you say, "Oh, he just doesn't like anyone near him when he eats"?

DOMINANT DOGS

To be content, some dogs need strong leaders, and in the absence of leadership, they will step into that role. They have to, because in the world of dogs it is all about who falls where in the group. To a dog, a group without a strong leader is inconceivable.

Some sweet, easygoing dogs can be the leader with no fuss or aggression. They just happily go about their lives in the belief that they are calling the shots. Other dogs become the leaders and start asserting their authority. This can and does lead to aggression. Following is a list of behaviors that can tell you whether or not you have a dominance problem brewing.

If she steals food or picks something up, can you take it away easily?

If not, this can be a sign that a dog is headed for trouble. The exception to this is a dog who has been punished after she has dropped the item. Wisely, the dog resists dropping the item and may become aggressive in her own defense. Please see the information on teaching the "out" command, starting on page 81.

Can you take away a toy while he is playing with it?

This includes chew toys, rawhides, and so on. In a dominant dog, worrisome signs involve freezing when approached, moving his head over the object, making direct eye contact, or mouthing your hand as it moves toward the toy. Crisis signs include growling, snarling, snapping, or any intensity level that gives you serious pause. We always tell owners, Trust the hair on the back of your neck. If it goes up, believe it.

Can you handle her collar?

The back of the neck is an area with much significance to dogs. If you watch two dogs meet, frequently the dominant dog will lay her head over the neck/shoulder area. A dog who ducks away or freezes when her collar is grabbed may well be giving strong signals of soon-to-arrive aggression. (The exception to this is a dog who has been dragged or beaten. This dog may freeze from fear when the collar is grabbed.)

Will he lie down on command?

Lying down on command is an act of mental submission. A dog who has been taught to respond to a few basic commands but "just doesn't like to" or "won't" lie down for his owner is making a clear statement of perceived rank. Downing for treats does not count, as the dog clearly sees the benefit to this activity. To discover your dog's attitude, work without treats. Work with food gets quick results and is a terrific way to teach, but it cannot be relied upon to change a dog's perception of his owner.

Can you brush her?

Being groomed requires that a dog submit to the owner's plans as well as to having several highly charged body areas handled. These areas include the back of the neck, the haunches, and the shoulders. If your dog struggles to get away,

mouths you, growls, or snaps when being groomed, these may be signs of a serious problem. As the leader, you should be able to handle your dog any place, any time, anywhere on his body.

Where does he sleep?

The higher-ranked dogs sleep in the best locations. Dogs with any sort of behavior problem should not be on the bed. Dogs who resist getting off the bed on command are giving a clear signal of what they perceive their rank and privileges to be. Any dog who growls (or worse) when moved from "his" spot needs immediate intervention from a qualified professional.

Does she move out of the way when you approach?

Subordinate animals give way to the leaders in the group. You can see this in a group of dogs. A higher-ranked animal will step in front of a lower-ranked one, blocking her path. The blocker may stand stiffly, tail slightly raised, staring at the other dog, who will usually move to the side.

All our dogs are number one in our hearts, but if you think yours may be number one in your home, you should seek the help of a qualified trainer or behaviorist. (Please see page 115 on finding professional help.) This is a *serious* problem that can lead to aggression toward you and your family—do not delay. While you are waiting for professional help to arrive, follow the suggestions in "Six Steps to a Better-Behaved Dog" (page 151) and do the following:

- **Neuter your male dog.** Intact male dogs bite the most often and cause the most damage when they do bite. While not all intact males do bite, any with a dominance issue are best sterilized immediately.

- **Ignore your dog when he isn't working for you.** He's not the center of the universe; best let him know that now.

- **Avoid contests of will.** Leave a lead on him when you are home so you can guide him away from difficult situations. Alternatively, call him or, last-ditch effort, ring the doorbell. No matter what, do not engage him in a battle—he'll probably win.

- **Remove coveted items.** Any toy he growls over disappears, at least for now.

- **Heap on the praise for good behavior.** Keep it warm and brief but sincere; you want him to be clear about what you want. Reward works, so use it any time you see a behavior you would like to see again.

- **Exercise your dog.** The more change/stress in your dog's life, the more exercise he needs.

- **Trust your instincts.** If you feel something is dangerous, or a situation is just making you feel uneasy—*stop!*

- **Take action!** Aggression does not go away on its own, it gets worse. And it can kill your dog. Waiting to "see if he grows out of it," thinking that "he didn't really mean it" or "was just upset by X," or declaring that "it only happens when . . ." can cost you your dog as surely as cancer. At the first signs of aggression—stiffening, growling, fast head swings at your hands—find skilled professional help.

Continuing Education

Basic training has been done (if it hasn't, please go back to the previous chapters and start there), so why not continue on in something both you and your dog will enjoy? Training does not have to be serious or formal to be effective. If teaching your dog to turn on a light switch, push the elevator button, carry the mail, roll over, or crawl like Lassie amuses you, find out how to teach your dog these "tricks." One of the secrets to successful training is practice, and one of the secrets to prac-

tice is enjoying it. Almost any training can reinforce the "I call the shots, you do something, we have fun," so unless you're wrestling with a serious behavioral problem, there's no reason not to indulge your whims. Having a good time is very reinforcing, for both of you.

Who knows what training can bring? Here Sarah and Caras work with the director on a TV shoot— what will you and your dog do?

TONI KAY-WOLFF

NO HUGGING ALLOWED?

Does your dog jump, whine, or try to get between you and your partner when you hug? If yes, this is a sign of a serious confusion in your dog's mind about who's in charge of this group. If your dog is behaving in this way, please follow the instructions in "Dominant Dogs," page 247, and review the list under "How to Create a Monster Dog" on page 96 to see if any of it looks familiar. Redirect your dog to a down or to move when he does this. Keep a lead on him so you can follow up calmly and easily if he says, "Not now, I'm busy." But since this is a sign of a relationship confusion, straighten that out first, then deal with this particular symptom.

With a hairy, large dog like this Briard, a good understanding of "off" is critical.

"OFF" FOR THE ADULT DOG

Jumping usually continues to be a problem because people get focused not on the behavior they want (sitting), but the one they don't want (jumping). What you need to do is tell your dog what you want. Start with all the methods outlined earlier in the book. Try those for several weeks. If at the end of that period you are still struggling, then you might want to add a correction.

With your dog on lead and whatever collar you are using (this is not the method for head halters or no-pull harnesses), approach a friend your dog often jumps on. Stay relaxed. As you reach your friend, command, "Sit." If your dog sits, reward and walk away from your friend. Repeat. If your dog is sitting well, seize the moment and practice success!

But if your dog jumps up, give a quick snap with the lead horizontally off to one side while saying, "Off." Do not pull the dog off. Do not yank hard. Most dogs are unsteady on their hind legs, and even a small pressure to the side forces them back onto all fours. The moment the dog is off, reward abundantly. Direct to a sit and reward again. Walk away and repeat.

STAY—CONTINUED

Basic work is completed, and your dog will sit (or down) on command and hold that position for a few seconds until you return to her side. Now, we start stretching out the time between the stay and the shoulder tap release. There are three things you work on with stay: duration, distraction, and distance. Work on duration and distraction before you tackle distance.

To increase duration, try any of these:

• **Have her down/stay as you prepare her meals.** Reward her with small bits of her dinner several times throughout the preparation. Frequent rewards will help her learn to hold her position. If she gets up, replace her without anger, comment, or reward. Replacement in and of itself is a correction; you don't need to add anything else to it.

• **Have her stay during commercial breaks.** Move around the room or kitchen. Return to her frequently with slow strokes, calm words, and the occasional unexciting treat (if any treat is unexciting to your dog).

If you and your dog are bordering on arguing about it (she's getting up, you're guiding her back down repeatedly), just try to end on a positive note, then quit for the time being. Don't try to force things when they aren't going well.

Next, add distractions slowly, a little at a time, and expect that your dog will be confused. Try squatting in front of her. Most dogs will get up immediately, as this is a friendly position and, as far as they are concerned, stay means stay only when you are standing. Place her back in position.

Try squatting only partway. Support her with calm praise. Return to her and give a few gentle strokes. Over several repetitions, you can squat more deeply until she stays in position regardless.

To introduce a ball, you could start simply by picking it up. If your dog gets up, replace her. Put the ball down and pick it up again. Repeat until she holds her sit or down. When she does, release her and bounce the ball. Since she wants it, why not use it as the reward? Any time your dog is highly motivated by something, try to figure out a way to use it as a reward.

Having run the long line behind the lamppost, Brian gives the "down" signal.

Once down, he gives the "stay" signal. This is a nice solution for dogs who creep forward, because moving ahead is impossible.

COME—CONTINUED

"Come" is a command that always needs work. While your dog is on lead, start periodically calling him away from things he loves. Let a friend say hello to him, then call him. The minute you say, "Come," have your friend stop petting him. Be ready with open arms to praise him enthusiastically. Repeat.

Or, with your dog on lead, open the front door as he shoots out of it, say, "Come!" and back away. Or, while walking down the street, back up and say, "Come." Do this when he sees a squirrel. Do this as you round a corner. If you ever hope to have control in those situations, you must start by getting it under control on lead. If a friend will help, have him restrain your dog as you walk away (a retractable lead is great for this game). Get your dog as excited as you can, then call him to you. When he arrives, reward.

The reason so few dogs really come reliably is that we usually don't practice it nearly enough. Try to sneak in five or more separate "come when called" exercises a day, and you'll be amazed to see how much your dog's response improves in a month.

OPPOSITION REFLEX

Put simply, the opposition reflex simply means that pressure in one direction makes a dog react in the opposite direction. If you pull back on the lead, the dog leans forward. If you try to shove a dog into a sit, the dog braces upward. If you try to pull the dog toward the bathtub for a bath . . . he pulls back. This can be avoided either by choosing not to use steady pressures in training or by using techniques that lure/reward the dog for moving with the pressure rather than against it.

A friend holds this Rhodesian Ridgeback for the owner . . .

. . . who gives a good clear "Come!" and praises as the dog runs to him.

"Sit" is added at the end (we're not fans of the finger point, but we won't be picky).

This dog's favorite reward? Not a treat for this dog—he prefers to run with his person!

This happy Black Russian Terrier pup demonstrates the classic opposition reflex. As his person pulls him back, he pulls forward.

PULLING ON LEAD

One of the most universal problems, pulling on lead is magnified in the city, where the dog has to get walked several times every day. Methods that rely on not moving forward unless the lead is slack are not always practical.

Exceptions Cause a Problem

We've watched clients allow the dog to drag them toward a fire hydrant without comment when they've just spent fifteen minutes complaining about pulling.

When asked why they just rewarded pulling by following after the dog, the answers are something like this: "Oh, he had to go to the bathroom."

If you make exceptions to your own rules, expect your dog to be confused. It is hard enough for a dog to learn not to pull, but forget teaching him "Don't pull except when . . ." One of the most potent motivational methods in the world is variable reinforcement, meaning sometimes you win and sometimes you don't. Every casino in the world knows that it is a recipe for serious compulsion.

When you allow the dog to pull some of the time, you are creating a dog who will pull more often and more intensely than before. (Keep in mind that punishments [losses] don't deter gambling behaviors as long as he sometimes gets what he wants—meaning, losing money doesn't deter a gambler if he wins occasionally. Nor will yanking on the leash deter your dog if he occasionally is allowed to pull you where he wants. He has to stop winning altogether [that is, stop making it gambling] for the behavior to fade.)

Your dog is never allowed to drag you. He can look at a squirrel. He can look at a fire hydrant. Or you may decide to say, "Leave it, let's go," because he has already urinated plenty for one walk. But in both cases you are consistent and your dog waits for your direction rather than dragging you over.

Your dog should adore your trainer. If that isn't true, something is wrong. Here, Sarah gets a kiss from a fan.

BRIAN KILCOMMONS

METRODOG

Things to Try On Your Own

A head halter and a no-pull harness are worth trying on your own if any appeal to you. Nothing works for every dog/owner team, but these are two of the easier-to-use tools.

Methods to Learn from a Trainer

If you elect to try a lead and collar method (something we've used with great success), you should learn how from a trainer. A small class or individual work is best. Look for someone upbeat and pleasant to work with who can offer you a variety of approaches.

WHY NOT YANK?

Yanking straight back or upward on the lead and saying, "Heel," in a harsh tone is a common approach. This seems so logical to us humans, right? Yank and tell her what you want: "Heel." The problem is that your dog has no clue what you want. How does she know when she's right? We already know that she has no clue what "heel" is (because if she did, she'd be heeling), so repeating it is not instructive.

What would you think if we were walking down the street and I hit you in the arm and said, "Trigap!" Would you have a clue what I wanted? What if I did that a hundred times, hitting you harder, saying it louder? Practice does not make perfect if you practice something in a way your dog finds incomprehensible (and she will demonstrate this by not learning the lesson). If our dog doesn't understand what we are trying to convey, it is our fault, not the dog's.

Here's a good rule: "If the behavior you are trying to change stays the same or gets worse—stop!" It's as simple as that. Find a new approach, find a new teacher, find a new way to motivate, but keep looking till you find a way that works. Think of all training as creating ways to reward your dog for doing something right. If an approach does not create those opportunities, the dog probably won't improve.

CHAPTER 6

The Older Metrodog
(Age Seven Onward)

Age can come on slowly or seem to happen overnight. Your companion—vigorous, playful, full of vitality—is slightly slower, a little grayer. She pauses a moment before gathering herself to hop onto the bed. She moves slowly down the stairs and may carry herself at an angle as she descends. And when she rests her head against your leg, you notice that the flesh and muscling are slightly changed by time and gravity. You gently stroke that skull you've stroked a million times; you cannot imagine what comes next.

If you're like us, you refuse to imagine.

SLEEP

As dogs age, they sleep more often and more deeply. I am reminded of this as our nine-year-old German Shepherd Dog, Julia, snores quietly next to me on her comfy dog bed. She never used to snore, but now the rhythm of her breathing keeps me company as I write. Sometimes I find that I have unconsciously matched my breathing to hers, and we breathe along together for a while. Such deep, frequent sleep is normal.

Life Expectancy

Life expectancy varies from breed to breed and individual to individual. Some breeds are devastatingly short-lived. Most of the giant breeds, the Great Danes, the Mastiffs, are considered ancient if they get into the double digits. Females normally live longer than the males, sometimes by several years. But in a recent poll of some Scottish Deerhounds, average life span of both sexes was under seven years.

Sadly, it is not just the giants. Boxers, Flat-Coated Retrievers, and Golden Retrievers can, too often, be gone before a decade passes. Seven or eight years old may be a more reasonable expectation. This is hard to comprehend, as all three breeds tend to be boisterous beings, bursting with energy and joy. But cancer now haunts their genetics, and no good medical answers yet exist.

In general, the smaller the dog, the longer the life. A Toy Poodle, Schipperke, or Chihuahua may guard your home and lap well into his teens. But whenever age arrives, there are changes you need to prepare for.

  METRODOG

This late-teens poodle likes
to nap with an old friend.
Toy dogs can live a long time,
but eighteen is old
by any standards.

CHRISTINE PELLICANO

CANCER?

Older dogs get lumps and bumps that have nothing to do with cancer, so don't scare yourself unnecessarily. But dogs do get cancer, and older dogs get more of it. Certain breeds can be prone, with Boxers, Flat-Coated Retrievers, Irish Wolfhounds, and Golden Retrievers topping the list. There are many symptoms for cancer because there are many types, but watch for limping that does not go away, lumps and bumps, rapid weight loss, depression, lethargy, difficulty breathing, wounds that don't heal, and smelly discharge from any opening.

BRIAN KILCOMMONS

With great dignity, this older
Pomeranian takes place in the
annual Blessing of the Animals
at St. John the Divine
in New York City.

Physical Changes

Noticing change is a key to caring for your older dog. Watch for increases or decreases in sleep, eating, drinking, panting, coughing, and lumps. Ask friends if they see anything different in your old dog. Sometimes people who don't see the animal every day will notice something you can't, like a weight trend. The sooner changes are noticed, the better the chances are of resolving whatever it is that is causing the change. Make sure you have a veterinarian you like, because you'll probably be seeing more of her.

ARTHRITIS

Aging certainly can affect your dog's joints, making your dog stiff upon waking, lag when out walking, and generally unwilling to do what were once normal activities. Medications and food supplements that can help a great deal are available. Some forward-thinking food companies are even adding one or more of these supplements to their senior foods, with people reporting noticeable results. Talk to your veterinarian about what is currently available.

Signs to watch for: When getting up from lying down, dogs prop their front feet up first and then lean forward and pull up their rear. They don't jump up on people or things anymore. Sitting can be more of a chore, so they either stand or lie down. They are stiff in the morning and after long naps. Snapping can be a sign as well, as pain begins to cause them to react to normal petting or to your children's presence with defensive aggression. They're not trying to be "mean," they just don't want to be hurt.

BOWEL AND BLADDER CONTROL

The urge to urinate becomes more pressing as some dogs age. If your normally clean dog starts having accidents, the first step is to have her thoroughly checked out by your veterinarian to make sure it is not an infection or some other physical problem.

  METRODOG

The paper towels tucked under this dog tell us that he leaks urine, but his person looks happy to have his company anyway.

If all is well, increase the number of walks per day. Go back to a puppy schedule of four to six walks rather than three. If this is not sufficient, consider putting down papers or putting on panties—either one can work, depending on your dog and your tolerance level.

If your dog is urinating in her sleep (you can tell this because her bed and/or haunches will be wet), there are medications that can usually help with this. So ask your veterinarian about that as well.

Signs to watch for: Whining, restlessness, puddles or piles in the home, wet dog beds, wet haunches. This problem can be extremely distressing to an older dog who has been clean all her life, so please do not become angry with her. If she could help it, she would.

This older dog is frightened. She never used to be. The owner needs to take action now, including tightening that collar. It could slip off.

CONFUSION AND LOSS OF MENTAL SHARPNESS

Also known as "cognitive dysfunction," this condition can be responsible for new behaviors in your dog's twilight years. It can be hard to sort out what may be growing deafness (or other physical changes) from the mental deterioration of an aging brain no longer working as effectively as it once did. Fortunately there are now medications that can help combat the symptoms of this latter aging process. If you suspect your dog is having these problems, discuss your options with your veterinarian.

Signs to watch for: Your dog barks at odd times, loses his housebreaking (though there is nothing physically wrong), seems disoriented in his own home, doesn't seem to recognize you, or wanders about aimlessly.

HEART PROBLEMS

As the heart ages, the valves that separate the heart's chambers get worn and stop closing properly, so heart murmurs develop. These murmurs may or may not be serious. Several other types of heart disease can develop, some of them treatable and some not. Talk with your veterinarian about the specific risks your dog may be facing (if any).

Because heart problems can develop as your dog ages, keeping him lean and fit is one of the best ways you can show your love and concern.

Signs to watch for: Coughing, fluid buildup in the belly, bluish gums, weakness, labored breathing, and no desire to exercise.

HEARING LOSS

As dogs age (as any of us age), hearing may dim. This, too, is a normal part of aging, though not all dogs will become deaf. If yours does, simply keep her on lead when in an unfenced area. Even well-known haunts can become dangerous if she gets distracted and wanders off.

Signs to watch for: It may be that your dog responds a bit slower to your commands, does not come when called immediately, or fails to greet you at the door when you come home. She may respond more slowly to the doorbell or to the sound of food being prepared and may seem to be sleeping more deeply.

  **METRODOG**

Kidney Failure

Dogs may start to lose kidney function as they age. They have to work harder to keep processing more water through the system. More water means more urine.

Signs to watch for: Increased thirst, urinating in apartment, needing to go out frequently, foul-smelling breath, weight loss, no appetite.

Obesity

Many older dogs get just plain fat! A dog's weight can sneak up on you as he ages, a combination of less activity, slowing metabolism, and unchanged diet. Carrying too much weight can shorten your dog's life by contributing to heart disease, diabetes, and other ailments. If you love him, get him lean!

Signs to watch for: He pants a great deal. He rarely runs or plays. Run your fingers from along your dog's side, from his shoulder to his rear; you should feel (but not see) his ribs as you pass over them. As you look down from above, his body should become thinner behind his ribs at his waist. As you look sideways at your dog, his waist should tuck up after his ribs. Both of these are somewhat dependent on breed.

If your dog is shaped like a watermelon or sausage, it's time for a change. Keep him on a good-quality senior or maintenance diet, but cut back the amount a little. Instead of biscuits and other treats, try raw carrot or apple slices, or let him chew on sterilized bones or nylon bones. Many dogs like ice cubes, and if you tell yours how special they are, he'll think they are wonderful treats. Increase his exercise a bit—maybe take another slow lap around

GWEN BARBA

Obesity sneaks up on all of us, but you won't find the ribs on this beloved Doxie. Especially with long-backed dogs, lean is good!

the block. If you have any questions or doubts, talk to your veterinarian before proceeding.

SIGHT LOSS

All the senses can dim with age, and sight is no exception. Some breeds are more prone to cataracts than other breeds, so do a little research to see if that may be a problem. Eyes can become a bit clouded. This happens with old age and does not necessarily affect vision.

Signs to watch for: Bumping into objects, dislike of going out at night, has a hard time locating you when you call, overreaction to objects that are familiar to her, hesitating when going down stairs or jumping on or off something, steering clear of shadows (which may look like dark holes in the ground to aging eyes), and eyes clouding (although some changes are a normal part of aging and do not affect the vision of your friend).

STAIR CARE

If your dog has to tackle several flights a day, he may need your help as he ages. If you use a harness and lead, you can then easily support his body and prevent an accident. A folded towel that is slung under his belly allows you to support a weakened rear end. Last, specially made slings are available for easy support when out walking. There are almost always advertisements for these in *Dog World*, *Dog Fancy*, or the other major dog magazines. Of course, going more slowly will help, and if the stairs are in your home, make sure they have good traction. Put a carpet runner securely in place if you have hardwood stairs. This will make life easier for your older friend.

An older dog can stay plenty active; he just needs to proceed more slowly.

Making Life Easier

Older dogs tend to love comfort and warmth. A nice cushy dog bed in a warm spot is just the thing. As our pack is aging, we have several thick foam beds scattered around the apartment that are almost always in use.

If your dog has always hopped on and off the bed or couch, you may want to stop that or provide a sturdy stool that gives her a halfway option. If you have an aging long-backed dog (such as a Basset Hound or Dachshund), please stop any such jumping immediately! For these dogs, installing sturdy ramps may be a good compromise. You may have been lucky so far with her back, but that luck can change for the worse in a second.

Consider putting nonskip runners down your halls and any place where the flooring is slippery, as older dogs can struggle with footing. Also, keep toenails and long hairs between the paw pads trimmed for better traction.

Health Care

Regular veterinary care becomes increasingly important as your dog ages. Consider having baseline bloodwork done at seven to eight years old so that changes can be tracked and compared later on. Dental care becomes critical, as a cracked

THE OLDER METRODOG

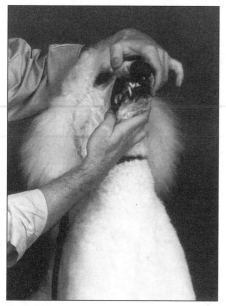

Caring for your dog's teeth
is part of being a good caretaker.

SARAH WILSON

tooth or an infection can lead to heart problems if the infection spreads through the blood.

Holistic care that helps maintain your companion's health is an excellent idea throughout his life and now is no exception. Acupuncture can ease an older dog's aches and pains. Massage and canine chiropractic care can do the same.

DIET

If there is one thing you can do to ensure your dog's health and longevity, it is feed him the best-quality food you can find and afford. Senior or diet foods can leave your dog ravenous (we do not know why, but we've seen this enough to know it happens), so proceed with caution. Sometimes half low-fat and half good-quality maintenance is enough to stop this pattern. Regardless of what you choose to feed, keep an eye on your dog's weight. Both sudden weight loss or rapid weight gain can signal trouble.

Games and Activities for the Older Dog

Once your dog starts showing her age, it is time to stop the joint-jarring, leg-twisting games of youth. Throw out the Frisbee, steer clear of the youthful gang

A room with a view may be all she asks for, but that doesn't mean that's all she can enjoy. Why not try something new?

at the dog run, and take up some easier activities. But being more conservative doesn't mean doing nothing. There are many activities you and your older dog can enjoy. Here are just a few ideas:

WALKING

If you've jogged or biked with your dog through the years, it may be time to slow things down. A brisk walk is a fine thing for a dog of almost any age (or owner). The exception is in hot weather, when all dogs (but short-nosed breeds in particular) should be kept indoors.

For this older Leonberger, daily walks are an important part of staying fit and healthy.

Every year, dogs of all ages die from heat exhaustion following obediently behind their beloved owners in the blazing summer heat. Don't risk it—exercise in the cooler early morning hours or switch to swimming during the hot months.

SWIMMING

This is the ultimate in low-stress workouts and an excellent means of exercise *if* your dog enjoys swimming. If not, don't force it. This is all supposed to be fun for you both.

TRICKS

We're past jumping through hoops and dancing on hind legs, but bringing in the mail, carrying things for you, getting the TV remote or TV guide on command, and playing "find it" or "hide-and-seek" are all well within your dog's grasp. Have fun! Be creative! Teach him things that make you laugh and him wag his tail.

CHRISTINE PELLICANO

These two appear to be singing together, and why not? That is surely time well spent.

Pet Therapy Visits

If your gentle, well-trained dog loves people, then becoming a therapy dog may be a delightful option. This is a team activity, where you and your dog work with populations in need. Nursing homes, special education programs, psychiatric wards, halfway houses, and more all benefit from this service. Having done it myself, I can say it is both rewarding and pleasant, with both staff and clients being universally positive. Please see page 207 for more resources on pet therapy.

More Training?

At this stage, the only goal is to have fun and enrich your dog's world as his physical and sensory abilities wane.

Expectations: That a lifetime of living together gives you unparalleled insight into how your dog thinks and what she enjoys. You use that insight for pure, unadulterated fun.

Watch out for: If she does not come when called, consider that her hearing is dimming. She may not even know you are calling her. You need to start watching her again as if she were a puppy. She can't go off lead if she can't hear you call. Dog runs may be out if she cannot see or hear other dogs coming at her and is no longer quick enough to get out of their way. Children, previously treasured playmates, may now hurt her if she has arthritis or frighten her if her sight and hearing dim.

Commands: She can learn anything explained in the previous chapters and much more. She will get great pleasure from making you laugh, so teach her all manner of tricks. Please refer to the resources section for books and videos on trick training.

This older Boxer and young Yorkshire Terrier make a happy pair. This is a big size difference, but it clearly works well for them.

New Puppy?

Many older dog owners wonder if they should get a pup. Would it be a nice addition, or would the older dog feel displaced? What is right for you and your older dog depends on both of you. Does your dog like other dogs? Is he playful with them or more aloof? If he's always liked other dogs, then an opposite-sex smaller-breed pup who's been raised with adult dogs might fit in nicely.

In general, a pup of the opposite sex will produce a less tension-filled pairing for both animals than a same-sex pup. So if you have a male, consider a female pup, and vice versa.

Also, a smaller breed or mix will be less overwhelming to your older dog as the new whippersnapper matures. Pups generally do harass the older dog to some extent, and this way the pup won't be equal or larger in size than your possibly somewhat frail older friend.

Getting a pup who's been raised with adult dogs is nice *if* those adults set clear boundaries. A pup kept with his mother for at least seven weeks (and if she was a no-nonsense type) has already learned to respect when an adult says: Enough!

Does all this mean that if you get a "same sex, larger breed, less time with Mom" pup, it will be a disaster? Not at all. It's just more likely to have problems than what we describe, and our job is to give you the best bets.

WHEN HE GOES . . .

Everyone has a unique way of coping with loss. One person wants to be cremated as her pets were, then wants to have their ashes mixed together before burial. Another keeps her dogs' ashes in special urns on the mantel. If she's thinking of a pet who's gone, she may take the urn to a favorite walking spot they shared together. Burial was an option for another who laid his dog's body down on his bed surrounded by his favorite toys and pictures of the things and people he loved. Another told of a Japanese tradition of bathing the pet after death, then laying it down in a bed of flowers. We all have our own ways; respect yours.

When the Time Comes

Choosing to end your dog's life is one of the great gifts we can give our companions as well as a huge burden on our own shoulders. When is it time?

First of all, in many cases there is no ideal time. Life just starts getting difficult. Pain starts to creep in stronger and more often. The luster goes out of the eyes. They may be confused and not themselves. Housebreaking may disappear, much to everyone's dismay, including your companion's.

People use all sorts of criteria to determine when the right time is—trust yours. You love your dog more than anyone else in the world. You'll make the decision that is right for you both.

That decision may not always make sense to anyone else. If you hang on as long as you can, carrying the dog in and out, diapering him, hand feeding—some will say you've waited too long. If you decide to end it because the inevitable is coming but has not yet ravaged your companion, others may say you did it too soon.

Look into those loving eyes, think back on the years you've had together, and

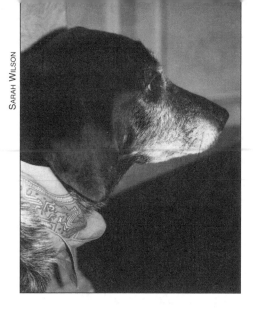

SARAH WILSON

His noble face, your heavy heart,
and an impossible decision.
No matter what your choice (or when),
he will love you.

decide by using all that you know of the animal, yourself, and your life. Those are the things to consider, not what others will say or think.

As a rule, listen only to people who have had to grapple with the same situation—everyone else just has opinions based on what they hope would be true, what they hope would be their actions. But hope and reality do not always overlap, so trust your decision.

HELPING CHILDREN SAY GOOD-BYE

This may be the first death a child faces. Ways to help her cope include the following:

- Reading children's books on pet death.
- Making scrapbooks of your dog's life, favorite things, and so on.
- Writing down stories you remember about your dog.
- Having your child draw pictures.
- Writing poems about her friend.

These are a few of the ways you can cope together with one of life's most inevitable events. If your child seems deeply upset or you are concerned, seek some professional advice from a counseling professional.

What Will Happen?

The things you need to know are that it is painless, and it is quick. Make payment arrangements before the euthanasia is done, as you will probably not be able to talk sensibly afterward. Some veterinarians will come to your home, but in most cases you will go to the clinic.

You will go into an exam room as you have many times before. The veterinarian will come in. The needle will be slipped in, and before the plunger is fully depressed, your animal will likely be gone.

In rare cases the body will fight on after the spirit has gone. The automatic nature of things continues with a few deep breaths or a leg jerking. This is disconcerting and can be upsetting, so it's important to know that your companion is gone by then. This is just the last curtain coming down on a strong spirit.

Death itself comes startlingly quickly. Say your good-byes as calmly and lovingly as you can. Let the last words he hears be loving ones. Let the last touch he feels be yours. That is the gift you can give your old friend. The price of that gift is high, and you will pay it for days, weeks, months, and even years to come.

The grief you feel can be overwhelming. You may feel isolated if family and friends don't understand the connection you felt. But you are not alone. There are Web sites, books, and groups that can help. Our resources section has a list; start there.

Ever onward.

CONCLUSION

In a world that can seem increasingly isolated, dogs give us connections. When we walk our puppy down a city block, people smile and nod. Some may stop to chat, and we connect. When our dog stands, vibrating with excitement at the tenth squirrel he's seen this day, we see the squirrel, too. We feel his enthusiasm, we remember nature amid all the urban brick and concrete. And when we unclip our dog's lead in the dog run, four friends smile and greet us. We don't know their last names. We don't know anything about them, but we are a member of an instant club. The club of dog lovers. It's one of the nicest clubs there is.

We hope this book allows the experience of cherishing your Metrodog to be easier and more joy filled. We'd like to make that gift to you. We're just passing along the gift our dogs have given to us.

Contact the authors: Brian and Sarah can be found on-line at www.GreatPets.com.

Selection

Paws to Consider: Choosing the Right Dog for You and Your Family
Brian Kilcommons and Sarah Wilson
Warner Books
New York
1999

We discuss breeds we've worked with and know well. Book is divided by need, not breed, with chapters on the city dog and the family dog, among others. Includes in-depth information on how to locate your dog and interview breeders.

Mutts: America's Dogs
    Brian Kilcommons and Michael Capuzzo
    Warner Books
    New York
    1996

Has good information on how to select a puppy or adult dog from a shelter. Mutts and purebreds are treated no differently.

The Puppy Report
    Larry Shook
    Lyons & Burford
    New York
    1992

This book will scare you straight! A true-to-life, carefully researched book about the puppy industry, genetics, and responsibility. Well worth a thoughtful read before you set out puppy hunting. Even though the book is getting dated, sadly, things haven't changed much.

Understanding Puppy Testing
    Suzanne Clothier
    Flying Dog Press
    P.O. Box 290
    Stanton, NJ 08885
    Phone: 1-800-7FLY-DOG
    E-mail: clothier@eclipse.net
    Internet: www.flyingdogpress.com

Ms. Clothier's booklets are easy to read, sensible, and short. You won't go wrong ordering any in her wide selection.

General Training and Behavior

Good Owners, Great Dogs
Brian Kilcommons and Sarah Wilson
Warner Books
New York
1992

With over two hundred thousand copies sold, we are pleased to report that sales are still going strong. Packed with sensible information, a fun read, well designed with great pictures. Has a good section on how to test a puppy.

The Canine Good Citizen: Every Dog Can Be One
Jack and Wendy Volhard
Howell
New York
1994

Nice, sensible, comprehensive book that can help any owner understand and live with his dog in harmony.

Childproofing Your Dog
Brian Kilcommons and Sarah Wilson
Warner Books
New York
1994

If you have children in your life, you need to read this small but information-packed book. Prevent problems before they arise!

Tails from the Bark Side
Brian Kilcommons and Sarah Wilson
Warner Books
New York
1997

Fun-filled stories, guaranteed to make dog lovers giggle. If you look at them as instructional guides on what not to do, it can even help with your new dog. Otherwise, just read it for the fun of it.

INTERNET

Brian and Sarah's Web site, www.GreatPets.com, is staffed by training and behavior professionals. You can get your individual questions answered there in a friendly, professional manner. At GreatPets we're just as nice to the people as we are to the dogs. Come join us.

Rescue Resources

The North American rescue network is extensive. The Internet is one of the great resources for contacts in almost every breed. Here are two sites worth checking out when you start looking for a rescue dog:

www.petfinders.com

www.AKC.org

(Look at the National Breed Club Rescue page.)

Games to Play with Your Dog/Tricks

Dog Tricks Step by Step
    Mary Ann Zeigenfuse and Jan Walker
    Howell Press
    New York
    1997

Fun and Games with Your Dog
    Gerd Ludwig
    Barrons
    1996

How to Love Your Dog: A Kid's Guide to Dog Care
    www.geocities.com/~kidsanddogs/trickspage.html

Clicker Training

Don't Shoot the Dog
    Karen Pryor
    Bantam
    1999

    Short, sweet, and to the point, this is a must-read for anyone with a dog. You will never look at your interactions with your dog (or spouse or child or boss) in quite the same way again.

Doing a Net search on "clicker training" will get you dozens of Web sites. Here are the sites of the two people who really launched this idea in the United States:

Karen Pryor's Clicker Training: www.clickertraining.com
Gary Wilkes Click and Treat Training Home Page: www.clickandtreat.com

Herbal and Nutritional Supplements

If you are curious on how nutrition, supplements, homeopathy, or herbs might help your dog, check out these resources:

American Holistic Veterinary Medical Association
2218 Old Emmorton Rd.
Bel Air, MD 21015
Phone: 1-410-569-0795
Fax: 1-410-569-2346
E-mail: AHVMA@compuserve.com

For a list of holistic practitioners near you, access the Web site www.altvetmed.com/ahvmadir.html.

Pet Loss Support

There is support out there when you need it. Here are just a few of the resources available:

Lists of grief counselors by state: www.superdog.com/petloss/counsel.htm
American Veterinary Medical Association:
www.avma.org/care4pets/losspetl.htm

Iowa State University Pet Loss Support Hotline
Hours of operation:
September–April: Seven days a week, 6:00–9:00 P.M. CST
May–August: Monday, Wednesday, Friday, 6:00–9:00 P.M. CST
Phone: 1-888-ISU-PLSH (1-888-478-7574) toll-free any time of day
E-mail: isuplsh@iastate.edu

Dog Magazines

The *AKC Gazette*
The Official Journal for the Sport of Purebred Dogs
5580 Centerview Dr.
Raleigh, NC 27606-3390
Phone: 1-919-233-9767
Fax: 1-919-233-3627
Internet: www.akc.org

Dogs in Canada
89 Skyway Ave., Suite 200
Etobicoke, ON M9W 6R4
Canada
Phone: 1-416-798-9778
Internet: www.dogsincanada.com

Dog Fancy
P.O. Box 53264
Boulder, CO 80322-3264
Phone: 1-303-786-7306
Internet: www.dogfancy.com

Dog World
29 North Wacker Dr.
Chicago, IL 60606
Phone: 1-312-609-4340
Fax: 1-312-236-2413
E-mail: dogworld3@aol.com
Internet: www.dogworldmag.com

DOG CAMPS

If taking a vacation to the country with your dog(s) sounds like an ideal vacation, look into dog camps. Here you both get to learn new skills, dabble in a few dog sports, hang out with people as dog involved as you are, and generally feel right at home. New camps spring up all the time. Here is one of the great Internet sites for all sorts of dog sport/event/activity information: www.dog-play.com/camps.html. Now, go have fun!

adolescent dogs, 149–97, 200
  commands for, 152–53, 159, 161–62, 184–97
  exercise and, 129–30
  interactions between children and, 171–73
  overly sensitive, 174
  proper social etiquette for, 159–71
  reading body language of, 153–58
  steps to better-behaved, 151–53
  training and, 151, 185–97
  training equipment for, 175–85
  what to expect from, 150–51
adult dogs, 199–259
  adoption of, 8, 199
  commands for, 205, 210, 232–34, 237, 240,
    245–59
  exercise and, 129, 131, 202–9
  fears of, 242–45
  health care for, 200–201
  at home alone, 209–15, 231, 235–36
  in-store manners for, 221–24
  introducing new pups to, 30–32
  making them work for a living, 210, 235
  mentally troubled people and, 224
  off leash on sidewalks, 225–27
  solutions to problems with, 227–46

  taking them to work, 215–17
  taxicabs and, 217–19
  tethering them near stores, 220–21
  treating them as number one, 31
aggression, 96, 149–50, 173, 193, 197, 218–19
  commands and, 81
  demanding behavior and, 232
  dog selection and, 4–5, 7–8, 15
  and dogs off leash on sidewalks, 226
  dominant dogs and, 247–50
  exercise and, 126
  and introducing new pups to other pets, 31–32
  late-developing, 243, 245–46
  and lunging and barking at other dogs or people,
    239
  and making rural dogs into Metrodogs, 11
  neutering and, 131–32
  older dogs and, 264
  reading canine body language and, 155–57
  social etiquette and, 160, 162, 165–66, 168–70,
    222–23
  and steps to better-behaved dogs, 152
  training equipment and, 179, 181–82
  see also biting
agility, 202–4

American Cocker Spaniels, 5, 66
American Kennel Club (AKC), 166, 203–5
anthropomorphizing, 247
apartments, 2, 5–6, 18–19, 106
arthritis, 264, 273
assertiveness, 149–50, 152
  reading canine body language and, 156–57
  social etiquette and, 159, 165, 168
Association of American Veterinary Medical
    Colleges (AAVMC), 118
Australian Shepherds, 3, 171–72, 204–5, 243

bark collars, 234–36
barking, 132, 173, 231
  confinement and, 38–41, 235
  and dealing with different temperaments, 68
  dog selection and, 4–6, 10
  exercise and, 127
  FRAP and, 43
  good habits and, 59–60
  handling common fears and, 97, 104
  housebreaking and, 24
  indoor activities and, 122
  and leaving adult dogs at home alone, 212–13,
    235–36
  and making rural dogs into Metrodogs, 11
  normal behavior and, 88
  and obedience in distracting settings, 139
  by other dogs, 238
  at other dogs or people, 239
  sensitiveness and, 174
  social etiquette and, 170
  solutions for, 233–36
  and taking your dog to work, 217
barriers, 230
Basset Hounds, 4, 269
Bearded Collies, 3
beards, dirt on, 3
beds, bedding, 45
  confinement and, 36–38
  housebreaking and, 23–24
  see also dog beds
begging, 64
behavior, impossible vs. normal, 88–89
behaviorists, 115–16, 118
Bichon Frise, 3, 102
Bishop, Becky, 152, 193

biting:
  dog selection and, 10, 15
  and dogs off leash on sidewalks, 226
  dominant dogs and, 249
  on leads, 147
  neutering and, 131
  normal behavior and, 88
  social etiquette and, 168–70, 221–22
Black Russian Terriers, 257
bladder control, 264–65
body language, 153–58, 166–68, 170, 186
bold behavior, 70
  exercise and, 127
  and first week of walks, 89
  handling common fears and, 101–2
  and obedience in distracting settings, 139
  social etiquette and, 167
  and steps to better-behaved dogs, 152
bones, 54–55, 66, 103, 167, 200, 267
boundaries, setting of, 151
Bouvier des Flandres, 24, 187, 219
bowel control, 264–65
Boxers, 126, 208, 262–63, 274
breeders, 13, 15
breeds, selection of, 3–7, 15
Bulldogs, 74
buses, 218

Canadian Kennel Club, 205
cancer, 262–63
Canine Freestyle Federation, 206
Canine Good Citizen (CGC) test, 204
carrying puppies out, 110
cataracts, 268
cat-treats game, 33
cat poop, dogs snacking on, 32
cats, introducing new pups to, 32–34
Cavalier King Charles Spaniels, 6, 19
Cepero, Elizabeth R., 215
check it out game, 102
chewing, 212–13, 231
  adult-onset fears and, 243
  dog selection and, 4–6
  dominant dogs and, 248
  good habits and, 65–66
  health care and, 200–201, 269–70
  and leaving adult dogs at home alone, 212
  at night, 46

normal behavior and, 88–89
quarantine and, 54–55
trainers and, 115
Chihuahuas, xvii, 262
Childproofing Your Dog (Kilcommons and Wilson), 29
children:
    adolescent dogs and, 171–73
    older dogs and, 264, 273, 276
    puppies and, 28–30
city services, 115–22
cleanliness, cleanups, 3, 5
    confinement and, 36–37
    and getting puppies to go outside, 109, 112–13
    housebreaking and, 22, 24
    leg lifting and, 240
    and taking your dog to work, 216–17
    see also grooming
clickers, 44, 57, 69–70, 179
clips, 184
cognitive dysfunction, 265–66, 275
collars, 62, 73, 96
    barking and, 234–36, 239
    and dealing with different temperaments, 70
    doggie day care and, 121
    dominant dogs and, 248
    exercise and, 208
    and first week of walks, 92
    introduction of, 56–59
    and obedience in distracting settings, 133–35,
        138, 140–43, 145
    older dogs and, 265
    practice handling of, 143
    social etiquette and, 169
    taxicabs and, 218
    and tethering near stores, 221
    and training for adolescent dogs, 189
    and training for adult dogs, 252, 259
    types of, 175–80, 182, 230, 234–36
come command, 82–85, 142–43, 192
    for adult dogs, 232–33, 237, 246, 255–56
    closeness for, 142
    collar handling for, 143
    demanding behavior and, 232
    late-developing aggression and, 246
    not coming and, 237
    and obedience in distracting settings, 141–43
    older dogs and, 273
    quick response to, 142–43
    social etiquette and, 162, 168

and steps to better-behaved dogs, 152
    training equipment and, 184–85
commands, 71–85
    for adolescent dogs, 152–53, 159, 161–62,
        184–97
    for adult dogs, 205, 210, 232–34, 237, 240,
        245–59
    barking and, 233–35
    dog sports/events and, 205
    dominant dogs and, 248–49
    and first week of walks, 90, 92–93
    late-developing aggression and, 246
    new, 143–47, 192–97
    and rules to live by, 73–74
    saying them once, 152
    see also obedience; training; *specific commands*
competitive obedience, 205
confinement:
    barking and, 38–41, 235
    couch hopping and, 228
    crates for, *see* crates, crating
    gates for, *see* gates
    housebreaking problems and, 240
    and leaving adult dogs at home alone, 212–14
    moderate, 213
    for puppies, 19–21, 23, 31–46, 60
    tethering and, *see* tethering
confusion, 62, 265–66, 275
correction, corrections:
    good habits and, 57
    and obedience in distracting settings, 137–40
    rules for, 139–40
    and training for adult dogs, 253
couch hopping, 227–30
counterconditioning, 91
covering puppies up, 110
Crabtree, Jenny, 50
crate door rushing, 39
crates, crating, 19–20, 25–26, 36–41
    barking and, 235
    doggie day care and, 120–22
    FRAP and, 43
    and getting puppies to go outside, 106–7, 109,
        112
    good habits and, 60, 63, 67
    housebreaking and, 36–37, 241
    and introducing new pups to other pets, 31–34
    introduction to, 38
    as inviting, pleasant places, 213–14

(*crates, crating, continued*)
  and leaving adult dogs at home alone, 212–14
  leg lifting and, 240
  and making rural dogs into Metrodogs, 11
  at night, 44–46
  types of, 37
  when to stop, 209, 212
crazy person game, 187
curbs, 111

Dachshunds, 267, 269
dancing with dogs, 205–6
death, 13, 275–77
defecating:
  and getting puppies to go outside, 105–14
  older dogs and, 264–65
  scooping and, 93–94, 111
  see also housebreaking
deferring, 8–9
Delta Society Pet Partners Programs, 207, 216–17
demanding behavior, 231–33
dental care:
  for adult dogs, 200–201
  for older dogs, 269–70
diet, *see* food
distance down command, 188–89
distraction, distractions, 110, 253
  obedience and, 132–47
Doberman Pinschers, 6, 90, 203
dog beds:
  couch hopping and, 228–29
  dominant dogs and, 249
  as inviting, pleasant places, 213–14
  and obedience in distracting settings, 144–46
  older dogs and, 261–62, 265, 269
  and training for adolescent dogs, 192
dogfights, 127, 166–71
doggie day care, 2, 14, 103–4, 120–22
dog runs, 210, 271, 279
  dog size and, 2
  and getting puppies to go outside, 106
  guidelines for use of, 126–31
  and obedience in distracting settings, 133
  quarantine and, 52
  social etiquette for, 166–71
dogs, sizes of, 2, 5–6
dog sports/events, 202–9
Dogue de Bordeaux, 180

dog walkers, 2, 20
  confinement and, 36
  dogs walked at same time by, 119–20
  and getting puppies to go outside, 107
  in-store manners and, 221–22
  when they pick up other dogs, 120
dominant dogs, 247–50
doors, 19, 39, 231
down command, 78–79
  for adolescent dogs, 186–90, 192
  for adult dogs, 232, 240, 246, 248, 252–54
  advanced, 186–87
  confinement and, 40
  demanding behavior and, 232
  distance, 188–89
  dominant dogs and, 248
  enforced, 135–36
  FRAP and, 43
  good habits and, 63
  in-store manners and, 222
  late-developing aggression and, 246
  leg lifting and, 240
  for non-food motivated pups, 79
  and obedience in distracting settings, 134–36, 147
  and steps to better-behaved dogs, 152–53
  when moving, 189–90
downtown areas, 52
Duford, Donna, 64

ears, 3, 154, 167
electric collars, 182
electric pads (scat mats), 229–30
elevators, social etiquette in, 159–60
enforced down command, 135–36
English Springer Spaniels, 3, 5
Establishing a Dog Park in Your Community, 166
euthanasia, 13, 277
exchange game, 82, 137
exercise, 87, 173
  adult dogs and, 129, 131, 202–9
  confinement and, 36
  and dealing with different temperaments, 69
  dog selection and, 4–6
  dog size and, 2
  dominant dogs and, 250
  and getting puppies to go outside, 107, 113
  good habits and, 65
  guidelines for, 125–32

late-developing aggression and, 246
and leaving adult dogs at home alone, 209, 212
mental, 123–25, 227
neutering and, 132
older dogs and, 266, 271–72
social etiquette and, 162, 170
exercise pens, 19, 35

family life, 29
fear, fears, 96–104, 173
  adult-onset, 242–45
  barking and, 234
  of certain places, 244–45
  dealing with, 67, 69–71, 97–104
  and dogs off leash on sidewalks, 225–26
  dog walkers and, 120
  dominant dogs and, 248
  exercise and, 127–28
  and first week of walks, 91
  and getting puppies to go outside, 105
  and obedience in distracting settings, 136, 139–40
  of objects, 102–3
  older dogs and, 265, 273
  of other dogs, 103–4
  of people, 100–102
  and quitting while you're ahead, 103
  reading canine body language and, 155, 157
  sensitiveness and, 174
  social etiquette and, 160, 162, 167, 223–24
  and training for adolescent dogs, 187
females, 7–8
find it! game, 53, 272
flat buckle collars, 175–76
Flat-Coated Retrievers, 262–63
flyball competition, 206
flying disk (Frisbee) competition, 206
following through immediately, 152
follow the leader game, 196–97
follow the lure game, 59
food, 18, 20–21, 23–29, 244
  and dealing with different temperaments, 70–71
  dog walkers and, 119
  health care and, 200–201
  homecoming and, 28
  housebreaking and, 21, 23–24
  and leaving adult dogs at home alone, 214–15
  normal behavior and, 89
  older dogs and, 266–67, 270, 275

social etiquette and, 159, 163, 167
  see also lures; rewards, rewarding; treats
food cubes, 53, 214–15
FRAP (frenetic random activity period), 43
freestyle obedience, 202, 205–6
Frisbees, 206, 270–71
frozen rope bones, 55, 89
furniture, 19
  hopping on, 227–30
  late-developing aggression and, 246
  leg lifting and, 239
  off command and, 190–92

gates:
  couch hopping and, 228
  and leaving adult dogs at home alone, 213
  puppies and, 19–21, 23, 31–34, 40–42, 60
German Shepherd Dogs, 6, 42, 115, 126, 174, 262
get busy command, 108
Golden Retrievers, 4, 66, 115, 262–63
good habits, 55–67
Good Owners, Great Pets, 227
Great Danes, xvii, 6, 126, 262
greetings, 279
  dog sports/events and, 204
  exercise and, 127
  and first week of walks, 92–93
  and getting puppies to go outside, 106
  handling common fears and, 103
  older dogs and, 266
  reading canine body language and, 154–56
  social etiquette and, 161–62
grooming:
  dog selection and, 5–6
  dominant dogs and, 248–49
  good habits and, 63–64
  taxicabs and, 218
  see also cleanliness
guard dogs, selecting watchdogs vs., 9–10

handling, 9, 63–64
hand signals:
  and obedience in distracting settings, 134–35
  and training for adolescent dogs, 186, 189–90, 193–95
head halters, 173, 175, 179–81
  adult-onset fears and, 245

(*head halters, continued*)
barking and, 234, 239
and dealing with different temperaments, 70
evaluation of, 180–81
exercise and, 208
and obedience in distracting settings, 138
social etiquette and, 159
taxicabs and, 218
and training for adult dogs, 252, 259
health care, 23
for adult dogs, 200–201
for older dogs, 269–70
hearing loss, 266, 273
heart problems, 266–67
Helstein, Kim, 49
herding breeds, 6–7
hide and go seek! game, 123, 272
high fiving, 124
Hill, Chris, 217
home, leaving adult dogs alone at, 209–15, 231, 235–36
homecoming, 28–29
housebreaking, 20–27, 213
and catching puppies in the act, 21
cleanups and, 22, 24
crates and, 36–37, 241
doggie day care and, 120
first steps in, 20–26
and getting puppies to go outside, 106–7, 109, 112–13
in-store manners and, 223
leg lifting and, 239–40
older dogs and, 266, 275
paper training and, 21–26
problems with, 240–41
sample schedule and, 25–26
straight, 24–25
taxicabs and, 218
trainers and, 115
see also walks, walking
Hoye, Cheryl, 142
hugging, 251
hurry up command, 108, 112
hyperactivity, 36, 43, 227

illnesses, 23, 106, 125, 129
adult-onset fears and, 243
housebreaking problems and, 241

older dogs and, 262–67, 270, 273
quarantine and, 46–47, 49–52
independent behavior, 71, 149–50
indoor activities, 122–25
indoor electronic units, 230
indulgence, confusing love with, 231
injuries:
confinement and, 37, 42
doggie day care and, 121
and dogs off leash on sidewalks, 226
exercise and, 125–26, 129, 208
at night, 45–46
quarantine and, 51
social etiquette and, 169–70
training equipment and, 181
inquisitive strangers, 113–14
Irish Wolfhounds, 263

J and J Dog Supplies, 184
jaw jousting, 165
Juarbe-Diaz, Soraya, 228
jumping, jumping up:
commands and, 85
doggie day care and, 121
dog selection and, 5
and first week of walks, 92–93
good habits and, 60–63
ignoring, 60–61
indoor activities and, 122
and leaving adult dogs at home alone, 212
and obedience in distracting settings, 139–40
older dogs and, 269
and redirecting with food lures, 61–62
social etiquette and, 159
and stepping on leads, 62
trainers and, 115
and training for adult dogs, 251–52

Kay-Wolff, Toni, 61, 94, 124
keep off/keep away products, 229–30
kidney failure, 267
Kong toys, 54–55, 65–66, 214

Labrador Retrievers, 4, 43, 63, 72, 104, 154, 158, 166, 174, 188, 220
leads, 158, 172–73, 210, 279

barking and, 234
biting on, 147
commands and, 73, 78, 82–83, 237
and dealing with different temperaments, 69–70
doggie day care and, 121
dog walkers and, 120
dominant dogs and, 250
evaluation of, 183–85
exercise and, 126–27, 208
and first week of walks, 90, 92–93
and getting puppies to go outside, 106, 109, 112
good habits and, 56–59, 62–63, 67
handling common fears and, 98, 103
homecoming and, 28
housebreaking and, 21–22, 25, 27
and introducing new pups to other pets, 30–31, 33
introduction of, 56–59
leg lifting and, 240
and making rural dogs into Metrodogs, 10
and obedience in distracting settings, 133, 136, 138–41, 143–45, 147
older dogs and, 12, 266, 268, 273
pulling on, 5, 115, 196–97, 257–59
retractable, 109, 162, 173, 181, 184–85, 194
social etiquette and, 159, 162–63, 166, 168, 223
trainers and, 115
and training for adolescent dogs, 186, 189–96
and training for adult dogs, 252, 255–59
walking on sidewalks without, 225–27
leave it command, 40, 80–81
and dogs off leash on sidewalks, 226
and obedience in distracting settings, 136–37, 139, 147
social etiquette and, 161–62, 168
leg lifting, 156, 239–41
Leonbergers, 271
let's go command:
for adolescent dogs, 196–97
and dogs off leash on sidewalks, 226
and obedience in distracting settings, 146–47
social etiquette and, 161, 223
Lewis, Barbara, 226–27
life expectancies, 262–63
limited admission shelters, 14–15
loud noises, fear of, 243–44
love, confusing indulgence with, 231
love my crate! game, 38
lunging, 238–39

lures, 59–62
and dealing with different temperaments, 70
and obedience in distracting settings, 134–36, 142, 145
rewards vs., 60
and steps to better-behaved dogs, 152
and training for adult dogs, 255
see also treats

McCue, Linda, 50
males, 7–8
Maltese, 6, 114, 161, 234
man-made testicles, 132
manners, see social etiquette
martingale collars, 176–77
medications, 116, 118, 231
adult-onset fears and, 243–44
for older dogs, 264, 266
mentally troubled people, 224
mental sharpness, loss of, 265–66, 275
Metrodogs:
advantages of, xvii
cruelty to, 1
selection of, 1–15
standards of behavior for, xvii–xviii
Miniature Poodles, 3, 166
mixed breeds, 3, 7, 205
monster dogs, creation of, 96
mounting:
good habits and, 62–63
reading canine body language and, 154
social etiquette and, 165–67
mouth, stick in roof of, 158
move command, 192–93
mute swans, 163
muzzles, 180–81, 245

National Capital Air Canines, 206
neighbors, nasty, 233
neutering, 63, 96, 131–32, 156
dog selection and, 13–14
dominant dogs and, 249
leg lifting and, 240
reasons for, 131
social etiquette and, 159, 167
and training for adolescent dogs, 193
when to do it, 132

night, making it through the, 44–46
noise, noises, 40–41, 242–44
nonsporting breeds, 6
no-pull harnesses, 181–82, 252, 259
North American Dog Agility Council (NADAC), 204
North American Flyball Association, Inc., 206
nutrition, *see* food

obedience:
adult-onset fears and, 245
competitive, 205
in distracting settings, 132–47
freestyle, 202, 205–6
linking things your dog enjoys to, 152
magic tools for, 141
and rules for corrections, 139–40
social etiquette and, 159, 162
and steps to better-behaved dogs, 151–53
and taking your dog to work, 216–17
see also commands; training
obesity, 267–68
odor neutralizer/eliminators, 20, 22, 24
off command, 140, 190–92, 252
older dogs, 261–77
adoption of, 11–12
death of, 275–77
games and activities for, 270–73
health care for, 269–70
life expectancies and, 262–63
making life easier for, 269
physical changes of, 264–68, 273
puppies with, 274
training for, 273–74
open admission shelters, 13–14
opposition reflex, 255–57
oral papillomas (warts), 129
orthopedic problems, 106, 125
out command, 81–82, 95, 137–38, 147

paper, paper training, 18, 87–88
confinement and, 36–37
dog walkers and, 119
and getting puppies to go outside, 106–7, 109, 112–13
housebreaking and, 21–26
older dogs and, 265

for scooping, 93–94
straight, 23–24
parking meters, 160–61
parks, 2, 52, 170–73
social etiquette in, 162–66, 170
and training for adolescent dogs, 186–87
Pellicano, Christine, 114, 241
people:
fear of, 100–102
inquisitive, 113–14
lunging and barking at, 239
mentally troubled, 224
pet-treats game, 34
pet shops, 15
pet therapy, 207, 273
place command, 144–46, 192–93
pointers, 5
poisons, 163–64
Pomeranians, 263
ponds, 163–64
positive associations, 172–73
prong collars (pinches), 175, 178–79
puppies, 279
city services for, 115–22
commands they should know, 71–85
confinement for, 19–21, 23, 31–46, 60
dealing with different temperaments of, 67–71
from end of quarantine to seven months, 87–147
first week of walks for, 89–94
FRAP of, 43
getting them to go outside, 105–14
good habits for, 55–67
homecoming for, 28–29
housebreaking for, 20–27, 106–7, 109, 112–13
impossible vs. normal behavior of, 88–89
indoor activities for, 122–25
introducing other pets to, 30–34
at night, 44–46
obedience in distracting settings for, 132–47
with older dogs, 274
providing leadership for, 94–96
from same litter, 7
sample schedule for, 25–26
selecting adult dogs vs., 8
from seven weeks to end of quarantine, 17–84
two same-sex, 7
water for, 26–27
puppy kindergartens, 50–51
puppy playgroups, 121

handling common fears and, 103–4
quarantine and, 49–52

quarantine:
  duration and reasons for, 46–55
  puppies from seven weeks to end of, 17–84
  puppies to seven months from end of, 87–147
  sanity savers during, 53–55
  socialization and, 47–52
quiet time, 54

rain, 90, 108, 113
rawhides, 54, 248
reactive behavior, dealing with, 69–70
redirection, 61–62, 233–34
rescue/draft dogs, 6
rescue groups, 15
retained puppy teeth, 88
retractable leads, 109, 162, 173, 181, 184–85, 194
retreating, retreats, 29, 172
  exercise and, 128
  handling common fears and, 103–4
  in-store manners and, 222
retrievers, 4
rewards, rewarding, 172
  adult-onset fears and, 243, 245
  barking and, 234–35
  clickers and, 44
  demanding behavior and, 232
  doggie day care and, 121
  dominant dogs and, 250
  enthusiasm in, 153
  and first week of walks, 90, 93
  and getting puppies to go outside, 105, 108, 112
  housebreaking problems and, 240
  indoor activities and, 124
  and lunging and barking at other dogs or people,
    239
  lures vs., 60
  and obedience in distracting settings, 135–36,
    138–40, 143–44, 146–47
  social etiquette and, 159–60
  and training for adolescent dogs, 186–89, 192,
    195
  and training for adult dogs, 252–56, 258
  types of, 72, 74
  see also treats

Rhodesian Ridgebacks, 256
role models, role modeling, 55, 98, 100
rolling on the back, 156–57
rope toys, 55, 66, 89
Rottweilers, 6, 224
rude human behavior, 97
running, 126–27, 208
rural dogs, making them into Metrodogs, 10–11

Sagal, Judy, 216
Saint Bernards, 6, 150, 225
say hello! game, 101–2
scent-based no-bark collars, 236
scent hounds, 4
schedules, 25–26, 214
scooping, 93–94, 111
second dogs, selection of, 8–9
sensitiveness, 67–69, 97, 174
separation problems, 231
setters, 5
sexes, 7–8
shock-based no-bark collars, 236
Siberian Huskies, 6, 65, 181
sidewalks, 111, 225–27
sight hounds, 4
sight loss, 268, 273
sit command, 73–77
  for adolescent dogs, 152–53, 186, 192
  for adult dogs, 205, 210, 232–33, 252–53, 255–56
  advanced, 186
  confinement and, 41
  demanding behavior and, 232–33
  dog sports/events and, 205
  and first week of walks, 93
  FRAP and, 43
  good habits and, 63
  indoor activities and, 124
  and leaving adult dogs at home alone, 210
  and obedience in distracting settings, 133–35,
    139–41, 143–44
  and steps to better-behaved dogs, 152–53
sleep, 213
  older dogs and, 262, 264–66
  of puppies, 28, 38, 44–46
slip collars (chokes), 177–78, 180
social etiquette:
  for adolescent dogs, 159–71
  doggie day care and, 120

(*social etiquette, continued*)
 for dog runs, 166–71
 dog sports/events and, 204
 in elevators, 159–60
 in parks, 162–66, 170
 in stores, 221–24
 on street, 160–62
 trainers and, 115
socializing, socialization, 150
 confinement and, 36
 doggie day care and, 120
 and getting puppies to go outside, 105–6, 113
 handling common fears and, 103–4
 quarantine and, 47–52
Soft-Coated Wheaten Terriers, 5, 130
sound-based deterrents, 230
sound-based no-bark collars, 236
spaniels, 5
stable behavior, 71
stair care, 268
stay command:
 for adolescent dogs, 162, 184–85, 189, 193–95
 for adult dogs, 232, 252–54
 training equipment and, 184–85
Stern, Geoff, 50
Sternberg, Sue, 187
stop, then go game, 58, 196
stores, 220–24
 manners in, 221–24
 tethering near, 220–21
straight housebreaking, 24–25
straight paper training, 23–24
street, social etiquette on, 160–62
structure, 12
submissive urination, 66–68, 103, 131
subways, 218
success, setting yourself up for, 153
support, 110
swimming, 272

taxicabs, 217–19
teeth, 88
 of adult dogs, 200–201
 of older dogs, 269–70
 see also chewing
teething, 88–89
temperaments:
 dealing with, 67–71

dog selection and, 8–9, 14–15
and obedience in distracting settings, 132, 139
 testing of, 8, 14–15
terriers, 5
tethering, 42–43
 at night, 45–46
 near stores, 220–21
Therapy Dogs Incorporated, 207
thunderstorms, fear of, 242–44
toy breeds, 6, 26–28, 63, 113–15, 221
 confinement for, 41–42
 dog walkers and, 120
 exercise and, 126
 health concerns of, 23
 housebreaking of, 27, 113, 241
 at night, 45
 safety tips for, 170
 teeth of, 88
 training equipment and, 182
Toy Poodles, 262–63
toys, 19–20, 150, 172
 barking and, 235
 commands and, 79, 82–84
 confinement and, 38–39
 couch hopping and, 229
 demanding behavior and, 232–33
 dominant dogs and, 248, 250
 exercise and, 127
 and first week of walks, 92
 good habits and, 57, 59, 62, 65–66
 handling common fears and, 103
 health care and, 201
 homecoming and, 28
 housebreaking and, 21
 indoor activities and, 123–25
 and leaving adult dogs at home alone, 213–15
 naming of, 123–24
 at night, 45
 normal behavior and, 89
 and obedience in distracting settings, 136, 139, 147
 quarantine and, 53–55
 social etiquette and, 167
 and steps to better-behaved dogs, 152–53
 and training for adult dogs, 253
Trader, Linda, 32
trainers, 20, 115–17, 127, 259
training, 149, 199–200
 adolescent dogs and, 151, 185–97

adopting older dogs and, 12
confinement and, 35–36, 38
and dealing with different temperaments, 69, 71
doggie day care and, 121
dog selection and, 6, 8–10, 13–14
and getting puppies to go outside, 108–9, 112, 114
good habits and, 56, 59
handling common fears and, 99, 101, 103
indoor activities and, 122
and introducing new pups to other pets, 32–33
and leaving adult dogs at home alone, 210, 212
and making rural dogs into Metrodogs, 11
for older dogs, 273–74
providing leadership and, 94
quarantine and, 50–51
taxicabs and, 218
when to start, 73
see also commands; obedience
training equipment, 175–85
treat retreats game, 58–59, 128
treats, 96, 172–73
    adult–onset fears and, 244–45
    barking and, 235, 238
    commands and, 73–85
    confinement and, 38, 40–42
    couch hopping and, 229
    dominant dogs and, 247–48
    exercise and, 127–28
    and first week of walks, 91–93
    FRAP and, 43
    and getting puppies to go outside, 105, 108–10
    good habits and, 57–62, 64, 66–67
    handling common fears and, 98–99, 101–3
    in-store manners and, 222
    and introducing new pups to other pets, 31, 33–34
    late-developing aggression and, 246
    and leaving adult dogs at home alone, 213
    and obedience in distracting settings, 133, 135–36, 138–43, 145
    quarantine and, 50, 53–54
    social etiquette and, 159
    and steps to better-behaved dogs, 153
    and taking your dog to work, 216
    training equipment and, 177–78
    and training for adolescent dogs, 187, 189–90, 195
tricks, 123, 272–73

trusting your dog, 225
Walter Turken Training for Adoption Program, 11

United Kennel Club, 205
United States Dog Agility Association (USDAA), 204
urination, urinating, 239–41
    and getting puppies to go outside, 105–14
    older dogs and, 264–65, 267
    in-store manners and, 223
    reading canine body language and, 154, 156–57
    submissive, 66–68, 103, 131
    and training for adolescent dogs, 197
    see also housebreaking

vaccinations, 46–47, 49, 51–52, 87

wait command:
    for adolescent dogs, 159, 161, 193–94
    late-developing aggression and, 246
    and leaving adult dogs at home alone, 210
    and obedience in distracting settings, 143–44
    social etiquette and, 159, 161
walk and stop, 197
walks, walking, 241
    brief, 89
    controlled, 146–47
    doggie day care and, 120–22
    and dogs off leash on sidewalks, 225–27
    first week of, 89–94
    and getting puppies to go outside, 105–7, 109–10, 112–14
    guidelines for, 126
    and leaving adult dogs at home alone, 211–12
    and making rural dogs into Metrodogs, 10–11
    midday, 211–12
    and obedience in distracting settings, 141, 146–47
    older dogs and, 265, 267–68, 271–72
    quiet areas for, 90–91
    social etiquette and, 161–62
    and taking your dog to work, 216
    and training for adolescent dogs, 196–97
    when to go for, 25
    see also dog walkers; housebreaking
walk-ups, 106
warts (oral papillomas), 129

watchdogs, 4, 9–10
water, 26–27, 164, 241
  confinement and, 36
  exercise and, 208
  and getting puppies to go outside, 108, 112
  housebreaking and, 21, 23–24
Weimaraners, 5
West Highland White Terriers, 5
which hand? game, 53–54

Whippets, 4
Wirehaired Terriers, 5
Woodhouse, Barbara, 190
work, taking your dog to, 215–17
working breeds, 6

yanking, 259
Yorkshire Terriers, 6, 150, 274